COLLECTED ECONOMIC ESSAYS

Volume 3

ESSAYS ON ECONOMIC POLICY I

COLLECTED ECONOMIC ESSAYS
by Nicholas Kaldor

ESSAYS ON ECONOMIC POLICY I

I. Policies for Full Employment
II. The Control of Inflation
III. The Problem of Tax Reform

NICHOLAS KALDOR

HOLMES & MEIER PUBLISHERS, INC.
New York

Second impression published in the United States of America 1980 by
Holmes & Meier Publishers, Inc.
30 Irving Place
New York, N.Y. 10003
First edition published 1964
Copyright © 1964, 1980 by Nicholas Kaldor

Library of Congress Cataloguing in Publication Data

Kaldor, Nicholas, 1908–

   Essays on economic policy.
   (His Collected economic essays; v. 3–4)
   Includes bibliographical references.
   CONTENTS: v. 1. Policies for full employment.
The control of inflation. The problem of tax reform'
– v. 2. Policies for international stability. Country
studies.
   1. Economic policy – Addresses, essays, lectures.
2. Full employment policies – Addresses, essays,
lectures. 3. Inflation (Finance) – Addresses, essays,
lectures. 4. Taxation – Addresses, essays, lectures.
5. Economic stabilization – Addresses, essays,
lectures. I. Title. II. Series.
HD82.K3   1980   338.9   80–18155
ISBN 0 8419 0453 7 (v. 1)

Printed in Great Britain by The Anchor Press Ltd
and bound by Wm Brendon & Son Ltd
both of Tiptree, Essex

ESSAYS ON ECONOMIC POLICY—Volume I

CONTENTS

INTRODUCTION

THE papers collected in these two volumes belong to the field of "applied" rather than "pure" economics—they concern the application of economic theory to issues of economic policy. As compared with the theoretical essays published in the two earlier volumes, their presentation has involved far more problems of choice and selection. Papers in "pure" theory may retain interest for the economist even when they become dated; they may still serve to illuminate the processes by which ideas develop, and the way in which the focus of interest is gradually shifted, as a result of further thought, from certain aspects of the economic mechanism to others. But the particular issues of economic policy, and the manner in which economists tackle them, are even more ephemeral than the theoretical ideas that form their background. Moreover, their consideration often involves a detailed analysis of the economic situation of some particular country at some particular time, which makes their perusal tedious reading once that situation has passed into history.

For this reason I tried to confine the selection to papers which deal with live issues—such as full employment, inflation, tax-reform, the problems of international trade and the balance of payments—and to discard those (such as papers on war economics) which would only be of interest today (and, one hopes, in the future) to a narrow group of specialists in economic history. Nevertheless, I have included in the second volume, under the heading "Country Studies," a group of specialised papers relating to the problems and policies of individual countries; in most cases these are the results of special assignments abroad, and, though their subject may not be of general interest to readers of other countries, I feel they may serve a useful purpose in broadening the outlook of students and bringing home the relativity of our basic ideas.

This process of discarding and selection has meant that most of the papers finally included are relatively recent. Exception was made in the case of two papers concerning full employment policies—the first and the second essays printed in the present volume—for special reasons which require explanation.

The first, on "Wage Subsidies as a Remedy for Unemployment," which was written in the early part of 1935, is reproduced
here as exemplifying the application of "pre-Keynesian" economics to the general problem of unemployment. There is nothing
wrong with the particular proposal for curing unemployment by a
general subsidy on wages paid to employers; if it had been tried
in the circumstances of the 1930's, it might have had spectacular
results.[1] Indeed, as will be evident to the readers of the last (and
most recent) essay printed in this volume, I still consider this
suggestion a fertile one, though for purposes rather different from
those which prompted the 1935 paper. But while the conclusions
were sound, the elaborate argument by which they were supported
was not—which perhaps shows that in matters of economic
policy, the intuitions of an economist may run ahead of his "tools"
and his methods of analysis. On the one hand, the argument of the
essay ignored almost entirely the macro-economic factors which
determine the level of effective demand for goods and services
and which, in turn, govern the aggregate volume of employment
in the short period. On the other hand, the whole analysis was
based on the notion of the "elasticity of demand for labour in
industry as a whole, which is a weighted average of the elasticities
of demand in individual industries" (p. 5)—without inquiring
whether any such curve exists, and, if it does, whether it is consistent with the postulate of the marginal productivity theory of
distribution.[2] If the case for a wage subsidy were re-stated in

[1] It *had* been tried, as I afterwards discovered, for a brief period by von Papen in
Germany, albeit much too late to save that country from Hitler; indeed, by inducing a
recovery of employment in the latter half of 1932 it caused a sudden fall in the electoral
popularity of the Nazi Party, which may have hastened the "unholy alliance" which
led to the takeover in January 1933.

[2] This demand curve postulates that the volume of employment will always be such
as to make the real wage equal to the marginal product of labour—which can only be
the case under conditions in which an increase in employment is associated with a fall
in the *average* product of labour, so that the marginal product is necessarily smaller
than the average product. In the converse case where the marginal product exceeds
the average product—as will be the case in most industries in the short-period, if only
because a considerable proportion of the labour employed is "overhead" labour—the
real wage is necessarily *lower* than the marginal product (since the wage cannot, in
any circumstances, exceed the *average* product) and the elasticity of labour's productivity curve provides no guide whatever to the employment consequences of a reduction in "real labour cost" brought about by a subsidy on wages. (Nor, I need hardly
add, does its neo-classical twin the "elasticity of demand for the product of the
individual firm" since this particular elasticity, as implied in footnote 2 on p. 5, does
not come in at all with regard to the effects of *general* reductions in the cost of labour to
employers.)

terms of Keynesian economics it would run on entirely different lines—in terms of the increase in the propensity to consume, engineered through the redistribution of income in favour of labour, which a general subsidy on wages would necessarily entail—provided only that the subsidy is not financed by such other taxes as would reduce the purchasing power of labour by an equivalent amount.[1]

In recent years it has become fashionable in certain circles, particularly in the United States, to decry Keynes' achievement and to suggest that on mature reflection, the *General Theory* did not contribute anything fundamentally new.[2] I submit my 1935 paper on wage subsidies as counter-evidence. I doubt that Professors Johnson, Friedman, Fellner and Co. would really argue that the "neo-classical" method of analysis employed in that paper is fundamentally sound, or that the employment consequences of the introduction of a scheme of wage-subsidies could be adequately analysed by the use of such techniques.

By contrast, the second essay, my memorandum to the Beveridge Committee on Full Employment, which was written eight years later, tackles the full employment problem in a thoroughly Keynesian way: and the difference in analytical method of these two papers is a demonstration of the revolutionary effect of Keynes' *General Theory* on the economist's mode of approach. The main principle which it enunciates—that "the fiscal policies of the State must be so regulated as to secure adequate total outlay for the community as a whole"—is no longer a controversial one, at any rate in Britain; the last Budget speech of Mr. Maudling (April 1963) reads almost like a classroom exercise in

---

[1] It may be worth mentioning that, in a letter written to me in 1935, Keynes denied that a general subsidy of labour is capable of increasing the aggregate volume of employment—for the reasons for which he thought that a general reduction in money wages was incapable of securing this result. He evidently overlooked the fact that whilst a general reduction in wages would normally tend to leave the price/wage relationship unaffected (at any rate in a closed economy), a general subsidy on wages cannot fail to reduce prices relatively to wages, and thereby increase effective demand.

[2] Cf. for example, Harry Johnson, "The General Theory After Twenty-five Years," *American Economic Review*, vol. li 2, May 1961. This "counter-revolution" started, in fact, earlier, with the publication of Don Patinkin's book on *Money, Interest and Prices* in 1956, which was hailed for a time as a "refutation" of Keynes. (However, subsequent controversy, particularly in the *Review of Economic Studies*, effectively answered any such claim. Cf. Archibald and Lipsey, "Monetary and Value Theory—A Critique of Lange and Patinkin," *Review of Economic Studies*, vol. xxvi, October 1958, and "A Symposium on Monetary Theory," *ibid.*, vol. xxviii, October 1960.)

the application of Keynesian principles to fiscal policy. But when "Appendix C" was first published, the principle was far from generally accepted; and its confident tone in asserting that the Government can ensure full employment through budgetary techniques by any one of four "routes" (or a combination of them), was much criticised.

To be fair, criticism was directed at the "optimistic" forecasts of the post-war situation, presented in the second part of the paper, more than at the analysis of what a full-employment policy would have involved under the pre-war conditions given in the first part.[1] The value of this exercise lay more in the method used in the analysis than in the actual forecasts: it was the first attempt to build up comprehensive estimates from a large number of separate forecasts (and assumptions) within the framework of a consistent econometric model.[2] If the number of econometric models that have been constructed since is any guide, the method has certainly established itself as a working tool, even though the basic short-coming of all such estimates (which lies in assuming that the future will be like the past in all relevant matters, except those in which there is evidence of dissimilarities, as stated on p. 46) can never be wholly overcome by more extensive statistical knowledge or further theoretical refinement.

In retrospect, I must concede that the assumptions made in 1943 concerning a hypothetical "1948" proved too optimistic. In one respect at least this was due to a deliberate "policy-decision" rather than mistaken judgment: I was requested by Beveridge to *assume* that post-war prices would be no more than 33⅓ per cent. above pre-war (which in turn involved the assumption that the rise in money wages would be no greater than 54 per cent.), however unlikely this may have seemed even in 1943.[3]

[1] Cf., in particular Sir Hubert Henderson, *The Uses and Abuses of Economic Planning* (the Rede Lecture of 1947), Cambridge University Press, pp. 28ff.
[2] The nature of the underlying model and the method of analysis followed was systematically set out in Stone and Jackson, "Economic Models with Special Reference to Mr. Kaldor's System," *Economic Journal*, December 1946, pp. 554–67. Cf. also A. G. Hart, "Model Building and Fiscal Policy," *American Economic Review*, September 1945, pp. 531–58.
[3] The reason was that all the calculations of the Beveridge Report on Social Security, published a year earlier, were based on the assumption of post-war prices being only 25 per cent. above pre-war, and Beveridge, for understandable reasons, did not wish to have his previous estimates on the cost of social security to be thrown out while the proposals were still under discussion. Since the rise in prices had already reached over

In actual fact, hourly wages more than doubled between 1938 and 1948, and the level of prices rose by 90–100 per cent.

However there were two other important errors in the forecasts which I can only attribute now to youthful exuberance. The most important of these was the assumption (in paragraph 30) that the "transition period" following the war (this was assumed to end "somewhere in the middle of 1945"—which suggests that military forecasts are easier to make than economic ones!) would only take 2½ years, after which the normal peacetime relationships between consumption and savings would have re-established themselves and the pre-war productivity trend would have been regained. In fact, the pre-war productivity trend was not regained until around 1951, while the pre-war savings ratios were not re-established until 1955 or 1956.[1] The wartime dislocations caused a considerable fall in productivity which I had not appreciated in 1943. The year 1948 did in fact show a very considerable improvement against earlier years, but this only meant that the pre-war *level* of productivity was (broadly) regained in that year; the 13 per cent. improvement forecast was not really attained until 1951 or perhaps 1953.

The other main error was in assuming that the terms of trade would be the same as in 1938 (which happened to be a year of recession in the prices of primary products). In fact the terms of trade of 1948 were 14 per cent. worse than in 1938; and if the estimates had been related to 1950 or 1953–5 the deterioration would have been 26 per cent. As a long range forecast, the assertion that a "prolonged period of scarcities in foodstuffs and raw materials" was unlikely because "the forces of technical improvement which made for the surpluses of the last two (pre-war)

30 per cent. by the time my memorandum was prepared, I was allowed to change the 25 per cent. assumption to 33⅓ per cent., but no more. (In the event the post-war inflation did not make much difference to the cost of the Beveridge Plan—but this was because Beveridge's original postulate concerning a "minimum standard" in pensions and other benefits was not adhered to.)

[1] Net *private* savings (including undistributed profits of enterprises but after deduction of depreciation and stock appreciation) were zero or negative until 1951, largely on account of the virtual absence of personal savings in the early post-war years. The pre-war relationship between gross domestic investment and the G.N.P. was regained by 1948, but, owing to the relatively greater price increases for capital goods, the volume of real investment was 10 per cent. lower, (while the real G.N.P. was 4–5 per cent. higher) and the pre-war volume of investment was not regained until 1950. *Net* investment did not reach the target of 25 per cent. above pre-war (Plan I of Table 22) until 1954.

decades do not appear to be in any way exhausted" proved to be correct. But partly as a result of the Korean war and the extensive stockpiling that followed it, these forces did not begin to make themselves felt until after the mid-'fifties.

These two factors explain the discrepancy between the 20 per cent. rise in real national income that was forecast and the 4 per cent. increase which actually occurred,[1] and this in turn was responsible for the erroneous conclusions on taxation. For the forecasts on public expenditure were not too low, when allowance is made for the difference in the price level. Indeed, total consolidated expenditure of public authorities (net of subsidies) was slightly less than forecast in Table 17.[2] On the other hand, there was a considerable surplus in the consolidated budget (which made up for the low private saving) so that the net total raised in taxation (in real terms) was 10 per cent. greater than estimated. This, together with the fact that private incomes in real terms were 16 per cent. lower than forecast, made the burden of taxation (again, net of subsidies) some 34 per cent. of private incomes, instead of 25 per cent.

The third essay, written in 1950, is concerned with the international aspects of full employment policies and thus deals with problems that are still very much in the forefront of interest. It was written at the time when the "chronic dollar shortage" and the dangers of an American business recession loomed very large. Though these particular fears proved groundless, the basic proposition of this paper—that the pursuit of full employment policies by individual countries may be incompatible with the maintenance of an international régime of fixed exchange rates —is one that has received strong support from subsequent

---

[1] The other assumptions set out in paragraph 33 turned out to be more or less accurate. The working population was somewhat higher than expected, hours of work somewhat shorter, unemployment somewhat less, but these differences cancelled out, so that the forecast of total labour input was broadly correct. The assumption on the division of the labour force between civilian employment and the armed forces turned out to be right, and so did the estimate of the fall in income from foreign investment.

[2] Adding 50 per cent. on account of the rise in prices, public expenditure on goods and services (in real terms) was almost exactly as forecast, but transfer expenditures were somewhat less, as the saving in national debt interest and social insurance payments (again, in real terms) more than offset higher expenditure for war damage compensation.

experience. As this paper emphasises (p. 85), under a régime of fixed exchange rates, fluctuations in employment represent the major mechanism for restoring equilibrium in the balance of payments when that balance is disturbed for any reason. If such fluctuations are prevented from occurring by the use of internal compensatory measures, the mechanism of adjustment is suspended and something else must be put in its place. What that something else should be is still a matter of dispute and argument. My own subsequent contributions to the discussion will be found at the end of the present volume (pp. 290–3) and in the following volume. While the provision of additional liquidity may be an appropriate remedy for dealing with temporary disturbances, there is no reason to suppose that the important disequilibrating tendencies operating under a régime of fixed exchange rates are, in the main, temporary in nature. Some way will therefore have to be found, sooner or later, to make it possible for individual countries to adjust their general level of costs and prices in accordance with international requirements, other than through pressures on money wages, exerted by a contraction in effective demand.

The next essay, written in the mid-'fifties for a foreign audience, reviews the results of the full employment policies pursued in Britain in the first post-war decade. It discusses why fiscal measures alone proved insufficient to deal with the instabilities caused by speculative movements in commodity stocks and the balance of payments crises engendered by them. It also expresses scepticism as to the effectiveness of the "monetary controls" employed by the Conservative Government—a scepticism which was amply justified by the experience of the subsequent five years. This theme is developed more thoroughly in my memorandum submitted to the Radcliffe Committee three years later (reproduced on pp. 128–53 of this volume) and in the Report of the Radcliffe Committee itself which is reviewed in a paper written for an American audience in 1960 (reproduced on pp. 154–65).

The paper on "A Positive Policy for Wages and Dividends," printed here for the first time, was written as a memorandum to Sir Stafford Cripps in the summer of 1950. It argues the case for a more permanent "incomes policy." At that time both wages and dividends were "frozen" by a voluntary scheme which could clearly not remain effective for more than a temporary period (and indeed broke down in the following year). The paper suggests that, as the need for income restraint in a full employment economy is a permanent need and not a temporary one, it requires a system of flexible and continuing restraints on both wages and dividends and goes on to elaborate a possible method for both. As regards wages, the paper emphasises that the major task of an incomes policy is not just to limit annual wage increases to some target percentage, but to provide a mechanism for bringing the scale of relative wages into harmony with the net advantages of different kinds of work—indeed, without a mechanism for adjusting relative wages it is unlikely that any policy of restraining the increase in aggregate wages would work. On the side of dividends, the paper emphasises that, while a rigid dividend limitation is incompatible with the efficient functioning of a private enterprise economy, it is possible to regulate the percentage growth of aggregate dividend payments in a way that does not interefere with economic incentives.

When, in November 1951, the Labour Government was replaced by a Conservative Government, the whole idea of an "incomes policy" was rapidly dismissed. The Conservative politicians and some of their economic advisers believed that the proper way to deal with the problem of a wage-price spiral was by operating on market forces, "damping down demand" through monetary measures; income restraint, like planning, was held to be inconsistent with their basic economic philosophy. It took ten years of frustrating experience with monetary controls before the Government went back on this view; and when Mr. Selwyn Lloyd (in June 1961) did go back, his new incomes policy took over only the wages-part of the old Cripps policy: the control of dividends was conveniently forgotten. This new approach, as reflected in the establishment of the National Incomes Commission, presumably rested on the ground that profits, being residual income, cannot be restrained or controlled in the same manner as wages. This is true but it is also beside the point. The proper *quid pro quo* for wage restraint is not profit restraint, but dividend restraint;[1] and, as my paper argues, it is perfectly possible to devise a scheme which ensures that the proportionate increase in total dividend disbursements does not exceed the proportionate increase prescribed for wages and salaries, without imposing any rigid limitation on the dividends paid by individual companies. It is quite feasible to devise a workable scheme which is "fair" to both parties. But it is idle to expect that the trade unions will accept an "incomes policy" which is merely a euphemism for a one-sided control on wage increases.[2]

My 1950 scheme for a flexible dividend restraint, under which companies would be free to increase dividends so long as their dividends did not exceed some standard percentage of earnings, was strongly criticised in official quarters on the ground that it would be "unfair" as between companies, particularly as between those with differing ratios of preference to ordinary capital. This seemed to me a wholly insufficient ground for rejecting a proposal that would have made it possible to put a policy of income-restraint on a more permanent basis. In the event, the Government opted (in the summer of 1951) for a complete (statutory) dividend limitation for a three year period, a scheme which may have been "fair" as between companies—in so far as any scheme which just freezes the existing situation satisfies the ordinary man's sense of fairness—but which would have certainly stored up inflationary trouble for the future if it had been adopted.[3] In the intervening 13 years, wages, dividends and prices went on merrily rising, but as far as I can judge, no intellectual advance has been made on the question of how to conduct a successful "incomes policy," despite the recent emergence of many converts. Looking back on what I wrote, I still feel that something on the lines of this paper

[1] Some people might dispute this on the ground that shareholders benefit in the form of capital gains, and not only in the form of dividend increases. However, share values invariably reflect *expected* dividend payments; a long-term control on dividend increases will therefore reduce the rate of accrual of capital gains as well as of dividend income.

[2] Between 1955 and 1961, both total wage payments and average earnings a head in manufacturing industry increased at a compound rate of 6 per cent. a year. Over the same period, dividends on ordinary shares of non-nationalised companies increased at a compound rate of 10·5 per cent. a year. If wage increases are to be reduced to 3·5 per cent. a year, as the Government suggests, clearly something needs to be done to ensure that the increase in aggregate dividend disbursements is also reduced to this percentage—if necessary by imposing some restraint on the proportion of current earnings that are distributed.

[3] As a result of the return of the Conservatives in the October election, the proposals were never adopted.

(the general idea both as regards wages and dividends is capable of course of a great many variations)[1] is probably the most hopeful approach to this problem in a democratic society; and if I were asked to review the problem afresh I doubt if I would have anything very different to offer—though I might not put the objective of attaining *complete* price-stability quite so high as I did then.

My subsequent change of view on this question was due to the recognition that, in a capitalist economy, a *"gently* rising price level" is probably the best of possible alternatives: unless the economy is a highly dynamic one, enjoying a high rate of growth of productivity, a policy of stable prices and a very moderate rate of growth of money incomes may not yield sufficient profit to sustain the process of investment and growth. This theme is developed in the memorandum to the Radcliffe Committee (pp. 137–9) and at more length in the second of the two lectures on growth and inflation (pp. 184–90). On both occasions I referred to the original contribution of D. H. Robertson who, in his 1922 book on *Money*, was the first economist to perceive this clearly. However, Robertson, who became an inveterate anti-inflationist in his later years, resented my references to his early writing as mischievous—a "poisoned kiss."[2] This was sad for, however much we came to differ in recent years, I never ceased to admire the way in which he could appeal to both reason and imagination in masterly prose. The passages reproduced on p. 188–89 give an excellent example of his style.

The two lectures on "Economic Growth and The Problem of Inflation" drew on the new dynamic theories of growth (as of 1959) to analyse the highly topical issue of the causes and consequences of the continuing rise in the price-level. These theories are summarised in the first lecture.[3] The second argued that, while a

[1] It would be possible, for example, to tie the maximum of permitted dividend increases to some percentage of the *increase* in profits available for distribution, irrespective of the initial relationship between dividends and earnings.

[2] *Growth, Wages, Money* (the Marshall Lectures for 1960), Cambridge University Press, 1961, p. 25.

[3] The one important respect in which I would now amend the exposition of the theory given on pp. 171-176 relates to the assumption of constant (short-period) prime costs. I did not realise then that this assumption—which makes a constant "mark-up" equivalent to a constant *share* of profit in income—was not just a simplification, but was definitely misleading. In industry, short period labour costs per unit of output are not constant, but falling (mainly on account of the influence of "overhead labour"); as a result of this, changes in the ratio of investment to output can elicit corresponding

certain degree of inflation stimulates growth (by stimulating investment), economic growth in turn stimulates inflation—because a
rise in production involves a rise in profits which, in turn, leads to
a rise in wages; the rise in wages causes profits to rise even faster.

This is consistent with both a "cost-push" theory and a
"demand-pull" theory of wage increases; according to the former,
the rise in money wages is governed by the bargaining power of
labour, which is in turn dependent upon the rise in profits;
according to the latter, it is governed by the competitive bidding
for labour by employers, which is dependent upon the degree to
which labour is scarce (as measured by unemployment). Since
the policy implications of these two hypotheses are very different,
it is a matter of considerable importance to know which of them
(if either) is correct. In the lecture (pp. 190–4) I came down
strongly in favour of the "cost-push" theory and advanced various
reasons why A. W. Phillips' historical findings in support of the
"demand-pull" theory are not conclusive. Since that time, a
number of empirical studies have been made[1] and, in the light of

changes in the *share* of profits (and hence in the savings ratio) even if the "mark up" is
constant; it follows from this that it is not *necessary* to assume full employment in order
that the "Keynesian" mechanism of adjusting the savings ratio to the investment
coefficient should operate. (Cf. R. R. Neild, *Pricing, Employment and The Trade Cycle*,
Cambridge University Press, chs. 4 and 6, particularly p. 52.)

[1] Cf. R. G. Lipsey and M. D. Steuer, "The Relation between Profits and Wage
Rates," *Economica*, May 1961, pp. 137–55; R. J. Bhatia, "Unemployment and the
Rate of Change of Money Earnings in the United States, 1900–1958," *Economica*,
August 1961, pp. 286–96; "Profits and the Rate of Change in Money Earnings in the
United States, 1935–1959," *Economica*, August 1962, pp. 255–62. Joint Economic
Committee, U.S. Congress *Staff Report on Employment, Growth and Price Levels*, ch. 5,
and also Study Paper No. 21, *Postwar Movement of Prices and Wages in Manufacturing
Industries*, by Harold M. Levinson, Washington, U.S. Government Printing Office,
24 December 1959 and 30 January 1960.

Lipsey and Steuer found that the "unemployment" theory provides a better explanation than the "profits" theory for the post-war period in the U.K. (and probably
also for the pre-1913 period) whilst the profits theory provides the better explanation
for the inter-war period. Bhatia found that the unemployment theory does not fit the
data for the United States, least of all for the post-war period; on the other hand, both
the level of profits and the rate of change of profits have been closely associated with the
rate of change in wages, assuming a two-months' lag in the response of wages to
profits. Levinson (for the U.S. Joint Economic Committee) found that for 19 U.S.
industries in the 1947–58 period, changes in money earnings showed a strong correlation with profits, lagged one year, but no significant relationship was found between
changes in earnings and changes in employment, productivity, or total output.

More recently, A. G. Hines' investigations gave strong support to the "cost-
push" theory. He found that the level of unionisation and changes in the rate of unionisation give a far better statistical explanation of the rate of change in money wages in
the U.K. than either the level or the rate of change of unemployment. (Cf. his paper,
"Trade Unions and Wage Inflation in the United Kingdom, 1893-1961," to be published in a forthcoming issue of the *Review of Economic Studies*.)

these, I would now concede that my condemnation of the Phillips theory was too sweeping and that, in times of acute labour shortage, the "demand-pull" theory *may* provide a better explanation of the mechanics of wage inflation than the "cost-push" theory. On the other hand, both the Lipsey-Steuer findings for the interwar period, and Bhatia's (and Levinson's) findings for the U.S. in the post-war period are sufficient to invalidate Phillips' conclusions that the wage-spiral can be avoided merely by maintaining a modest percentage of unemployment; they tend to confirm my conclusion that, so long as the economy is growing and not stagnating, the profit-wage spiral will cause wages to rise in excess of the rise in productivity, even when no shortage of labour prevails. Indeed the present general acceptance of the need for an "incomes policy" is sufficient evidence that "damping down" is no longer regarded as an effective method for combating inflation, if stagnation is to be avoided.

The last group of essays printed in this volume arises from my role as a tax specialist—a role which I assumed, rather belatedly and unexpectedly, as a result of the minority report of the Royal Commission on Taxation and my book on *An Expenditure Tax*. This role took me to many faraway lands and exotic places to assist in the universal quest for more public revenue; and, since I invariably urged the adoption of reforms which put more of the burden of taxation on the privileged minority of the well-to-do, and not only on the broad masses of the population, it earned me (and the governments I advised) a lot of unpopularity, without, I fear, always succeeding in making the property-owning classes contribute substantial amounts to the public purse.

The main reason for this—as indicated in the paper I wrote at the request of the American journal, *Foreign Affairs*, reproduced on pp. 255-65—undoubtedly lay in the fact that the power, behind the scenes, of the wealthy property-owning classes and business interests, proved to be very much greater than the responsible political functionaries (whether Presidents, Prime Ministers or Ministers of Finance) suspected. Thus when the Finance Minister of India, Mr. T. T. Krishnamachari, made an honest and determined attempt, in his April 1957 Budget, to bring the tax system of India more into conformity with the "socialist pattern of society," which was so loudly proclaimed as the major political objective of the Congress Party, he faced the most bitter opposition, first in the Cabinet and then in Parliament, and was forced into a Parliamentary battle which can have few historical parallels, apart perhaps from Lloyd George's famous fight following upon the 1909 Budget. But, unlike Lloyd George, he failed, in the end, to carry his scheme into law, except in a much truncated and emasculated form. In the case of Ceylon, Mr. Solomon Bandaranaike's Government was strong enough to get the tax-reform proposals, relatively unscathed, on the statute book; but the Governments which succeeded him after his tragic death (he was murdered, I am relieved to know, by some fanatical Buddhist monks, on a racial issue, and not by enraged millionaires) were not powerful enough (or perhaps desirous enough) to enforce them. In two other countries whose Governments requested my advice—Mexico and Turkey—and which were more in need of an honest tax reform than any of the others, the proposals put forward were blocked long before the legislative stage: in Mexico, I believe, on account of the reluctance of the President and his Cabinet; in Turkey, mainly on account of the violent opposition of the landed interest, which caused the collective resignation of the top officials of the State Planning Organisation.

Finally, in two countries which adopted my proposals—Ghana and British Guiana—the presentation of the Budget led, almost immediately, to an ugly political situation, with an attempt, in each case, to overthrow the Government through strike action.[1] In both, the organisers of the strike made the introduction of a scheme of compulsory savings the main ostensible ground for their action, despite the fact that almost none of the workers on strike were affected by it.[2] These events have shown that in under-

[1] For an account of these events in Ghana, cf. *Statement by the Government on the Recent Conspiracy*, Accra: Government Printing Department, 11 December 1961. For the account of the events in British Guiana, cf. *Report of the Commission of Inquiry into Disturbances in British Guiana in February*, 1962, Colonial White Paper No. 354, London, H.M.S.O., 1962.

[2] The proposals for compulsory savings provided for a deduction of 5 per cent. on wages and salaries, repayable with accrued interest after 7–10 years; but in each case there was an exemption limit high enough to relieve all but the highly paid skilled workers from the charge. For an account and appreciation of the British Guiana Budget, cf. paragraphs 43–5 of the *Report of the Commission of Inquiry*, quoted above.

developed countries the moneyed interest is capable of exerting its influence in strange and unexpected ways: if not through the Cabinet, or through Parliament, or through the revenue administration, then in the last resort, through organised labour.[1] It also operates (as more recent events in British Guiana have shown) through the deliberate fomentation of racial antagonism.

My experience as a tax adviser has thus brought me face to face with the realities of *power*, in a setting that is not normally within the province of an economist. In retrospect, I do not think that the advice I gave was wrong.[2] In most underdeveloped countries, where extreme poverty co-exists with great inequality in wealth and consumption, progressive taxation is, in the end, the only alternative to complete expropriation through violent revolution. It is the only alternative instrument for curbing the power of wealth, for mobilising resources for development, and for loosening the paralysing hold of traditional social and economic relationships. The progressive leaders of underdeveloped countries may seem ineffective if judged by immediate results; but they are the only alternatives to Lenin or Mao Tse-Tung. We must offer them advice on the best means of achieving their social and economic aims within as democratic a framework as their circumstances permit. And experience has reinforced my conviction that it is only if they persist, undaunted by setbacks, in their efforts to change the socio-economic profile through tax reform that they can hope to succeed.

Of the five essays reproduced here, the first, a lecture given to a group of chartered accountants, deals mainly with the tax system of Britain. The second analyses the tax reform adopted in India in 1957, following on the recommendations I had made in the

---

[1] Thus the "T.U.C." of British Guiana demanded the withdrawal of the anti-avoidance provisions concerning the taxation of business profits, and of the tax on advertising, as one of the "conditions" for calling off the general strike. Similarly, the railway unions of Ghana demanded the withdrawal of the new income tax provisions on *foreign* companies, of the property tax, and the purchase tax on luxury goods—none of which affected the workers in whose name these demands were put forward.

[2] The political problems would have been a great deal easier if in some instances—notably Ghana and British Guiana—the political situation had been more stable, and if the exigencies of the financial situation had not made it necessary to raise indirect taxation sharply in the same budget in which the reform of the direct tax system was introduced. The simultaneous action on two fronts made it possible for the élite, which disliked the basic reform of the direct tax system, to misrepresent the budget as one mainly aimed at the poorer classes—which, of course, it was not.

previous year. The third, prepared for a Conference on Fiscal Reform by the Organisation of American States in Santiago, Chile, sums up the lessons derived from my experience, and sets out the major requirements of an efficient system of taxation in such countries, as I see them. The fourth, already referred to, after describing the same problem more briefly for a general audience, deals with the political and social obstacles to tax reform.

The last paper, entitled "A Memorandum on the Value-Added Tax" is of a rather different character. It was written recently at the request of the Richardson Committee on Turnover Taxation, and it mainly deals with the long controversial issue of the incidence and economic effects of taxes on business profits in "advanced" countries, like the U.K. and the U.S. The merits of a value-added tax should be judged, not in isolation, but in relation to the effects of other taxes which it might replace or of the subsidies which it would be capable of financing. The essay will be mainly of interest to economists for its approach to price theory. However, in its final section it deals with the more specific question of how adjustments in the tax system could serve to make exports more competitive and improve the balance of payments.

Three of the papers printed in this volume have not been published previously and two others have only appeared in publications that are not easily accessible. For the rest, I am indebted to the authors or editors of the publications (the names of which are given in a footnote at the beginning of each essay) for permission to reprint them. I should also like to express my thanks to Mrs. Dorothy Hahn, who both assisted in the selection of these papers for publication and saw them in their various stages through the press.

NICHOLAS KALDOR

KING'S COLLEGE
CAMBRIDGE
December 1963

PART I
POLICIES FOR FULL EMPLOYMENT

1

WAGE SUBSIDIES AS A REMEDY FOR UNEMPLOYMENT[1]

I

ANY discussion of unemployment policy must begin by distinguishing between what I should like to call "partial" and "general" unemployment. In so far as unemployment is only *partial*, i.e. is restricted to certain industries or certain geographical areas while there is at the same time a scarcity of labour in other industries or geographical areas, the existence of unemployment is merely an outcome of a maldistribution in the supply of labour; and a permanent remedy for this kind of unemployment can only consist in the correction of this maldistribution. Such a correction is brought about—in time—automatically, through the operation of the forces of the market; and all that the State or any other authority could do is to speed this process of adjustment (by schemes of labour transference, etc.). Any other measure in this case would merely represent a palliative, not a solution of the problem, and would retard the essential readjustment.

The case is different when unemployment is *general*, i.e. when, at a given general level of wages, even the optimum redistribution of the labour force between different industries and geographical areas would not reduce to a significant extent the volume of unemployment. In this case unemployment must be the result of either a reduction in the marginal productivity of labour relatively to other factors or an increase in the cost of labour; and whatever the cause, the remedy will always involve either an increase in marginal productivity or a reduction in labour cost.[2]

Methods of reducing unemployment by increasing the productivity of labour can be grouped under three headings:

---

[1] This is a revision of a paper read at the New York meeting of the Econometric Society, December 1935, reprinted from the *Journal of Political Economy* (University of Chicago), December, 1936.

[2] One should distinguish, furthermore, between temporary and permanent causes: between "cyclical" and "technological" unemployment; but this is less important for the purposes of the present paper.

1. State employment of labour (public works), which will increase labour's marginal productivity in so far as a unit of expenditure by the State causes a larger net demand for labour than the expenditure of private individuals which it replaces.[1]

2. State stimulation of production by tariffs or subsidies, which will also increase the marginal net productivity of labour in so far as the stimulated industries have a larger relative demand for labour than the unstimulated industries which will bear the burden of the State policy.[2]

3. The acceleration of real investment through a reduction in the rates of interest. Under this heading fall all "monetary" ways of relieving unemployment (as well as an increase in the rate of capital accumulation which does not involve monetary expansion, if such is possible), irrespective of whether the monetary expansion is due to State policy or is merely the "natural" effect of "recovery".

The methods of reducing unemployment by reducing the cost of labour give us two further possibilities:

4. A reduction in the level of wages.

5. A general subsidy on wages.

All possible ways of eliminating unemployment could be brought under these five headings; and theoretically, at any rate, it should be possible to eliminate unemployment by any one of these methods, although there may be insuperable practical obstacles to carrying out some of these policies to the necessary extent. It is the purpose of this paper to show that, as between all these different methods, the one most neglected by economists and politically the least favoured,[3] a subsidy on wages, possesses, from a theoretical point of view, a distinct superiority over most of the others.

[1] I am assuming that the State expenditure in this case is covered by taxation or "non-inflationary" borrowing. In so far as it is expected to be covered by monetary expansion, it ought to fall under (3).

[2] Other things being equal, the imposition of an appropriately selected tariff can always increase the volume of employment at a given wage level—a point which is generally conceded by intelligent free-traders.

[3] The only economist of distinction, known to the present writer, who has given serious consideration to the question of wage subsidies is Professor Pigou. Cf. *The Economics of Welfare* (4th ed., London, 1932), Part IV, chap. vii, and *The Theory of Unemployment* (London, 1933), Part III, chap. iv. The only practical instance of a policy of wage subsidies on a considerable scale is the "Papen Plan" in Germany in 1932 which remained in operation only for six months.

II

Let us begin by comparing the relative effects of a given percentage reduction in wages and a subsidy on wages of an equivalent amount. For the moment we shall ignore the question of how the cost of the subsidy is raised. Then the cost per unit of labour for individual employers will be reduced by precisely the same amount in both cases; and we can only conclude that the effects on employment will also be identical, depending in both cases on the elasticity of demand for labour.

This conclusion is undoubtedly correct if we take into account the effects of an isolated wage reduction, or wage subsidy, in a single industry. When, however, a *general* wage reduction or wage subsidy is considered, certain complications arise.

In the first place, a general wage reduction by a certain percentage or amount is only feasible if there is a sufficient unemployed reserve of labour within each "non-competing group"[1] to meet the increase in the demand for labour, for wages can only be reduced up to the point at which the total available labour supply becomes employed. For the same reason, a general wage subsidy of a given percentage or amount will lead to an increase in wages, rather than an increase in employment, in those non-competing groups where the amount of unemployed labour is less than the increase in the quantity of labour demanded at the previously prevailing rate minus the subsidy. It is only by assuming that this is not the case that we can measure the effects of a given wage subsidy on employment by the elasticity of the demand for labour in industry as a whole, which is a weighted average of the elasticities of demand in individual industries.[2]

---

[1] A "non-competing group" consists of a group of industries or firms (situated in the same district for example, and using the same type of labour) within which labour is highly transferable.

[2] The elasticity of demand for labour in each industry (or non-competing group) will be different, of course, according to whether the reduction in wages only refers to the labour available to the industry (the wages in all other industries remaining constant) or whether it implies an equivalent percentage of reduction in wages for all industries. The elasticity of demand for labour in industry as a whole is obtained by taking the elasticity of the second type of demand curve for each industry and weighting it according to the amount of labour employed in each industry. It is important to bear in mind that the elasticity of the second type of demand curve is normally always larger, and may be very considerably larger, than the elasticity of demand curves of the former type (cf. Pigou, *The Theory of Unemployment*, pp. 61-76, for an analysis of this question). Roughly speaking, it is equal to what the elasticity

We shall consequently assume that a general wage subsidy is only granted in such circumstances and only to such an extent as would make a general wage reduction of an equivalent amount *technically feasible*—in other words, a general wage subsidy which

of the former type of demand curve would be, if the demand curves for all commodities were infinitely elastic. It approximates therefore the elasticity of the marginal productivity curve of labour.

Fortunately, this enables us to reduce the problem to simpler dimensions for determining the actual magnitude of this elasticity. For we know that the elasticity of the average productivity curve is always equal to

$$\frac{\text{Average product}}{\text{Average product—Marginal product}}$$

i.e. it depends on the ratio of wages to net output per head. We also know that the elasticity of marginal productivity curve is greater than, equal to, or smaller than, the elasticity of the average productivity curve, according to whether the elasticity of this latter curve is rising, constant, or falling. Finally, we can determine independently, from the ratio of wages to net output per head, the elasticity of the marginal productivity curve when it is linear, i.e. when its elasticity is falling so rapidly as to make the slope of the curve constant. In this case the elasticity of the marginal productivity curve is equal to

$$\frac{\text{Marginal product}}{2\ (\text{Average product—Marginal product})}$$

Constant elasticity curves—where the elasticities of both marginal and average curves are equal at a given level of employment—would imply that an increase in output, associated with an increase in employment, would leave the ratio of wages to output per head unchanged. A linear curve would imply that the ratio of wages to output per head is falling at a faster rate, following upon an increase in employment, than the rate of increase in employment itself. Available statistical material appears to indicate that, while an increase in employment, in the short run at any rate, is normally associated with a decrease in the proportion of labour incomes in the social dividend, this decline is not so rapid as would be required by the hypothesis of a linear marginal productivity curve. It therefore appears probable that, while the elasticities of the productivity curves are falling rather than rising, the curves are nevertheless, over the relevant range, concave (upward), i.e. that the actual value of the elasticity of labour's marginal productivity curve, and thus of the demand curve for labour as a whole, must fall between the values indicated by the hypotheses of constant elasticity and of linearity. These considerations enable us to determine the limits within which the actual value of the elasticity must fall merely from the knowledge of the relation of wages to net output per head. If, on the average, wages are three-fourths of the value of output per head, the elasticity of the demand curve for labour should fall between 4 and $1\frac{1}{2}$; while if wages are two-thirds of the value of output per head, it should be between 3 and 1; if they are only one-half, it must lie between 2 and $\frac{1}{2}$. On the whole, it appears fairly safe to regard 2 as the most probable value of this elasticity.

The foregoing calculation refers, of course, to changes in real wages (or rather, real labour-cost). It ignores the possibility of the rates of interest changing in consequence of an increase in employment, which however, as we shall see later on, is not likely to be important. It also neglects the fact that in many industries, owing to lack of competition, prices are higher than marginal costs, while in the foregoing calculation wages were regarded as being equal to the value of the marginal product of labour. This factor is not likely either to call for significant correction. For while the fact that wages are lower than the value of the marginal product of labour tends to make the ratio of marginal to average products lower, and thus the value of the elasticity of demand lower, than it really is, it also ignores the fact that increases in employment may be associated with a decline in the ratio of wages to the value of the marginal product of labour. These two factors tend to cancel each other out.

leaves the relative level of wages in different non-competing groups unaffected.[1]

In the second place, a general wage reduction will always cause some reduction, temporary or otherwise, in the demand for consumption goods, and will thus reduce, or tend to reduce, the price level of consumption goods. A given reduction in money wages will therefore be unlikely to cause the same percentage of reduction in real wages and, in consequence, will generally cause a smaller increase in the volume of employment than a given percentage of reduction in real wages. In Professor Pigou's terminology, the elasticity of the money demand for labour will be smaller than the elasticity of the real demand for labour.[2] In times of deep depression it is even possible that the effects on employment of a general reduction of money wages will be zero or negative, while the effects on employment of a reduction in real wages must always be positive.

Now, in the case of a general wage subsidy, as distinct from a wage reduction, the demand for consumption goods cannot be reduced, but only increased, as a result of the subsidy. For the money incomes of workers already in employment will be unaffected, while the money incomes of additionally employed workers will be necessarily increased. A given reduction in money labour cost, caused by a wage subsidy, will therefore necessarily lead to an equivalent or greater reduction in "real labour cost"— in other words, the elasticity of money demand for labour, in respect to wage subsidies, must be equal to, or larger, than the elasticity of the real demand for labour. We can now establish our first conclusion: that a *general subsidy on wages will, especially in times of economic depression, have far greater effects on employment than an equivalent general reduction in money wages.*[3]

---

[1] This is always much more likely to be true for small changes in labour cost than for larger changes.

[2] *The Theory of Unemployment*, pp. 100-6.

[3] The foregoing argument holds true for all monetary systems where the money rates of interest are not regulated in such a way as to keep aggregate money incomes constant (where, therefore, aggregate money income is some function of aggregate real income). It holds true, in particular, in the case where the money rates of interest remain unaffected by the change in wage rates (or the wage subsidies); and also in the case where the reduction in money wages is not offset by a sufficient reduction in the money rates of interest. Translated into Mr. Keynes's new terminology (*The General Theory of Employment, Interest and Money* (London, 1936), chap. iii), it implies that a general subsidy on wages is capable of bringing about a shift in the aggregate

The type of subsidy contemplated in the foregoing is a flat rate (either some percentage of wages or a lump sum per worker) payable on all labour and equal in all industries. It is probable that a graduated subsidy (varying in different industries and places according to the percentage of unemployment or the elasticity of demand for labour) will lead to much better results per unit of cost to the State. On the other hand, such a graduated subsidy will have effects similar to a tariff in distorting the productivity relations between different industries; and in addition it will tend to prevent necessary adjustments in the distribution of the labour supply. It should therefore only be resorted to when there is no possibility of transferring unemployed pools of labour from one industry (or place) to another; when a state of chronic unemployment is regarded as a social evil in itself; and when it is improbable that the increased output, created by the absorption of the unemployed, will merely reduce the price of exports without increasing the real income of the community. Even so, it is very much better to give a differential rate of subsidy to labour employed within certain areas than to labour employed in particular industries, for labour is generally much more highly transferable between different industries in the same area than between industries of different areas, whereas industries are often induced to move even under a slight stimulus.

It is more difficult to judge, *a priori*, the relative merits of a policy of subsidising all wages or a policy of subsidising "additional employment" only. Apart from the technical difficulties involved in administering subsidies of the latter type, it is by no means clear which of the two policies is more advantageous (from the point of view of the State) in the long run. For a subsidy on additionally employed labour alone cannot change the relative costs of production of different commodities, already produced; it can only affect the costs of additionally produced output. Nor can it affect the type of "machinery" which it is optimal to

supply function, relatively to the aggregate demand function, which, on Mr. Keynes's assumptions, is not possible in the case of a general reduction of wages. For the factor which is relevant in determining the volume of employment is not "real wages" but "real labour cost"; or rather, it is the former only on the implicit supposition that the former is always identical with the latter.

In so far as a general subsidy on wages is capable of causing a *rise* in the money rates of interest, the above conclusion may require some modification. The possibility of this is discussed below.

combine with labour already employed. In so far as the so-called "short-period elasticity" is small—which will be the case in boom times if the existing plant capacity is fully employed—the main way through which a change in labour cost will affect the volume of employment is partly through a change in the type of "machinery" used, partly through a relative increase—on account of the fall in relative costs—in the output of those commodities which contain relatively more labour. These latter effects, however, do not come into operation if only additionally employed labour is subsidised. In the long run, therefore, a given rate of subsidy on all wages will have much larger effects on employment than a subsidy on additionally employed labour, and the difference might even be so great as to make the net cost to the State (for a given amount of additional employment) ultimately less in the first case than in the second. This will be more likely the greater the amount of unemployment and the longer the period over which it has already persisted. It appears therefore that a policy of subsidising additional employment—apart from the technical difficulties connected with its administration—is more appropriate for dealing with the "cyclical" unemployment resulting from an industrial depression—when the short-period elasticity of the *real* demand of labour is large—while a policy of subsidising all wages is more appropriate for dealing with "chronic" unemployment which has resulted either from technological inventions reducing the marginal productivity of labour or trade union action raising the level of wages about the long-run "equilibrium" level. In the following we shall deal only with subsidies of the latter type, since all our conclusions as to the cost of these will hold *a fortiori* for subsidies of the former type.

III

We may now consider how far the foregoing conclusion is modified if the cost of the wage subsidy is taken into account. The consideration of this question will also enable us to judge the relative merits of a scheme of wage subsidies and of methods of alleviating unemployment through other forms of State expenditure.

Assuming that the expenditure involved in administering the

subsidy is not covered by borrowing (or monetary expansion), we have to consider, first, the net cost of a scheme of wage subsidies to the State and, second, the ultimate cost to the tax-paying community as a whole.

The net cost of the wage subsidy to the State, as we shall presently see, might be negative as well as positive; but in either case it will be smaller if the subsidy takes the form of removing an existing tax on wages (pay rolls) than in the case where the subsidy is a direct payment (of an equivalent amount), owing to the difference, in the two cases, in the volume of employment on which the tax, or subsidy is paid. The removal of existing insurance contributions paid by employers with respect to workers is therefore the optimal form of administering such a subsidy. The cost involved to the State in this case will be *negative as long as the elasticity of the demand for labour is equal to, or greater than, the ratio of wages to unemployment benefits.*

This can be proved in the following way: Let i be the rate of contribution per worker, w the rate of wages, b the rate of unemployment benefits, A the number employed at a wage rate w, h the number of additional unemployed created by increasing the cost of labour from w to $(w+i)$, e the elasticity of demand for labour. Then the condition under which the cost of the additional unemployment will be equal to the total revenue obtained from the employers' contributions can be written in the form:

$$i(A-h)=bh.$$

If $h>0$,

$$i\left(\frac{A}{h}-1\right)=b. \tag{1}$$

But since $e=\dfrac{w}{A}\cdot\dfrac{h}{i}=\dfrac{h}{A}\div\dfrac{i}{w}$,

$$\frac{A}{h}=\frac{w}{ei}. \tag{2}$$

Substituting (2) into (1),

$$\frac{w}{e}-i=b,$$

$$b+i=\frac{w}{e}.$$

Writing $b = wr$, where r is the ratio of unemployment benefits to wages,

$$e = \frac{1}{r + \dfrac{i}{w}} \cdot \qquad (3)$$

Hence

$$e < \frac{1}{r} \cdot$$

The cost of removing the contribution will therefore be negative if $e = 1/r$, since then the saving in the cost of unemployment will necessarily be larger than the loss of revenue. (This is the case, e.g., when $e = 2$ and $b = w/2$.)[1]

In the case where a direct subsidy is granted, analogous reasoning leads to the result that the elasticity of demand for labour must here be larger than ratio of wages to benefits, in order that the cost of the subsidy should be negative to the State.

Writing s for the rate of subsidy per worker, and h for the number of additionally employed, resulting from the payment of the subsidy, the cost will be zero if

$$s(A + h) = bh,$$

from which by analogous reasoning,

---

[1] In case the revenue from an insurance contribution is expected to cover the cost of maintaining those already unemployed (in addition to those who become additionally unemployed on account of the contribution), this will be possible only if

$$i(A - h) \geq b(H + h),$$

where H is the number of the initially unemployed. Assuming the two to be equal, and writing $r = b/w$, $k = A/H$, and $z = i/w$, the foregoing equation (3) becomes

$$e = \frac{1 - \dfrac{rk}{z}}{r + z} \cdot$$

On any reasonable assumption about the numerical values of r, k, z, this expression will either be negative or, if positive, will be very unlikely to be greater than 1. This method of financing unemployment insurance is therefore only possible if the elasticity of demand for labour is very small—otherwise the attempt to do so can only lead to a cumulative increase in unemployment and the total breakdown of the system. If, e.g. the initial unemployment is 10 per cent., the unemployment benefit 40 per cent. of wages, and the insurance contribution 5 per cent. (which are very conservative figures for a country like Great Britain, for instance), the elasticity of demand for labour must not be larger than 4/9. It must not be forgotten, of course, that in most countries actually only a small proportion of the cost of maintaining the unemployed is covered by employer's contributions. (In Great Britain only about 1/5 or 1/2·5, if the health insurance contributions are also included.)

$$e = \frac{1}{r - \dfrac{s}{w}} \; ;$$

hence

$$e > \frac{1}{r}, \text{ or } er > 1.$$

The percentage of increase in employment which can be created without imposing any net expenditure upon the State is:

$$\frac{h}{A} = er - 1,$$

for $\dfrac{h}{A} = \dfrac{es}{w}$, $s = b - \dfrac{w}{e}$, and $b = wr$.

It is clear from the foregoing that, on any reasonable assumptions about the elasticity of demand for labour and the cost of maintaining the unemployed, neither the removal of a pay-roll tax nor the imposition of a subsidy is likely to involve an appreciable burden upon the State; and it is possible, if not likely, that the cost will be negative to the State in both cases. The net result depends, of course, upon the elasticity of "real" demand for labour, a factor concerning which few estimates were made. We have already shown earlier[1] our reasons for supposing that 2 is the most probable value of this elasticity. According to Professor Pigou's more comprehensive calculations,[2] in periods of industrial depression, the numerical value of the short-period elasticity of real demand for labour cannot be smaller than 3; and even in the very short period, in a country like Great Britain, it is unlikely to fall below 2. The long-period elasticity would then be necessarily greater. If we accept these estimates as to the order of magnitudes involved, even if not necessarily as to the actual figure—which seems to be supported also by other researches in this field[3]—and if we further take into account that the average cost of maintaining the unemployed is likely to be as much as 40 per cent. of

[1] Cf. above, p. 6, footnote.   [2] *The Theory of Unemployment*, pp. 88-97, esp. p. 96.
[3] Paul H. Douglas, *The Theory of Wages* (New York, 1934), pp. 152 ff. Professor Douglas, by a different method, reaches the conclusion that it is 4. Professor Douglas' results appear to me to be rather exaggerated owing to his basic assumption of constant elasticity functions. Cf. on this question p. 5, n. 2, above.

wages and will, in most countries, probably fall between one-half and one-third of wages, we cannot be far wrong in assuming that the cost of such a subsidy scheme, even if positive, cannot be larger than a fraction of the amount actually distributed.[1]

IV

The foregoing results, however, become much more favourable once we turn to consider not the net cost to the State but the ultimate cost to the tax-paying community as a whole.[2] For even if, on account of either of two possible reasons—a small elasticity of demand for labour or a small rate of expenditure upon the unemployed—the cost of the wage-subsidy scheme is large, necessitating considerable additions to general taxation, the cost of the subsidy will still be negative to the tax-paying community

[1] In Great Britain the unemployment and health insurance contributions, paid by employers, amount to about 3 per cent. of wages and yield some £40,000,000. Their removal might easily increase the demand for labour by 6 per cent. within a period of two years (assuming the elasticity of demand to be 2), which would reduce unemployment by some 600,000 workers, *under the assumption that this amount of general unemployment still exists*. In that case the net cost to the State would not exceed £10,000,000. It is highly questionable, however, whether in Great Britain, at the present time, this amount of "general unemployment" is still available. If allowance is made for "normal unemployment", which is an inevitable feature of the labour market, the average unemployment in the relatively prosperous areas (south-east and south-west of England and the Midlands, which together employ about one-half of the insured working population) is probably not more than 1·5–2·0 per cent. The same measure, confined to the depressed areas (north-east and north-west England, Scotland, and Wales), where the average unemployment in excess of "normal unemployment" is still over 15 per cent., might, however, reduce unemployment by as much as 250,000–300,000 at no greater cost to the State than some £5,000,000–£7,000,000.

In the United States, the Social Security Act of 1935 provides for the gradual imposition of an aggregate tax on wages of 9 per cent., of which 6 per cent. will be paid by employers and 3 per cent. by workers. The effect of this on unemployment will depend partly on the extent to which the employers will be able to shift the incidence to the workers and partly on the phase of the business cycle which will be operative when the taxes come into operation. There is no need, of course, to assume that wages are "entirely rigid" in order that the imposition of the pay-roll tax should have a permanent effect on employment. Unless the elasticity of the supply curve of labour is actually zero—and such an assumption is certainly not warranted by experience—the employers can at best shift a part, but not the whole, of the tax burden in the form of reduced wages to the workers. Assuming that in the United States employers generally will be able to shift as much as one-half of the taxes in the form of wage reductions, and assuming that the elasticity of demand for labour as a whole is 2, the net effect of the pay-roll taxes imposed by the Social Security Act will be to decrease the volume of employment by over 2,000,000 below the level it would have reached otherwise.

[2] For simplicity we assume that the term "tax-paying community" comprises all classes other than wage-earners (which will be the case if, e.g. the sums required to finance wage subsidies are raised by means of the income tax). In case part of the additional taxation falls on wage earners (if, e.g. the scheme is financed by means of a sales tax), the balance of gain from the point of view of non-wage-earners will be still more favourable than in the results given above.

as a whole, since the wage subsidy will augment taxpayers' incomes by almost as much as the subsidy itself. With regard to that part of the subsidy which is paid on labour already in employment, the tax-paying community's income is augmented by precisely the same amount as the total amount of the subsidy, while on additionally employed labour, the loss to the tax-paying community is not likely to be larger than half the rate of subsidy per additionally employed worker,[1] without allowing for the saving in unemployment benefits. The net burden on the taxpayers as a whole will therefore necessarily be negative as long as the rate of subsidy per worker is less than twice the cost of maintaining the unemployed (the rate of unemployment benefit per worker), and this will certainly be the case under all conceivable circumstances.[2,3] This conclusion, moreover, is *independent*

[1] Since the value of the product created by additional employment cannot fall short of the cost of additional employment by much more than this amount. For the cost of additional employment will be hw; while the value created by additional employment is, under the assumption that the demand curve for labour is a straight line within the range of A and $A+h$, equal to the area of the trapezoid bounded by $w - A - (A+h) - (w-s)$, which is $(w+w-s)(h/2) = h[w - (s/2)]$. If the demand curve is concave (upward), it will be slightly more than this; if it is convex, it will be slightly less (cf. also Pigou, *Economics of Welfare* (4th ed.), p. 701). In the absence of purely competitive conditions the additional product associated with an h increase in employment will be necessarily larger than $h[w - (s/2)]$, and thus the balance of gain more favourable from the point of view of non-wage-earners.

[2] The total cost will be $s(A+h) - sA + h(w-s) - h[w - (s/2)] - bh = (s/2)h - bh$. The negative of this sum represents, therefore, the net gain in income accruing to all classes other than wage-earners as a result of the payment of the subsidy, while the net gain of wage-earners as a class will be $h(w-b)$. The net gain of *all* classes (the increase in the national dividend)—which, as we have seen, is $h[w - (s/2)]$—will be distributed therefore among wage-earners and non-wage-earners in the ratio of $[w-b]/[b - (s/2)]$. If we allow for the fact that a part of the additional product is likely to be made for export, an adjustment has to be made for the change in the real ratio of international trade consequent upon the increase in output. In that case the net increase in the social dividend will be, not $h[w - (s/2)]$, but $[h - hk(1/\eta)] \cdot [w - (s/2)]$, where k is the proportion of additionally employed workers engaged in producing export goods and η the elasticity of foreign demand for export goods. The balance of gain from the point of view of non-wage-earners will, however, still be positive so long as

$$k\frac{1}{\eta} < \frac{b - \dfrac{s}{2}}{w - \dfrac{s}{2}},$$

which is likely to be the case for most industrial countries.

[3] It is important to bear in mind that, contrary to appearances, the net cost to the tax-paying community as a whole will always be less if this subsidy is paid on all labour than if it is paid on additional employment only. For the cost of the subsidy paid for labour already in employment is exactly offset by the gain from the receipt of such a subsidy; while the cost of the subsidy paid on additionally employed labour will be all the more negative the larger the amount of additional employment created by any given rate of subsidy. We have seen above (p. 8) that in the former case this increase will always be larger than in the latter case.

of the elasticity of demand for labour as long as this elasticity is greater than zero. A scheme of wage subsidies will therefore always increase total output, and this will always partly augment the total income of labour and partly augment the total income of the rest of the community. The extent of this increase, following a given rate of subsidy, will also depend on the effect of the scheme (and of the methods adopted to finance it) on the "liquidity preferences" of individuals, i.e. to what extent it causes a net monetary expansion.

Suppose, e.g. that a certain wage subsidy is granted (say a lump sum per worker) in the form of a relief (or credit) from general income tax, proportional to the number of workers employed by the income or corporation taxpayer, while the general rate of taxation is raised to a corresponding extent so as to provide the same income to the State. For the time being, the total amount raised by taxation will be the same as before, while gradually, as the number of unemployed and the cost of unemployment diminish, the State will be in a position to lower the general rate of taxation. At the beginning, at any rate, some people will pay more, others less, in taxes (than before), but the net income of taxpayers as a whole will remain the same; and even the net income of every income class, taken separately, will be likely to remain unchanged. The only change will be a shifting in the burden of taxation from those who employ relatively much labour (per unit of income) to those employing relatively little labour, i.e. from "employers" to "rentiers". The relative increase in the yield of capital along those lines where investment involves a heavy pay roll will be the main factor tending to increase employment, in precisely the same way as in the case of a general reduction in real wages; the only difference being that, whereas in the case of a wage reduction the yield of all capital will increase, in the case of a wage subsidy financed by taxation the yield in some lines will increase, in others decrease; the change in relative yields, however, will be precisely the same in both cases.

This implies that if the rate of investment (per unit of time) is constant—which also carries with it that the effective quantity of money, MV, remains the same—the increase in employment created by a wage subsidy and financed by taxation will be the same as the one which would be brought about by an equivalent reduction in *real* wages. This is no longer necessarily true, however, if the monetary effects are taken into account, for one of the effects of a reduction of real labour cost is the enlargement of investment opportunities available at given rates of interest and the consequent increase in the volume of funds seeking investment. This expansion, on the other hand, can be assumed to be all the larger the greater is the increase in prospective yields *in general*. Since the immediate increase in the rate of taxation needed to finance wage subsidies is necessarily larger than the ultimate increase, while investors in calculating future yields—in so far as they deduct income taxes from the yield of capital—can be presumed to regard future rates of taxation as being identical with ruling rates, there is a prima facie case for financing the initial expenditure on wage subsidies by borrowing rather than by taxation (apart from any desire to stimulate monetary expansion)—at any rate, to the extent to which the initial rate of net additional expenditure exceeds the expected permanent rate of net additional expenditure, for such a policy is likely to reduce the permanent rate of expenditure itself.

It remains to examine the possibility of how far a scheme of wage subsidies could lead to a contraction, rather than an expansion, of the aggregate volume of investment. (This might be the case if the policy led to a rise in the long-term money rates of interest.) It will be sufficient to examine the situation in the limiting case, where the whole amount of the subsidy is financed by an increase in the general rate of taxation and where the whole amount raised by direct taxation is levied on entrepreneurs and property-owners, and none on the recipients of "earned incomes". In this case, as we have seen, the average income from capital remains the same as before,[1] while there will be an increase in the income from those types of investment which operate with relatively large expenditure of labour, and a fall in the income from

[1] This is true under the assumption that the money demand for consumption goods remains unchanged. But, as we have seen, in the case of a general wage subsidy, as distinct from a wage reduction, the aggregate money income of wage-earners necessarily increases; and thus the effects on the aggregate money demand for consumption goods can only be favourable. Thus, while general wage reductions tend to set up anticipations of a sort calculated to nullify the effect of the reductions on the labour market, a general wage subsidy should not greatly affect anticipations; and, in so far as it does, it is likely to do so in a favourable direction.

those whose wages bill is relatively small. Expressed in terms of the stock exchange, the price of Government securities would fall and the price of industrials rise. Any tendency toward "bearishness" created by the former will be offset by a tendency toward "bullishness" created by the latter. Even in this case, therefore, there seems to be no more reason to assume that the net effect will imply increased hoarding than to suppose that it will imply dishoarding. If we take into account, first, that not all income subject to taxation is capital income and, second, that the total amount of additional taxation will always be smaller (and may be very considerably smaller) than the amount distributed in subsidies—owing to the saving in the cost of unemployment—it becomes overwhelmingly probable that the imposition of such a subsidy scheme will lead to monetary expansion rather than contraction.

V

The argument so far has assumed that the subsidies leave the rate of wages everywhere unaffected, which will be true in so far as the rate of subsidy is not large enough to create an effective scarcity of labour in any of the "non-competing groups", and in so far as labour will not demand an increase in the rate of wages so long as unemployment is higher than "normal". It is, of course, difficult to say how far either of these assumptions is legitimate in practice. In so far as the subsidy creates significant increases in wages (or in a significant part of the system) the wage subsidy ceases to be an unemployment-relief measure and becomes a measure of socialistic income redistribution, for then the subsidy will not benefit employers but only workers. The political danger, therefore, arising out of such a scheme as a permanent measure is that it might lead to an ever increasing demand for a rise in the rate of wages paid, which individual employers might be willing to concede in the hope of recouping themselves by extorting from the State a corresponding increase in the rates of subsidies on wages. Such a development, pushed far enough, might reduce the net income from capital so seriously as to defeat its own end by causing capital consumption on a large scale. As a long-run measure, therefore, a scheme of wage subsidies is only feasible if the money rates of wages can be technically stabilised—in other words, if the State authority is powerful enough to make the payment of wage subsidies conditional upon the maintenance of a steady level of money wages.[1]

This latter problem, however, does not affect the argument in favour of a removal of existing taxes on wages, for the psychological expectations which might be created by a direct subsidy will not arise merely through a removal of a tax. There is, in fact, no feasible argument in favour of a policy of taxing wages or pay rolls—at any rate, while unemployment prevails. The ultimate reasons why such a tax is so much more pernicious in its effects than an income tax or a tax on other factors of production are twofold. In the first place, factors of production other than labour will only go out of use if their net productivity (minus the tax) becomes zero. Labour, on the other hand, has always a "reserve price", and will become unemployed even if its net marginal productivity is positive. In the second place, the existence of unemployed labour involves a special cost of maintenance upon the community, which must be deducted from the revenue which the taxes yield, which is not so in the case of "ultra-marginal" land or "ultra-marginal" machines. There can be no doubt that the policy manifest in the latest social security legislation of the United States is thus in flat contradiction to all canons of economic science.[2]

VI

We are now in a position to compare the relative advantages of subsidising wages or of relieving unemployment by any of the other methods, such as public works, the stimulation of production or interest reduction through monetary expansion.

1. It should be clear from the previous analysis that the creation of a given amount of additional employment through public works must involve a relatively larger cost to the community,

---

[1] This does not imply, of course, a stabilisation of the real income of labour. In so far as the real productivity of labour is increasing, the real income of labour will also increase, in the form of falling prices of consumption goods. It does imply, however, a monetary policy designed to stabilise the rate of money wages rather than the price level of consumption goods.

[2] In order to avoid misunderstanding, it should be pointed out that nothing said above was meant to provide an argument against social insurance itself. It is only the particular method adopted by various countries for financing social insurance which is held to be pernicious, both from a financial and an economic point of view.

unless (a) the excess of the cost of the employment per unit of labour over the value of the product, created by public works, is equal to, or smaller than, (b) half the rate of subsidy which secures the same additional employment. For we have seen reasons to assume that in the case of wage subsidies (a) is unlikely to exceed (b), irrespective of the elasticity of demand for labour.

Now the "product" created by public works is frequently of such nature that it is difficult to assign a definite "market value" to it. Nor is there any need to do so (in order to make such a comparison), as long as the "public works" in question are of a kind which ordinarily fall within the scope of activities of public authorities (such as road-building, etc.). There is every reason to concentrate such works in times of slack business. It is only when public works involve activities which are not ordinarily undertaken by public bodies—and which are only undertaken in order to relieve unemployment—that a comparison has to be made between the value created by such public works and the value which the same quantity of labour could have created if absorbed by private industry. In regard to the latter type of public works, there is an *a priori* reason to believe that the value created by them will be relatively smaller—unless the State authority is sufficiently wise to employ labour in precisely those "submarginal" uses for which labour would have been employed if a wage subsidy or a wage reduction had induced entrepreneurs to employ them. The increase in the social dividend created by an increase in public employment is likely to be smaller, therefore, than that caused by the same increase in private employment achieved through wage subsidies.

The same argument still applies when the prime motive behind a policy of public works is to stimulate monetary expansion. In so far as the difference between the cost of additional employment and the value of product created by additional employment is greater in the case of public employment than in the case of private employment, the same amount of stimulation must necessarily create a larger increase in the national dividend if it is spent in the form of subsidies on employment than if it is spent directly in the form of public works.

Moreover, there is an important technical reason why a policy of wage subsidies is preferable to a policy of public works—at any rate, when it is a question of evening out the fluctuations in employment due to the trade cycle. It should not be beyond the capacity of an efficient government so to regulate the rate of subsidy as to secure a stable volume of employment at a stable wage level. But even a very efficient government would find it difficult to produce public-works projects with sufficient rapidity and scope, and with sufficient elasticity in their proposed duration, to secure this effect. The necessity of forming an accurate judgment of the business situation at all times makes the prospects of success from such a stabilising policy somewhat doubtful in both cases. But even if we credit governments with the ability of forming such judgment, it is still very much easier—at short notice—to alter the rate of subsidy (or tax) than to alter the scope and extent of public works.

2. An argument similar to the foregoing can be applied to the question of tariffs or subsidies on production. It is easy to see that the effects of these two policies—a subsidy on wages versus a subsidy on output—can never be identical; and if they diverge, it is the cost of wage subsidies which is smaller, from the point of view of the community as a whole. Even if we assume the State authority to be sufficiently wise to stimulate precisely those industries which would be stimulated by a reduction in labour cost, the incentive to substitute labour for capital in production, within the same industry, will be absent; and consequently it will require a much larger degree of stimulation (in the second case) to produce the same effects on employment. (The two policies could yield identical results only if the technical coefficients were entirely rigid in all industries.)

The same point can also be put in a different way. A scheme of general wage subsidies (at any rate, within the limits of our assumptions as to the distribution of unemployment or the mobility of labour) will reproduce exactly the same effects as to the distribution of resources between different uses that would come about in an "ideally free" labour market, which, in turn—external economies or diseconomies apart—is always the arrangement which maximises the aggregate volume of output, measured in terms of value.[1] As Wicksell has pointed out,[2] if in a particular case the circumstances are such that the free operation of the forces of the market would tend to depress wages and the standard of living of labour, it is always very much better to subsidise wages than to restrict the scope of free competition.[3]

3. There remains the third possibility: to raise the equilibrium rate of wages through a reduction in the rates of interest. An adequate consideration of this alternative would lead us right into the centre of the controversial section of trade cycle theory and would far extend the scope of this paper. I shall therefore confine myself to a few cursory remarks.

There can be no doubt that, if the structure of interest rates could be permanently lowered, the volume of employment at a given wage level would also be permanently raised; in fact, this is one of the few conclusions on which economists of all shades of opinion seem to be agreed. Their disagreement refers rather to the question whether this effect is, in fact, attainable through the monetary policy of the State. The present writer is not one of those who believe that the maintenance of a lower level of interest rates necessarily involves a process of "cumulative inflation". Since the marginal productivity of investment is generally a diminishing function of the volume of investment, the cumulative effects of an "inflationary" monetary policy need not come into operation so long as there is unemployed labour to draw upon at a

---

[1] Under the assumption that the aggregate quantity of available labour can be regarded as given and differences in the relative attractiveness of different occupations can be disregarded.

[2] In the section on the effects of technical inventions on wages in *Lectures on Political Economy* (London, 1934), chap. i, p. 141.

[3] This is also the answer to the natural objection that the introduction of wage subsidies would retard economic progress by preventing the introduction of labour-saving inventions. It is true that wage subsidies might retard the introduction of some labour-saving inventions. But they do so only to the extent to which this is beneficial to the community (from the point of view of the maximisation of the national dividend). For wage subsidies, however large, can never reduce the effective cost of labour to employers below the level which would obtain in a "truly competitive" labour market (if they did the rise in wage rates would adjust this); and, as Wicksell has conclusively demonstrated (*ibid.*, pp. 133–41), the national dividend is only benefited by such technical innovations whose profitability is consistent with factor prices which secure full employment for the factors of production. The adoption of inventions which are only profitable if the cost of labour is higher than the level which secures full employment will reduce, and not increase, the national dividend. It is only by assuming that wage subsidies lead to a lengthening of hours wage-earners are willing to work (or prevent a reduction of hours which would otherwise have taken place) that the question of an unhealthy stimulation of "labour-wasting" methods of production could arise.

given level of wages.[1] It is thus conceivable that the State should, by a single well-chosen dose of inflation, permanently increase the capital equipment of the community. At the same time, such a policy, in order to be successful, would have to take into account the reactions which the policy itself creates upon the price expectations and the degrees of uncertainties felt by investors and entrepreneurs; and it must be in a position to compensate adequately for any changes in the demand for money which it creates. It is highly improbable that such a policy could be carried out by the methods at present available to central banking technique, which is confined to a regulation of the quantity of money either by rationing or by changing the short-term rate of interest (either through the policy of the discount rate or through open-market operations). This would only be sufficient if the short-term rate always stood in some rigid (or independent) relation to the various long-term rates. The monetary experience of recent years has clearly demonstrated that this is not the case: the one reacts upon the other, if at all, only through a considerable time lag.[2] A policy of regulating the "structure of interest rates" would therefore only be feasible through a vast extension in the scope of open-market operations so as to cover all types of long-term securities as well—in fact, through a regulation of the entire capital market.[3] It would be beyond the scope of this paper to examine further the technical feasibility of such a policy. For our purpose it will be sufficient to have demonstrated that the effects on production and employment which could be secured by an adequate regulation of the structure of interest rates can be equally achieved through a regulation of real labour costs by means of wage subsidies, leaving the question open as to which is more amenable to the regulatory powers of the State.

[1] A given reduction in interest rates will increase employment in two ways: primarily, through the expansion of investment, created by the fall in the interest rates; secondarily, through the further increase in investment created by the increase in the yield of capital goods, which is due to the increase in consumption associated with the larger volume of employment. If the reduction in the rates of interest is such that the sum of the primary and secondary effects involves a lesser addition to employment than the volume of unemployed labour available, the maintenance of the lower interest rates will not require a continuous credit expansion.

[2] Cf. Keynes, op. cit., p. 197.

[3] Moreover, if the "liquidity preference" of the public is such that they are unwilling to hold illiquid assets at all below certain prospective yields, no amount of monetary expansion can be sufficient to secure rates of interest lower than these minimal yields.

2

THE QUANTITATIVE ASPECTS OF THE FULL EMPLOYMENT PROBLEM IN BRITAIN[1]

1. The purpose of this memorandum is to examine what a full employment policy would involve, in terms of the revenue and expenditure of public authorities, assuming that the principle is accepted that the fiscal policies of the State are so regulated as to secure adequate total outlay for the community as a whole. Any such analysis of the quantitative aspects of the full employment problem requires a large number of hypotheses and assumptions resting on more or less firm statistical foundations. We shall set out these hypotheses and assumptions as fully as possible so as to enable the reader who has reason to differ from them to revise the estimate accordingly.[2]

2. We shall begin by giving a brief account of the nature of the alternative policies by which full employment may be secured, and showing their general implications. After this introduction, the actual statistical analysis will be tackled in two stages: first by examining the implications of the full employment policies in the circumstances of pre-war Britain; second, the nature of the problem in the conditions that will probably arise after the war.

I. ALTERNATIVE METHODS OF SECURING FULL EMPLOYMENT BY FISCAL POLICIES

3. There are many ways in which a Government desirous of ensuring full employment can so regulate the fiscal policies of the State as to ensure adequate total outlay for the community as a whole; but they can all be reduced to four distinct types. The first is by increased public expenditure covered by loans; the second is by increased public expenditure covered by taxation; the third is

---

[1] A memorandum prepared for Sir William Beveridge's Committee on Full Employment and published as Appendix C to *Full Employment in a Free Society* by Sir William Beveridge (London, 1944).

[2] I am indebted to Dr. T. Barna both for working out the statistical correlations involved, and for allowing the use of yet unpublished estimates regarding the incidence of taxation.

by increased private spending brought about through remission of taxation, and the fourth is by increased private spending brought about through changing the incidence of taxation or imposing a combined system of taxes and subsidies. The first two methods imply that idle resources are primarily absorbed for purposes that are determined by, or are under the control of, the State; the last two that they are absorbed in uses determined by private citizens. The first and the third (though not the second or the fourth) imply "deficit spending"—i.e. a state of affairs where aggregate State expenditure, for all purposes, exceeds total State revenue from taxation and public property, and where in consequence there is continuous public borrowing. We shall examine the implications of each of these policies.

4. An increase in the scale of public expenditure with given *rates* of taxation, will increase the total outlay of the community on home-produced goods and services by a greater amount than the rise in the public expenditure itself, since—on account of the increase in incomes and the increase in productive activity to which it gives rise—it will lead to increased private expenditures. The size of this secondary expansion will depend on three factors; first, on the way private citizens allocate the increase in their incomes (their "marginal" incomes) between taxation, savings, and consumption; second, on the extent to which increased spending by the Government, and increased spending by private citizens, leads to an increase in capital expenditures by industry (the increase in "private investment"); and third, on the proportion of the increased demand for goods and services of all kinds which goes to home-produced and to imported goods and services respectively. If by means of a policy of increasing public outlay, while keeping the existing rates of taxation constant, an expansion of demand is generated that is sufficient to absorb unemployed resources, (i) the total increase in the demand for goods and services will be *greater* than the value of the potential output of unemployed resources, since part of the increase in demand will be directed abroad; (ii) the increase in public expenditure will be *less* than the total increase in demand, since there will be a consequential increase in private consumption and private investment; (iii) the increase in public borrowing (the size of the

deficit) will be *less* than the increase in public expenditure, since the higher expenditure will increase the yield of existing taxation.

5. Full employment could be secured, however, by means of increased public outlay, even if the State expenditure is fully covered by taxation—for the reason that an increase in taxation is not likely to reduce private outlay by the full amount of the taxes paid. It may be assumed that all taxes have some influence on the savings of the individuals on whom they fall; taxes which fall on the poor have a relatively large effect on consumption and a relatively small effect on savings; with taxes paid by the rich it is probably the other way round. Hence an increase in public expenditure will cause a net addition to the total outlay of the community, even if it is covered by taxation; and this net addition is likely to be all the greater, the more progressive is the incidence of the extra taxation raised to cover it. But since the addition to total outlay brought about by a given expansion of public expenditure would in this case be necessarily much smaller than in the case where the rates of taxation are kept constant and there is an expansion in the rate of borrowing, the total expansion of public expenditure would have to be much greater.

6. The alternative approach to securing adequate total outlay, and hence an adequate total demand for labour, is to increase, not the State expenditure, but the expenditure of private citizens. Here also there are two different methods of procedure, according as the policy chosen involves "unbalanced budgets" or not. The creation of a budgetary deficit by the simple device of reducing taxation relatively to a given rate of expenditure will increase employment, since it converts the ordinary expenditure of the Government into "loan expenditure" which is an offset to savings. Since some part of the additional incomes made available through tax remissions would be bound to be saved by the recipients, the necessary deficit would always have to be larger, in this case, than in the case of increased public outlay; there are, on the other hand, no technical obstacles to making the deficit sufficiently large.

7. The financially orthodox method of raising private outlay relies on the stimulus given by changing the incidence of taxation: reducing the taxes falling on the relatively poor (who can be

expected to spend most of the additional incomes made available to them) and increasing the taxes falling on the relatively rich, and thereby reducing total savings at any given level of income. This can be done either by raising the degree of progressiveness of income tax and surtax at any given standard rate (increasing exemptions in the lower income brackets and graduation in the upper brackets) or by reducing indirect taxes and raising the standard rate of income tax. In order to secure an adequate expansion of outlay in this way, however, the required changes in relative taxation would have to be very large, while the scope for such changes—under the British system of taxation, which is fairly progressive in any case—is limited. To secure an adequate expansion under this method the State may have to supplement the reduction or abolition of particular taxes by the granting of subsidies (which are negative indirect taxes) either in the form of subsidies on the price of necessities (such as are given in war-time) or subsidies on wages paid to employees.[1]

In general, if considerable changes in the structure of income distribution are desired, it is better to tackle the problem directly —by forcing producers to sell at lower prices relatively to costs— than indirectly through changes in taxation or some combined scheme of taxation and subsidies. The main reason for this is that it is extremely difficult to devise a scheme where the consequential higher taxation on profits would not in itself have adverse effects on incentives and hence on employment.

8. It will be shown in Section II of this memorandum that in the kind of circumstances which existed in Great Britain in 1938, those of the above policies which did not involve loan expenditure would have been ineffective or impracticable. Full employment could have been secured (in principle) without deficit finance, either by enlarging sufficiently the range of public expenditure, or by changing (through taxation and subsidies) the distribution of

---

[1] A subsidy on wages paid to employers would—in so far as the benefit of lower wage costs is passed on to the consumers in the form of lower prices—have much the same kind of effect as subsidies on commodities or subsidies on earnings paid to employees. But in so far as, owing to rigidity of prices in some sections of the economic system, the cost-reduction cannot be relied on to result in corresponding price reductions in every case, a subsidy on wages paid to employers would be less effective as a means of raising employment than either subsidies on commodities or subsidies on wages paid to employees.

available incomes but, in either case, the policy would have involved such major changes in the social framework as to have made it—from a political and administrative point of view—very difficult to carry out. The practical alternatives therefore were either the creation of budgetary deficits through higher public outlay, or the creation of deficits through tax remissions.

9. It will be argued in Section III of this memorandum that in the circumstances of the early post-war years this will probably not be so; the needs of private industry after the war, together with the higher ratio of exports to imports, are likely to set up, for a number of years, a demand for labour that will be much more closely related to the available supply than was the case before the war. This might enable a full employment policy, for a time, to be consistent with budgetary surpluses, rather than public borrowing. But taking a longer view, there appears to be no reason why the employment problem should not again present itself in much the same aspects as in the 1930's; and once this stage is reached, the practical methods of maintaining full employment will again be the creation of loan expenditure, either by increasing public outlay, or by lowering taxation.

10. In Section III, dealing with the post-war situation, it will be assumed that (i) a rigid separation will be made in the public accounts between the ordinary running expenditures of the State and investment expenditures; (ii) that the Government will plan the rate of national investment as a whole, both privately and publicly financed; (iii) that the rates of taxation will be so adjusted as to secure continuous full employment with the planned rate of investment expenditure. It will thus be shown: first, what is the level of national investment consistent with full employment, assuming that the level of taxation is just sufficient to cover the ordinary expenditure of public authorities; and second, what are the adjustments in taxation necessary in order to secure higher levels of investment that may be more in accord with the objects of national policy. In Section IV, a brief examination will be made of the long-run aspects of the problem, with particular reference to the long-run effects of a rising National Debt.

II. THE FULL EMPLOYMENT PROBLEM IN 1938

11. In order to examine the implications of full employment policies, in the circumstances of 1938, in quantitative terms, it is necessary to make three kinds of estimate: (i) how the value of the national output would have been changed as a result of the change in employment; (ii) how the various types of income would have been changed, as a result of the changes in the value of the national output; (iii) how the various elements of the national expenditure—consumption, taxation, the level of imports and the Balance of Payments,[1] private savings and private investment outlay—would have been changed as a result of the changes both in the national output and in private incomes.

12. The estimates are based partly on the official estimate of the national income in 1938, as given in the White Paper on the National Income,[2] partly on a regression analysis of the relation between variations in the national income and its various components in the inter-war period, based on Professor Bowley's estimates of the National Income,[3] partly on other estimates relating to savings and the relation of undistributed profits to total profits.

13. The calculations throughout are in real terms, i.e. they assume constant rates of wages and prices. If a full employment policy had been associated with a rise in wages and prices, the resulting money totals (of the national income, consumption, Government expenditure, etc.) would have been higher but without necessarily changing, to any significant extent, the relative magnitudes of the various items.

The National Output in 1938

14. The estimate of the "net national income and expenditure at factor cost"—which is a measure of the value of the current

---

[1] By the term Balance of Payments, here and throughout this paper, we mean the balance of payments on income account—i.e. the net sum of the balance of merchandise trade, the balance of invisible exports and imports (shipping, insurance, etc.) and the net income from foreign investments. It excludes gold and capital movements.

[2] Cmd. 6520, 1944.

[3] *Studies in the National Income, 1924-38* (Cambridge University Press, 1942). Professor Bowley's series have been adjusted for a number of factors, in particular for over-assessments and business losses in the figures for profits.

national output of goods and services, plus the net income obtained on foreign investments—is given in Table 1. The

Table 1

NET NATIONAL INCOME AND EXPENDITURE IN 1938

	£ millions		£ millions
Rents	380	Personal expenditure on con-	
Profits and Interest ..	1,385	sumption	3,510
Salaries	1,100	Private net investment at home..	420
Wages	1,730	Balance of foreign payments ..	− 55
Pay of H.M. Forces	80	Expenditure of public authorities on goods and services out of revenue	725
		Government expenditure on goods and services out of loans	75
Net National Income ..	4,675	Net National Expenditure ..	4,675

Note.—The estimates are from Cmd. 6520, Table I, except that the figures for profits, private net investment at home and the net national income (and expenditure) have each been raised by £70 millions, to adjust them for the amount of "inventory losses" in profits, as this adjustment gives a more correct picture of the value of the national output at constant prices. The figures on the expenditure side are measured at factor cost of production, i.e. all indirect taxes are deducted from, and subsidies added to, the relevant categories. The estimates in the latest White Paper show separately the expenditures incurred in the transfer of property and the investment of savings, which are here included in the item "private net investment at home". This item is therefore composed of the following: net investment in fixed capital, £335 millions; net increase in working capital and stocks, £25 millions; cost of trans-ferring property, etc., £60 millions. The figures in this table are rounded off to the nearest £5 millions.

national income, on this definition, is smaller than the sum of the separate incomes of all individuals and corporations, since it does not include "transfer incomes" (i.e. National Debt interest, pensions, payments in respect of unemployment relief, etc.) which, though regarded as income by the individuals concerned, are not earned in connection with the production of goods and services. These "transfer incomes" amounted to £478 millions in 1938. Similarly, the expenditure of public authorities shown on the right hand side of Table 1 is not the total expenditure of public authorities in that year, but falls short of this amount by the £478 millions of transfer expenditures. The total amount of taxation paid by private individuals and corporations in 1938 was £1,176 millions, as shown in Table 4, p. 34, of which (after the deduction of £478 millions, which went to provide for transfer expenditures and £15 millions for subsidies) £683 millions were available to meet the expenditures on goods and services. This latter sum, together with £44 millions State-revenue from public property, makes up the £727 millions "public expenditure on goods and services out of revenue." Since the total expenditure of public authorities on goods and services was £802 millions, there was a net deficit of £75 millions, covered by borrowing. (This was by no means typical of the pre-war period, since in most years there was a net surplus on the consolidated public accounts.[1] The deficit in 1938 was solely due to the fact that 1938 was a re-armament year.)

The National Output under Full Employment

14. In 1938 there were, roughly, 14·5 million wage-earners aged 16–64, of whom about 1·7 millions were unemployed.[2] On the assumption that under "full employment" 97 per cent. of wage-earners are employed, the additional number of wage-earners to be brought into employment was 1·25 millions. On the assumption of constant returns (which seems well supported by the pre-war relation between variations of employment and output) the value of the additional net output of 1·25 million wage-earners in primary and secondary industries might be put at £375 millions.[3] We must also take into account, however, the consequential increase in the value of the output of "tertiary industry", i.e. in the distributive trades and in services. The value added by distribution can be taken (on the average) as 50 per cent. of the factory value, and since the increase in personal expenditure on consumption would have been about half the increase in output (see below) the incomes earned in the distributive trades could be assumed to have increased by some £95 millions, while a further £30 millions can be added on account of

---

[1] Cf. Clark, *National Income and Outlay* (Macmillan, 1937), p. 59.

[2] This figure was reached as follows. Of 13·7 million persons insured for unemployment under the general scheme, 1·8 millions were unemployed in 1938. Of the insured, about 2½ million persons were in non-manual occupations; and it was assumed that the general rate of unemployment was applicable to them. On the other hand, 3 million persons in manual occupations (1½ million men and 1½ million women) were in occupations outside the insurance scheme, such as agriculture, domestic service, etc. It was estimated that of these 3 millions, 200,000 were unemployed.

[3] On the basis of the 1935 Census of Production, but correcting for changes in wage rates, etc., net output per operative in 1938 can be put at £300.

the consequential increase in the income from professional services,[1] etc. The net result is that full employment would have increased the national output by £500 millions, or 11 per cent., over the £4,675 millions actually reached, thus making it £5,175 millions.

The same result can also be reached by the following considerations. As will be shown below, under pre-war circumstances, and in terms of constant wage-rates, 36 per cent. of any increase in the national output went into wages, which means that the increase in the national output was 2·78 times the increase in the wages bill associated with a given rise in employment. Since the additional employment of 1·25 million wage-earners would have added some £180 millions to the total wage payments,[2] it would have increased total income by £500 millions.

Incomes under Full Employment

15. We must next consider how the increase in the national output would have affected the different types of income. This is shown in Table 2. The average percentages of the different types of income relate to the actual income in 1938, and are taken from Table 1. The "marginal" percentages which show what would have been the share of each type of income in the increase in the national income, were estimated on the basis of the pre-war relation between the variations in the national income, wages, salaries and rent, and of the pre-war proportion of marginal profits put to reserve. This estimate shows that while the share going into wages out of an increase in incomes is only slightly less than the share of wages in the whole income, the share going into salaries is little more than half the average, while the share going into rent is nil. On the other hand, the share of profits and interest takes up 51 per cent. of any increase in income (as compared with 29½ per cent. in average income) and since 45 per cent. of this increase is put to reserve the share of undistributed profits in

---

[1] Equivalent to a 5 per cent. increase in services other than distributive services, and excluding the net output of dwellings and of services provided by the Government.

[2] Of the 1·25 millions, 1 million were adult men and 250,000 women or young men. The average weekly earnings of each category in 1938 have been obtained from the earnings inquiry of the Ministry of Labour. To obtain the annual wage bill, the weekly figures were multiplied by 48.

marginal income becomes 23 per cent. as against 7 per cent. in average income. These differences between the average and marginal profits (and, in particular, the high proportion of marginal profit going into undistributed profits) are chiefly responsible, as will be seen below, for the increase in savings, following on an increase in incomes, being so much larger than the proportion of savings in total income.

Table 2

SHARE OF DIFFERENT FACTORS IN THE NATIONAL INCOME

(*In Percentages of Total Income*)

	Average	Marginal
Rent	8	–
Distributed profits and interest	22½	28
Undistributed profits	7	23
Salaries	23½	13
Wages	39	36
Total	100	100

Note.—Average percentages based on Table 1. *Marginal* percentages were obtained as follows. Wages and home-produced national income, both deflated by an index of wage rates, were correlated for the period 1924-38, on the basis of Bowley's estimates of the National Income, corrected for various factors. Salaries, deflated by an index of salary rates, were correlated with wages, deflated by an index of wage rates. Rents did not fluctuate with employment. The share of undistributed profits in marginal profits is based on Radice, *Savings in Great Britain*, page 71. There was no trend in the share of wages during the period, but there was an upward trend in the share of rents and salaries.

The Level of Taxation

16. We must now consider the allocation of expenditures out of the different types of income between taxation, savings and consumption. We shall first estimate the amounts taken in taxation from the different incomes and then the allocation of income available after taxation between savings and consumption.

The proportions of average and marginal incomes paid in direct and indirect taxation in 1938 are shown in Table 3.

Applying these estimates to the distribution of incomes under full employment (which is shown in Table 6, p. 38), it is possible to estimate what the yield and the incidence of taxation would have been under full employment (assuming the 1938 rates of taxation in force) and how it would have compared with the

Table 3

TAXATION OF AVERAGE AND MARGINAL INCOMES
IN 1938

(*In Percentages of Incomes*)

	Average Incomes		Total	Marginal Incomes		Total
	Direct Taxes	Indirect Taxes		Direct Taxes	Indirect Taxes	
Rent, interest and distributed profits ..	23	8	31	35	4	39
Undistributed profits ..	25	3	28	33	2	35
Salaries	4½	14½	19	10	10	20
Wages	—	18	18	2	14½	17
Average	11	12½	23½	19	8	27

Note.—The percentages are largely based on the estimates of the incidence of taxation in an unpublished thesis by T. Barna. Social insurance contributions have been included in indirect, and not direct, taxation, divided between salaries and wages. Taxes on undistributed profits include income tax at the standard rate, a proportionate share of stamp duties, N.D.C. and of indirect taxes on production in general (allocated to this item because they fall on investment goods bought out of undistributed profits). Taxes falling on the pay of H.M. Forces and on social incomes are not included in the figures. For the yield of different kinds of taxes, in the actual situation and under full employment, see Table 4 below.

yield and incidence of taxation in the actual situation. This is shown in Table 4.

Consumption and Savings

17. As regards the distribution of the expenditure between consumption and savings from *available* incomes (incomes remaining after taxation), the estimates shown in Table 5 were based on the following considerations. Total net savings (at factor cost) amounted to £440 millions in 1938.[1] This, however, excludes that part of the savings (amounting to £90 millions) which is offset by death duty, etc., payments. From the point of view of estimating the saving propensities of different classes, these have also to be taken into account and therefore the average percentages in Table 5 refer to the £530 millions *gross* savings, which were allocated between the different types of income as follows:

[1] This is equal to the sum of the items private net investment at home, the balance of foreign payments, and Government expenditure out of loans, in Table 1, p. 29.

Table 4

ACTUAL AND FULL EMPLOYMENT TAXATION IN 1938

(*At the rates of taxation in force in 1938*)

	Actual Taxation						Taxation under full Employment					
	Direct Taxes		Indirect Taxes		Total		Direct Taxes		Indirect Taxes		Total	
	£Mn.	%	£Mn.	%	£Mn.	%	£Mn.	%	£Mn.	%	£Mn.	%
Rent, Distributed Profits and Interest	373	72	125	19½	498	43	418½	68	130½	19	549	42
Undistributed Profits	89	17	9	1½	98	8½	127	21½	11	1½	138	11
Salaries	50	10	160	25	210	18	56½	9	166½	24½	223	17
Wages	5	1	310	48	315	27	10	1½	336	50	346	27
Pay of H.M. Forces and Social Income	—	—	40	6	40	3½	—	—	40	5	40	3
Total	517	100	644	100	1,161	100	612	100	684	100	1,296	100

Note.—Social Insurance Contributions included among indirect taxes.

Table 5

PROPORTION OF AVAILABLE INCOMES SAVED

(*In Percentages*)

	Average	Marginal
Rents, distributed profits and interest	11	25
Undistributed profits	100	100
Salaries	9	15
Wages	6	10
Total Income	14	33

Note.—Average percentages were obtained by relating amounts saved to incomes received less taxation, but not deducting death duty payments, as the savings are gross of death duties. The large difference in the estimate of savings out of average and marginal total income is primarily due to the higher proportion of undistributed profits in marginal income, as shown in Table 2.

savings out of undistributed profits (i.e. undistributed profits, less taxes)[1] amounted to £230 millions, leaving £300 millions savings out of personal incomes. The total savings of persons with incomes below £250 a year can be estimated at about £120–£140 millions,[2] thus leaving £160–£180 millions as the total savings of those with incomes over £250 a year. It was assumed that the savings of persons with incomes below £250 were divided between wage-earners, salary earners and the recipients of other incomes in proportion to the amount of wages and salaries and other incomes earned; while the savings of persons above £250 were divided between salary-earners and other incomes (i.e. the recipients of rents, distributed profits and interest) in proportion to the amount of salary income and other incomes in the latter category.[3] On these assumptions £300 millions personal gross savings were allocated as follows:

					£ millions
Rents, interest and distributed profits				..	130
Salaries	..	..	..	..	80
Wages	..	..	..	..	90
Total personal savings	..	..	..	300

[1] Undistributed profits were adjusted for stock valuation.

[2] Based on the method employed by Radice, *op. cit.* chap. vi, making certain adjustments.

[3] Total personal incomes below £250 a year amounted to £2,600 millions, of which £1,810 millions were wages, £520 millions salaries and £270 millions other incomes. Personal incomes above £250 a year amounted to £1,900 millions of which £580 millions were salaries and £1,320 other income. (These figures include interest on the National Debt, but not other transfers, i.e. unemployment benefits, etc., which are excluded on the supposition that no savings were made out of the latter.)

These amounts were then applied to the incomes remaining after taxation in the respective categories and the results are as shown in Table 5. The estimate of the percentages of *marginal* income saved shown in the same table are based on the following considerations. The estimate of 33 per cent. for savings out of total available income (which is the equivalent of 24 per cent. of marginal income before deducting taxation) is based on the estimates of the "multiplier" before the war[1] which suggest that expenditure on consumption took up about one-half of an increase in income, while savings and taxation took up the other half. Since undistributed profits take up 23 per cent. of marginal income, and therefore 63 per cent. of marginal savings, only 37 per cent. of marginal savings are made out of personal incomes. These were allocated among the three categories of wages, salaries and distributed profits as shown in Table 5. The estimate of savings out of marginal wages and salaries is supported by estimates based on the movements of working- and middle-class savings.[2] The assumption that 25 per cent. of the marginal income out of distributed profits is saved, is supported by the facts (i) that the typical profit income is larger than either the typical wage or salary income and it is reasonable to suppose that a higher proportion of any increase of income is saved, the higher the income; (ii) that individual incomes from profits are more unstable than individual wage or salary incomes and therefore a higher proportion of any increase of income tends to be saved.[3] While pre-war statistics tend to suggest that the total savings of the capitalists out of *personal* incomes are not much more than the payments of death duties, this is quite consistent with the marginal savings out of profits being relatively high.

Full Employment Income and Outlay

18. The assumption made in paragraphs 15–17 above makes it possible to estimate the distribution of private incomes and outlay

---

[1] Clark, "The Determination of the Multiplier", *Economic Journal*, 1938, pp. 435 *et seq.*; R. and W. M. Stone, "The Marginal Propensity to Consume and the Multiplier", *Review of Economic Studies*, Vol. VI, p. 1.

[2] Radice, *op. cit.*, p. 66.

[3] It should also be borne in mind that while the increase in the wage and salary bill is largely due to the increase in the number of persons earning wages and salaries, the increase in profit incomes implies an increase in income per income recipient.

under full employment and the effects of changes in the rates of taxation. It follows from these assumptions and from Tables 2–5 (*a*) that an increase (or decrease) in the national income by £100 millions, the rates of taxation remaining unchanged, will increase (or decrease) consumption by £49 millions, savings by £24 millions and tax payments by £27 millions; (*b*) that at full employment level of income, a proportionate change in all tax rates, increasing (or decreasing) revenue by £100 millions would decrease (or increase) consumption by £73 millions, and savings by £27 millions; (*c*) that a similar change in the rates of *direct* taxation (excluding social insurance contributions) would decrease (or increase) consumption by £60 millions, and savings by £40 millions; (*d*) that a similar change in the rates of *indirect* taxation and social insurance contributions would decrease (or increase) consumption by £84·5 millions, and savings by £15·5 millions.

The distribution of private income and outlay under full employment, under the assumption that the actual tax rates of 1938 are maintained unchanged, is shown in Table 6.[1] The distribution of the national expenditure under policies that would involve changes in the 1938 tax rates is shown in Table 8, p. 42.

Imports under Full Employment

19. A correlation analysis of the movements of imports and the national income in real terms shows that under the conditions of the 1930's the marginal propensity to import was 15 per cent.— i.e. a £100 increase (or decrease) in the national income caused a £15 increase (or decrease) of imports. In 1938 visible and invisible imports exceeded visible and invisible exports plus the net income derived from foreign investments by £55 millions. This means that if the foreign demand for British exports is taken as given (irrespective of changes in the level of employment in Britain) the Balance of Payments under full employment would in the circumstances of 1938 have amounted to −£130 millions, since imports would have increased by £75 millions.

---

[1] It will be noted that the figures in Table 6 refer to the national income looked at as the sum of private incomes, i.e., it is equal to the net national income shown in Table 1, plus £478 millions transfer incomes, less £44 millions Government income from property.

In the calculations in paragraphs 22–24 below, it is assumed that British exports under a full employment policy would have been the same as in the actual case, while imports would have been

Table 6

PRIVATE INCOMES AND OUTLAY IN 1938

(£ *millions*)

	Actual Incomes (a)	Hypo-thetical Incomes under Full Employ-ment		Actual Outlay	Hypo-thetical Outlay under Full Employ-ment
Rent, distributed profits and interest ..	1,595	1,735	Personal expenditure on consumption (d) ..	3,510	3,755
Undistributed profits (b) ..	330	445	Savings (d) ..	440	560
Salaries ..	1,100	1,165	Taxation (e) ..	1,160	1,295
Wages and social income (c) ..	2,085	2,265			
Total Income ..	5,110	5,610	Total Outlay ..	5,110	5,610

Notes.—(*a*) Based on Cmd. 6520, with an addition of £70 millions to undistributed profits and total income, on account of adjustment for inventory losses.

(*b*) Includes, in accordance with the White Paper definition, "the savings held in the business accounts of traders, farmers and other individuals", in addition to the undistributed profits of companies.

(*c*) Includes £278 millions cash payments on account of social insurance and allied services. It was assumed that this item is identical under full employment, which means (since payments on account of unemployment benefit, at the ruling scales, would have been £70 millions less) that the scales of social benefit cash payments were raised by 33 per cent.

(*d*) At factor cost—i.e. after deduction of all indirect taxes.

(*e*) This is the total taxation falling on private incomes and differs from total tax receipts by the amount of taxation falling on public authorities.

allowed to increase freely with the increase in incomes. In paragraph 26, however, an estimate is made of the requirements of a full employment policy under the assumption that the adverse foreign balance is eliminated.

Private Investment Outlay

20. In 1938, net private investment at home[1] amounted to £420 millions which, together with £340 millions estimated

[1] In accordance with the definition adopted in the White Paper, this item includes all investment which is financed privately or which forms part of the capital expenditure of the Post Office and the housing and trading services of local authorities.

depreciation, made up the gross private investment of £760 millions. Gross and net private investment were made up of the various items as shown in Table 7.

Table 7

GROSS AND NET PRIVATE INVESTMENT IN 1938

	Gross Investment	Net Investment
	£ millions	*£ millions*
A. Outlay on fixed capital:		
Public Utilities	140	60
Buildings	350	245
Plant and Machinery	120	20
Other fixed capital	65	10
B. Net Increase in Working Capital and Stocks ..	25	25
C. Costs incurred in the transfer of property and the investment of savings	60	60
Private investment at home	760	420

Note.—The estimates are those of Cmd. 6520, Table D, except that they are in terms of factor cost and not market prices (i.e. deducting the proportion of general indirect taxes falling on them); the investment in working capital, etc., is the value of the change in stocks, and not the change in the value of stocks; and the item C has here been included under private investment. *Public utilities* investment includes capital expenditures of the railways and the London Passenger Transport Board, dock and harbour, canal, water supply, electricity and gas undertakings and the Post Office. *Buildings* includes all house building as well as other building, with the exception of those included in public expenditure or public utility investment. *Other fixed capital* includes merchant shipping and fishing vessels, roads, goods vehicles and public service vehicles and passenger cars bought for business purposes. The definition of "gross investment" here adopted differs from earlier estimates in that it excludes expenditure on repairs other than repairs to buildings. (This change of definition leaves, of course, the figure for net investment unaffected.)

In attempting to answer the question, "What would have been private investment under full employment?" we are confronted with the primary difficulty that the rate of investment varies not only with the level of output but to a large extent also with the changes in the level of output. Thus an *increase* in employment normally involves a considerable increase both in investment in fixed capital and investment in working capital. But the extra stimulus afforded to both these types of investment is to a great extent temporary; as time goes on, and employment is kept at a constant level, private investment would gradually fall again to a level determined by the rate of technical innovation and other long-run trends. It is impossible therefore to make any particular estimate for private investment under full employment without specifying how long the full employment policy was supposed to have been in operation.

In the subsequent calculations, the pre-war private investment outlay on fixed capital and working capital under full employment was taken as £400 millions instead of the actual £360 millions in 1938 (which means a total net investment—including the costs incurred in the acquisition and transfer of property—of £460 millions). This is not meant as an estimate of what private investment would have been in 1938 if output had suddenly been raised to the full employment level, but rather as an indication—not unreasonable in view of the general pre-war experience—of what the normal annual private investment outlay could have been expected to be, under a continuous full employment policy.[1]

Alternative Policies of Full Employment

21. We have now made all the assumptions necessary for exploring the quantitative implications of full employment policies.

As was shown in paragraphs 3–7, full employment could have been secured in four different ways; these are specified by the following "routes":

Route I: Assuming that the *rates of taxation* are maintained at the actual (1938) level and total Government expenditure is raised to the extent necessary to secure adequate total outlay;

Route II: Assuming that *revenue is kept equal to expenditure* (i.e. that there is no borrowing) while both are increased to whatever level is necessary to secure adequate total outlay;

Route III: Assuming that *total Government expenditure* is kept at the actual (1938) level and the total yield of taxation is reduced to the extent necessary to secure an adequate expansion of private outlay;

Route IV: Assuming that the total Government expenditure on goods and services is kept at the actual (1938) level, and revenue

---

[1] We shall also assume that the total outlay on private investment under full employment will be the same, irrespective of whether full employment was secured (primarily) by an increase in public outlay or an increase in private consumption outlay. It may be that the actual rate of capital expenditure by private industry would have been different in the two cases; but it is quite impossible to say—without making detailed assumptions about the objects of Government outlay—whether it would have been greater in the one case or in the other.

is kept equal to expenditure, but that the *structure of the tax system* (i.e. the rates of the individual taxes and subsidies)[1] is so altered as to secure an adequate expansion of total outlay.

22. In the case of Route I and Route II, it will be assumed that the increased Government expenditure is similar in character to investment expenditure, and hence does not react unfavourably on the proportion of income consumed by private individuals.[2] Routes II and III admit several solutions, according to the nature of the taxes which are raised or lowered in the two cases respectively. The necessary expansion of taxation in the case of Route II will be all the less, the more the additional taxation is concentrated on those who save a high proportion of their marginal incomes; while the necessary deficit in the case of Route III will be all the smaller the more the reduction of taxes benefits those who consume a high proportion of their marginal incomes. This means that—since the bulk of the incidence of direct taxation is on the higher income groups, while the bulk of indirect taxes falls on the lower income classes—Route II would involve a smaller expansion of expenditure and Route III a smaller deficit, if in the former case only direct taxes were raised, and in the latter case only indirect taxes were lowered, than if all taxes were proportionately raised or lowered, in each case. Accordingly two solutions are given for these two latter cases. "Route II" assumes a proportionate increase in all tax rates; "Route IIa" assumes that the increase is confined to direct taxation; "Route III" assumes that all taxes are reduced in the same proportion; "Route IIIa" that the tax reductions are confined to indirect taxation.

Similarly, in the case of Route IV, the actual solution depends on the precise nature of the changes of taxation. We shall assume that all direct taxes are proportionately raised and all indirect taxes are proportionately lowered, which makes Route IV a virtual combination of Routes IIa and IIIa.

23. It follows from the assumptions made above, particularly

---

[1] Government expenditure on subsidies (either on wages or commodities) is regarded as negative indirect taxes.

[2] This means that the objects of the increased Government expenditure are assumed to be either capital goods or goods and services for communal use, and not consumption goods destined for the individual use of private citizens. Subsidies on private consumption are treated as "transfer expenditures" and are covered by Route IV.

the estimates given in paragraph 18, that Route II would have implied an all-round increase in tax rates by 66 per cent.; Route IIa an increase in the rates of direct taxation by 94 per cent.; Route III an all-round reduction in the rates of taxation by 31 per cent.; Route IIIa a reduction in the rates of indirect taxation by 50 per cent.

The full results for Routes I–III are set out in Table 8. It must be borne in mind, in interpreting the estimates given in this Table, that all the calculations assume that the marginal propensities

Table 8

ACTUAL AND FULL EMPLOYMENT OUTLAY IN 1938

(£ *millions*)

	Actual Outlay 1938	Hypothetical Full Employment Outlay, 1938				
		Route I	Route II	Route IIa	Route III	Route IIIa
Private Consumption Outlay	3,510	3,755	3,135	3,410	4,045	4,045
Private Home Investment Outlay ..	420	460	460	460	460	460
Balance of Payments Abroad	− 55	− 130	− 130	− 130	− 130	− 130
Public Outlay out of Revenue	725	860	1,710	1,435	460	515
Public Outlay out of Loans	75	230	—	—	340	285
Total Outlay ..	4,675	5,175	5,175	5,175	5,175	5,175
Total Public Outlay ..	800	1,090	1,710	1,435	800	800
Increase in total public outlay as compared with actual amount	—	290	910	635	—	—

shown in Tables 2–5 above are constant over the relevant range; and that this assumption is all the more hazardous the more the hypothetical full employment situation diverges from the actual situation. There is greater uncertainty therefore concerning the estimates in Routes II and III—which involve more far-reaching changes in the amount of incomes available to the different classes—than is involved in the estimate for Route I. If, in particular, the marginal propensity to consume were found to be a diminishing function of available incomes and not a linear function, the estimates under Route II and II*a* would overstate the extent of the required increase in Government expenditure, while Routes III and III*a* would understate the amount of deficits required.

24. In the case of Route IV, which is not included on Table 8, since its salient features could not be shown in terms of the categories there given,[1] full employment could not have been secured by redistributing the burden of taxation between direct and indirect taxes alone, since the total abolition of indirect taxes, and their replacement by additional direct taxes, would only have reduced full employment savings by £160 millions, and increased the total outlay on home-produced goods and services by £350 millions instead of the required £500 millions. Hence to have secured an adequate expansion of outlay, the policy implied in Route IV would have required in addition the granting of subsidies on consumption goods, to an aggregate amount of some £250 millions. It would therefore have required an increase in the rates of direct taxation by 150 per cent., the total revenue from direct taxation (cf. Table 4), being raised from £612 millions to £1,562 millions. In interpreting this result, the limitation referred to in the previous paragraph should, of course, be borne in mind; in case the proportions of marginal incomes saved were not constant, but diminishing, the scope of the necessary changes in taxation would be smaller.

Full Employment and the Balance of Payments

25. The various solutions of the full employment policies given above were all worked out on the assumption that the Government adopted a purely passive attitude as regards the reaction of the higher outlay on the Balance of Payments. Hence, with the volume of exports actually obtained in 1938, the full employment *adverse* balance would have amounted to £130 millions instead of the actual figure of £55 millions.[2] As a long-run policy, however,

---

[1] In the case of Route IV, the various items shown on Table 8 are identical with those given for Route III, with the exception of the items of public outlay, which are identical with Route II.

[2] It should, however, be borne in mind that the assumptions in para. 13 above tend to make the situation appear too unfavourable for (*a*) they make no allowance for the fact that 1938 was an exceptionally bad year for British exports; (*b*) they do not allow for the effect of additional British imports on incomes abroad and hence on British exports.

it would have been neither desirable nor even possible to maintain an adverse balance of that magnitude. To eliminate it, measures would have had to be taken either to increase exports or, if that proved impossible, to cut imports by restricting purchases from abroad to those commodities which are essential and for which it is not easy to find substitutes in home production. In the circumstances of 1938 (on the assumption of constant terms of trade, i.e. a constant ratio of export prices to import prices) and under full employment, this would have meant either increasing exports by £120 millions, i.e. by 25 per cent., or cutting imports by £140 millions or 15 per cent.[1] below their hypothetical full employment level or adopting some combination of both methods. Either of these two methods of adjustment would have absorbed labour in Britain—though we cannot, of course, be certain that they would have done so to the same extent—and would thereby have made the required expansion in Government expenditure (or alternatively, the required reduction in the rates of taxation) very much less.

Table 9

ALTERNATIVE ROUTES TO FULL EMPLOYMENT IN 1938 WITH AN
EVEN BALANCE OF PAYMENTS

(*£ millions*)

	Route I*b*	Route II*b*	Route III*b*
Private Consumption Outlay	3,755	3,485	3,915
Private Home Investment Outlay ..	460	460	460
Balance of Payments Abroad	—	—	—
Public Outlay out of Revenue	860	1,230	640
Public Outlay out of Loans	100	—	160
Total Outlay	5,175	5,175	5,175
Total Public Outlay	960	1,230	800
Increase in total public outlay as compared with actual amount	160	430	—

26. In Table 9 the three hypothetical solutions of the full employment problem, given as Routes I, II and III, are worked out under the amended assumption that the adverse balance of payments is eliminated by an expansion of £120 millions in the volume of exports. This gives three variations of the original

[1] These estimates allow for the movements of the invisible exports (shipping and insurance) consequent upon a change in the volume of visible exports and imports.

routes which are described here as Routes I*b*, II*b*, and III*b* respectively.

It is seen that in Route I*b*—full employment secured by increased public spending, without changing the rates of taxation—the necessary expansion in public outlay is not £290 millions, but only £160 millions, and the resulting deficit is only £100 millions, that is, only slightly more than the actual deficit in 1938 with a *lower* level of public expenditure; while in II*b*—where full employment is secured without any deficit at all—the necessary expansion in public spending would amount to £430 millions, instead of £910 millions. What these figures show is that if Britain had secured 25 per cent. more exports in 1938—which was the expansion necessary for securing the level of imports appropriate to full employment without an adverse balance—she would, in doing so, have absorbed about one-half of her unused resources, and would thus have left less scope for other methods of utilising them.

27. Expanding exports would, of course, have been the more favourable method of eliminating the adverse balance; if Britain had to be content with securing an even balance via a restriction of imports, she could not have expected to enjoy the same real income from the use of her resources; nor would it have been certain that the expansion of home production consequent upon the restriction of imports would have given rise to the same increase in employment as an expansion of exports would have done. To the extent that the commodities no longer imported would have been replaced by home produced substitutes, the expansion in employment would have been greater; to the extent that the use of certain kinds of goods might have had to be foregone altogether, it might have been less. But in any case, the scope of the necessary Governmental measures under any of the alternative policies would have been much smaller than if the adverse balance of payments had not been eliminated.

III. THE FULL EMPLOYMENT PROBLEM AFTER THE WAR

28. The foregoing analysis referred to the full employment problem as it existed in Britain before the war. Its purpose, however, was not merely an historical one, but to provide the background

for an analysis of the conditions of full employment in the post-war situation. It is, of course, quite impossible to make forecasts about the future except on the hypothetical postulate that in all matters where the nature of changes cannot be definitely foreseen and taken into account, the future is assumed to be a continuance of the past. The subsequent calculations should be interpreted in this light; they are not put forward as prophecies of future events, but only as the joint outcome of the most reasonable hypotheses that can be made about post-war conditions in the light of present knowledge.

29. After the conclusion of hostilities there will be a period of transition and immediate reconstruction which, from the economic point of view, will have more affinities with the present war economy than with a peace economy. In order to examine the background of a post-war full employment policy it is best to ignore this transition period altogether, and to make forecasts of the relevant economic factors for a succeeding period, when the transition from a war-time to a peace-time economic structure will already have been largely accomplished—when the ordinary peace-time industries will have re-absorbed their labour, restored their pre-war output capacity and replenished their stocks. This does not mean, of course, that the period of reconstruction, as distinct from the period of transition, is assumed to have been completed. "Post-war reconstruction" is generally interpreted to mean the accomplishment of a large number of things which go far beyond the restoration of the pre-war economic structure. If the present plans as regards post-war housing policy, agriculture, transport, etc., are even partially adopted, the reconstruction period will extend over a large number of years; and during this period the requirements of the reconstruction programme and the requirements of a stable full employment policy will have to be fitted in with each other.

30. It is impossible to foretell with any exactness how long the immediate transition period will last.[1] In the following calculations

[1] After the last war, 1924 was generally looked upon as the first "normal" peace year, i.e. five years after the conclusion of hostilities. But this was partly because the big post-war slump of 1921-2 was erroneously regarded as a phase of the transition period; and the position was further complicated by the period of large-scale currency disorders in Europe and the British policy of gradually returning to the gold standard at pre-war parities.

it is assumed that the war will come to an end somewhere in the middle of 1945, and that this transition period takes $2\frac{1}{2}$ years. The hypotheses therefore refer to "1948"—this being taken as the first normal post-war year. We shall attempt to make estimates— in an analogous manner to those given above for 1938—of the national income and its distribution under full employment conditions in 1948; of the level of Government expenditure, and of taxation, consumption and savings, under alternative hypotheses.

31. It will be assumed, for the purposes of this analysis, that the pre-war economic structure will, in broad outline, have been restored and that the pre-war economic relations will continue to operate, except in those particular cases where there are definite reasons for assuming a change. This means that as far as the distribution of income between profits, wages, etc., and the division of the outlay of the various income groups between consumption and savings are concerned, the estimates will be based on an extrapolation of pre-war trends, without taking into account the war-time shifts in those factors.[1] In the case of the ordinary expenditures of the Government, allowance will be made for the effects of the war and for other changes unconnected with the war (such as the expenditure on education) to which the Government is already committed. It will be assumed that the Social Security Plan put forward in the Beveridge Report will have been adopted in full. In the case of foreign trade, it will be assumed that the terms of trade (the ratio of the prices of export goods to the prices of imported goods) will be the same as in 1938; but in the case of the income from foreign investment, allowance will be made for the war-time liquidation of assets owned abroad.

32. In one important respect the new setting of the problem calls for a change in procedure. Whatever justification there may have been for making a guess at the full employment level of private investment in the circumstances of 1938, it would clearly be idle to speculate on the corresponding magnitude of this

[1] The most important of these war-time shifts is, of course, in the proportions of income saved. The present enormous increase in the savings propensities of the public is due—apart from the patriotic appeal—to sheer inability to spend money owing to rationing and the complete disappearance of many objects of peace-time consumption. It is possible that the savings habits generated during the war will, to some extent, be retained afterwards (though this is not borne out by the experience of the last war). But it would be quite impossible to make an allowance for this factor.

item in the circumstances of 1948. For a considerable period after the war the demand for capital investment is likely to be considerably larger than that experienced in the 1930's. There will be the needs of the housing programme, the demand for new capital investment in industry, transport, agriculture, fed by a decade's accumulated backlog of technical invention and innovation; there will also be the need for capital expenditures arising out of Britain's participation in the reconstruction of Europe. In an unregulated economy—where the Government did not take positive steps to ensure that the total outlay of the community was adjusted to available man-power—the danger, for a number of years, might be more that of "inflationary gaps", with the consequent upward pressures on prices, than of "deflationary gaps", with large-scale unemployment.[1] If that proved to be the case, the Government might decide to limit private spending through the creation of budgetary surpluses (or the maintenance of rationing) and/or to limit the rate of private capital expenditures in accordance with a scale of national priorities. In a situation of this sort, the needs of public investment (whether that of the Central Government, of the local authorities or of public utilities) could not be treated as a "left-over", to be drawn on after the needs of private investment had been satisfied, but the Government would have to plan the allocation of the aggregate of resources available for investment purposes among investment of all kinds.

Hence in analysing the requirements of a full employment policy in 1948, we shall treat public and private investment together, and estimate the amount available for purposes of home investment of all kinds, assuming either (a) that there is an even balance of payments (i.e. the amount of exports is sufficient to pay for all imports) and that the level of taxation is just sufficient to cover the ordinary expenditures of public authorities (i.e. that there is no surplus or deficit on the current accounts of public authorities); or (b) that the resources available for investment

---

[1] It may be objected that the big slump of 1921-2 points to a different conclusion. But after the last war, long-term capital investment (in housing and industry) did not get going until much later; the boom in 1919-20 was essentially a re-stocking boom, and the slump of 1921-2 signified that both the period of war expenditures and the period of post-war restocking had come to an end.

purposes are augmented by heavier taxation (or other methods of restricting consumption), or by an adverse balance of payments.

The National Income in 1948

33. We shall estimate the full employment level of the national output in 1948 by assuming (a) that the working population will be the same as in 1938; (b) that the average hours of work per week will be the same as in 1938; (c) that the average unemployment rate will be 3 per cent.; (d) that the average real productivity per man-hour will have risen, over the period 1938-48, by 13 per cent.; (e) that the Armed Forces of the Crown will be maintained at double the strength of that of 1938, i.e. between 750,000 and 1,000,000 men; (f) that the real terms of international trade (the ratio of export prices to import prices) will be the same as in 1938; (g) that the income from foreign investment will have fallen to 40 per cent. of its 1938 amount; (h) that the average level of prices will be stabilised at $33\frac{1}{3}$ per cent. above the 1938 level.

The basic considerations behind the more critical of these assumptions (those relating to (a), (d), (e), (f), (g) and (h) above) are as follows:

(a) The net change in working population will be the resultant of the following factors: (i) the normal increase in the working population, due to the change in numbers and age composition which, in the absence of war, would have amounted to some 550,000;[1] (ii) the war casualties (killed and permanently disabled) which are put at 500,000;[2] (iii) the withdrawal of boys and girls from the labour market, due to the raising of the school-leaving age to 16, which implies a reduction of 850,000 juveniles (aged 14–15) at work; (iv) the addition to the working population due to the increase of the number of women in the labour market as a by-product of the war. To obtain the net change in the working population, each of these classes has to be weighted by its output per head, which may be assumed to be proportionate to the relative wages in 1938. Since the weekly wages of classes

---

[1] Obtained by interpolation from the Registrar-General's forecast of population. (Actual increase 1928-38 was 1,700,000.)

[2] War casualties (including civilians) killed and permanently disabled were about 250,000 in the first four years of war.

(i)–(iv) on the basis of Bowley's[1] and the Ministry of Labour's estimates were 50, 65, 13, and 32·5 shillings respectively, it would require an addition of 500,000 women under head (iv) to keep the aggregate working population unchanged. This last assumption is not unreasonable, in view of the fact that about 2½ million women were stated to have been drawn into industry and the Forces in the course of the present war; while after the last war, the number of women remaining in industry (up to the time of the slump of 1921, at any rate) was stated to have been about 30–40 per cent. of those additionally employed in the course of that war.

(d) As regards the average productivity per man-hour, the estimate of a 13 per cent. increase was arrived at as a result of averaging between (i) the actual rate of increase in productivity per man-hour over the period 1914–24; (ii) the rate of increase of productivity between 1924–38. The increase in hourly productivity, for the national output as a whole (including distribution and services) in the ten-year period covering the last war seems to have been around 10 per cent.,[2] while in the inter-war period it was at the rate of 1·5 per cent. per annum (which implies a rise of 16 per cent. over a ten-year interval). It appears fairly certain (from various statements made by responsible authorities) that the increase in productive techniques in the course of the present war is much more substantial than that of the last war; and it is by no means improbable that when peace returns the rise in productivity will be found to be even greater than what would have resulted from the mere continuation of pre-war trends.[3] The estimate of a 13 per cent. increase over the period should therefore be regarded as the minimum probable, rather than the most likely, figure of the rise in productivity.

(e) Our assumption is that by 1948 at any rate the war will have been concluded with Japan as well as Germany. At the

[1] *Studies in the National Income*, p. 67.
[2] Though the statistical estimates covering this period are not so extensive as for later dates, the estimate of a 10 per cent. increase in hourly productivity is supported both by Rowe's production index, divided by an index of employment and of hours, and of Bowley and Stamp's estimate (*The National Income*, 1924, p. 58) that home produced real income per head in 1924 was about the same as in 1914, while the length of working hours was about 10 per cent. less. Cf. also Clark, *National Income and Outlay*, p. 267.
[3] On the increase in productivity see also para. 56 below.

same time it would be idle to expect that the immediate post-war situation would enable the strength of the Armed Forces to be reduced to the pre-war level; the needs of military occupations, etc., will probably require the maintenance of a much larger number of effectives. In 1938, the complements of the Army, Navy and Air Force amounted to 400–450,000 men. For 1948, it will therefore be assumed to amount to (roughly) double that number, say between 750,000 and 1,000,000 men. This means (since the definition of the aggregate working population, which was assumed to be unchanged, included the Armed Forces) that the number available in industry, etc., will be about 400,000–500,000 less. It means also that the real increase in home-produced output over the 1938 full employment level will amount to, not 13, but only 11 per cent. (since the value of the output per head in the Armed Forces—represented by their pay and maintenance—is less than the output per head in industry).

(f) The assumption of an unchanged price of imports in terms of exports implies (roughly) that the world price level of foodstuffs and raw materials in terms of manufactured goods will be the same in 1948 as it was in the late 1930's. The experience of the aftermath of the last war was that of a considerable improvement in the terms of trade, so that Britain obtained the same amount of imports with about 20 per cent. fewer exports than before. There is no reason to suppose that this favourable experience will be repeated, but neither is there any definite reason for assuming the contrary. The policies of control adopted in the course of the present war have prevented the spectacular rise in the prices of primary products which was such a prominent feature of the last World War, and it may be assumed that the same policies will continue in force during the period of immediate post-war scarcities. There is no sign at present of the world entering a more prolonged period of scarcities in foodstuffs and raw materials; the forces of technical improvement which made for the surpluses of the last two (pre-war) decades do not appear to be in any way exhausted.

It is possible, of course, that in the effort to obtain sufficient exports to pay for imports, Britain may deliberately set out to lower the prices of her exports of manufactures, not only in terms of the foodstuffs and raw materials which she imports, but also relatively to the prices of manufactured goods of other countries. It is not possible to take account of this contingency in calculating the national income, but the nature of the balance of payments problem will be examined in paragraph 43 below.

(g) In the five years 1939–43 the total amount of disinvestment abroad (through the loss of gold and foreign exchange, the sale of foreign assets and the accumulation of debt) amounted to £3,073 millions.[1] Since in the years 1942 and 1943 disinvestment proceeded at an approximately constant rate of £650 millions per annum, the aggregate of disinvestment, up to the middle of 1945, may be put at £4,100 millions, the loss of income from which may be estimated as follows:[2]

	£ millions	
	Amount	Loss of Annual Income
Loss of gold and foreign exchange ..	700	—
Sale of securities	900	36·0
Sterling balances of foreign countries held in London and other loans ..	2,500	62·5
Total	4,100	98·5

On the other side, allowance must be made for the fact that the devaluation of sterling and the higher earnings of companies operating abroad (due to higher prices, etc.) would have raised the income from foreign investment, on the pre-war investments, considerably above the £200 millions obtained in 1938. If we allow for an increase of only some £10 millions on account of the last factor, the post-war income from foreign investments may be put at £110 millions at post-war prices or £80 millions at pre-war prices.

(h) The assumption made in the Beveridge Report on Social Services was that the average level of prices after the war will be

[1] Cf. Cmd. 6520, Table I, item 13.
[2] For sources of estimate cf. *Economic Journal*, June-September, 1943, pp. 261-2. It was assumed that since the securities sold consisted to a large extent of Indian, Canadian, and other Government bonds of a low yield, the average loss of income on securities can be put at 4 per cent. The loss of income due to the accumulation of sterling balances assumes that these balances are converted into long-term obligations with a yield of 2·5 per cent.

25 per cent. above pre-war. The latest official estimates suggest, however,[1] that unless there is a reduction in the general level of money wages (which is not likely) the allowance of 25 per cent. is likely to prove insufficient, and it is safer to reckon on post-war prices being 33⅓ per cent. above 1938. This assumption was therefore preferred and in the subsequent calculations the estimates for Government expenditure, and in particular the scales of benefit of the Social Security Plan, were adjusted accordingly.

The net result of these assumptions is that the net national output (including foreign income) in 1948 is estimated to be £7,450 millions, in terms of post-war prices, or £5,600 millions in terms of 1938 prices. This allows for a substantial reduction in the national money income below its current war-time level (the official estimate for 1943 being £8,172 millions) a difference to be explained by a number of factors, among which the larger occupied population and the longer hours worked in war-time are the most important. The comparison between the pre-war and the post-war national income is shown in Table 10.

Table 10

CONSTITUENTS OF THE NATIONAL OUTPUT IN 1938 AND 1948
(*£ millions*)

	1938 (Actual)	1938 (Full Employment)	1948 (Full Employment)	
			at 1938 Prices	at 1948 Prices
Home-produced output excluding the Forces ..	4,395	4,895	5,360	7,110
Pay and allowances of H.M. Forces	80	80	160	230
Net Income from Foreign Investments	200	200	80	110
Net National Income ..	4,675	5,175	5,600	7,450

Note.—The average prices of home-produced output are assumed to be 33 per cent. higher in 1948. In calculating the pay and allowances of H.M. Forces at 1948 prices, cash pay was assumed to rise at the same rate as the average level of wages (see below) and payments in kind in proportion to output prices.

34. The division of the net national income between the different types of incomes, shown in Table 11 (p. 54), is based on

[1] Cf. Cmd. 6520, pp. 7-8.

the following additional considerations. It was assumed that the
share of wages in wage-containing output will be the same in 1948
as it would have been under full employment in 1938. In other
words, allowance was made for the change in the share of wages
consequent upon full employment, but it was assumed—in
accordance with the pre-war experience[1]—that the change in
productivity leaves this factor unaffected. This implied that,
taking into account the rise in output prices and the increase in
productivity, the average level of wage rates was 54 per cent.
above that of 1938.[2] In calculating the total wage bill, allowance
was made for the transfer of men (as compared with 1938) to the
Forces. In the case of salaries, it was assumed that the average
level of salaries increases by 33 per cent., i.e. in the same ratio as
prices, while the number of salary earners will be the same as
under full employment in 1938. In the case of rents, the assumption was that there will be one million additional houses by

Table 11

NET NATIONAL INCOME IN 1938 AND 1948

(£ millions, at current prices)

	1938 (Actual)	1938 (Full Employment)	1948 (Full Employment)
Rents	380	380	450
Profits and Interest	1,385	1,640	2,400
Salaries	1,100	1,165	1,550
Wages	1,730	1,910	2,820
Pay of H.M. Forces	80	80	230
Net National Income	4,675	5,175	7,450

1948 and that the average level of rents will be 10 per cent. above
1938, on the presumption that the Rent Restriction Acts continue
in force, while agricultural and other rents not subject to restriction rise with the increase in the price level. The amount of
profits and interest was then obtained as a residue; it implies an
increase (in money terms) of 57 per cent. in home produced profits
and interest as compared with the 1938 full employment estimate.

[1] Cf. note to Table 2 above.
[2] The average increase in wage rates, up to the end of 1943, was 39 per cent. Our
assumption of a 54 per cent. increase up to 1948 implies that the average level of
wage rates rises at about 2 per cent. per annum over the next five years.

Private Incomes in 1948

35. To obtain the amount and the distribution of private incomes (as shown for 1938 in Table 6, p. 38) the figures in Table 11 must be adjusted for "transfer incomes" (consisting of National Debt interest, social security cash payments and war pensions) and for Government income from property, and an estimate must be made of the amount of undistributed profits.

We shall assume Government income from property to be £70 millions instead of the pre-war £44 millions.[1] For National Debt interest paid to private individuals and corporations (including accrued interest on National Savings Certificates, but excluding that part of the nominal interest burden which represents payments to public funds)[2] we allow £500 millions. This item was £200 millions in 1938 and £340 millions in 1943, having risen at a rate of about £50 millions per annum during 1942 and 1943. The assumption of £500 millions allows therefore for the continuation of borrowing on the present scale up to the end of 1945; it also allows for the conversion of £2,500 millions floating debt into long term debt bearing 2·5 per cent. interest after the war.[3] Social security cash payments—assuming that the Beveridge Plan is adopted in full, allowing for an upward adjustment of benefit rates owing to the assumption of a 33⅓ per cent. rise in the price level, and making a number of other adjustments, set out in the note to Table 15, p. 59—will amount to £470 millions, while war pensions are put at £100 millions, which allows for some £70 millions for the pensions arising out of the casualties of the present war. The resulting comparison of transfer incomes in 1938 and 1948 is shown in Table 12.

---

[1] For 1943, this item was officially estimated at £97 millions, but some of the revenues under this head (such as the receipts under the Railway Agreement) are temporary in character.

[2] But without deducting National Debt interest paid to foreigners, because this has already been deducted in calculating the net national income.

[3] Account must also be taken of the repayments on account of post-war credits on income tax (say £600 millions), the repayment of 20 per cent. of Excess Profits Tax less income tax (say £250 millions) and the post-war payments under the War Damage Acts. There are, on the other hand, the accumulated tax accruals (which will amount to at least £1,500 millions by the end of the war) to cover these items.

Table 12

TRANSFER INCOMES IN 1938 AND 1948

(£ *millions*)

	1938	1948
National Debt Interest	200	500
Social Income:		
Social Security cash payments ..	238	470
War Pensions	40	100
Transfer Incomes	478	1,070

36. In making the estimate for undistributed profits it was assumed—in an analogous manner to the assumptions about consumption and savings out of personal incomes, explained in paragraph 41 below—that over longer periods the share of undistributed profits in total profits varies not so much with the amount of profits, but with the level of unemployment. The high proportion of any increase in profits which is normally put to reserves is largely due to the policies of dividend stabilisation followed by businesses; as time goes on, and profits increase, the standard around which businesses stabilise their dividends is also raised. Hence it seemed more reasonable to assume that the proportion of undistributed profits in home produced profits and interest would be no higher in 1948 than it would have been at the full employment income of 1938.

Table 13

PRIVATE INCOMES UNDER FULL EMPLOYMENT, 1938 AND 1948

(£ *millions*)

	1938	(1938)	1948
Rent, distributed profits and interest ..	1,735	(2,315)	2,640
Undistributed profits	445	(595)	640
Salaries	1,165	(1,550)	1,550
Wages and pay, etc., of H.M. Forces ..	1,990	(2,650)	3,050
Social Income	275	(365)	570
Total Private Income	5,610	(7,475)	8,450

Note.—For the sake of comparison, the middle column was inserted to show what the 1938 incomes would have been at the 1948 level of money values. Thus the difference between the third and the first columns shows the change in money income, and that between the third and the second columns the change in real income, between the hypothetical full employment earnings at the two dates.

Public Expenditure and Taxation

37. In estimating the post war budgets of public authorities we shall assume the following principles: (i) that all ordinary expenditures will be financed out of taxation, but not capital expenditures which will be excluded from the ordinary budgets. (It is estimated that in 1938 capital expenditures included in the ordinary budgets of the Central Government and local authorities amounted to

Table 14

CONSOLIDATED BUDGETS OF LOCAL AUTHORITIES
IN 1938 AND 1948
(£ millions)

1938		1948	
Revenue	Expenditure	Revenue	Expenditure

Rates .. 211
Income from
  property .. 26
Contribution
of Central
Government 169
	Social Security
	  Services .. 68
	Other ordinary
	  expenditures 311
	Capital Ex-
	  penditure 20
		Rates .. 250
		Income from
		  property .. 40
		Contribution
		of Central
		Government 125
			Ordinary Ex-
			  penditure .. 415

	Total Expen- diture .. 399 Surplus .. 7		

Total Revenue 406	Total Expen-
	  diture and
	  Surplus .. 406
		Total Revenue 415	Total Expen-
			  diture .. 415

Note.—For 1938, the figures are those of Cmd. 6520 (Table IV, items 83, 87, 115, 95) except for the division of local authorities' expenditure among the three categories of social security services (which consist of services included in the Social Security Budgets, i.e. health services and public assistance cash payments), other ordinary expenditures and capital expenditure which is derived from other sources. For 1948, it is assumed that only the second category (ordinary expenditures other than health and public assistance) is financed locally out of revenue, and that the cost of these is increased by 33 per cent. as compared with 1938. The revenue from the 1938 poundage of rates in 1948 is based on the estimates of rent given in Table 11.

£40 millions, of which £20 millions were spent on new road construction); (ii) that all services provided by public authorities before the war will be maintained (and in the case of defence expanded) and, in addition, the services proposed in the Report on Social Insurance and Allied Services[1] and the Education Bill[2] will be provided in full, and a further allowance will be made for

[1] Cmd. 6404, 1942.   [2] Cmd. 6458, 1943.

other similar contingencies; (iii) that all social security services will be consolidated in a Social Security Budget, which will be financed by insured persons, employers and public funds in the proportions recommended by the Social Insurance Report, but that the whole burden falling on public funds will be borne by the Central Government, thus relieving the local authorities from the finance of social security services altogether; (iv) that the poundage of local rates will be maintained at the 1938 level, and that the Central Government contribution will be the amount necessary to balance the local authorities' budgets, on this principle; (v) that the taxation of the Central Government will be such as to balance the Central Government budget.[1] The estimated budgets for 1948 (together with the actual budgets of 1938) are shown in Tables 14–16 and the basis of the estimates of individual items is explained in the notes attached to the tables. Table 17 brings the accounts of all public authorities together and shows the amount of Central Government tax revenue that will be necessary to balance the accounts of public authorities.

38. Tables 14–17 show that after making full allowance for the additional commitments of the Government and for the higher expenditure due to the rise in prices, and making an allowance for unforeseen contingencies, the Central Government will have to raise £1,655 millions in taxation to balance the budgets of public authorities as a whole. To find out the rates of taxation that will be necessary to obtain this revenue we shall first of all estimate what the yield of the 1938 rates of taxation would be at the full employment national income of 1948. We shall assume the same taxes in force as in 1938[2] and the same *ad valorem* tax rates—which means that *specific* tax rates are deemed to have been adjusted for the rise in the general price level, and all allowances in direct taxation (i.e. the various income tax allowances, the surtax limits, etc.) to have been raised in the same proportion, so that the proportion paid in taxation out of any given real income is the same.

This estimate is given in Table 18. The first column in Table 18 shows the actual yield of the different taxes in 1938. The second column shows what the same taxes would have yielded under full

---

[1] On the question of sinking funds, see para. 48 below.
[2] I.e. war-time taxes other than National Defence Contribution—which was already in force in 1938—are not taken into account.

Table 15
SOCIAL SECURITY BUDGET IN 1938 AND 1948
(£ *millions*)

1938		1948	
Revenue	Expenditure	Revenue	Expenditure
Contributions:	Civil Pensions (e) .. 91	Contributions:	Social Insurance .. 315
Insured Persons (a) 55	Unemployment Payments (f) 90	Insured Persons (l) .. 176	National Assistance .. 47
Employers (b) 67	Public Assistance (g) .. 23	Employers (l) 124	Children's Allowances 107
Local Authorities (c) .. 68	Health Payments (h) 34	Central Government (m) 355	Cost of Administration of above .. 26
Central Government (d) .. 152	Workmen's Compensation 13		Health Services .. 160
	Cost of Administration (i) 20		
	Health Services (j) .. 49		
	Total Expenditure .. 320		
	Surplus (k) 22		
Total Revenue 342	Total Expenditure and Surplus .. 342	Total Revenue 655	Total Expenditure .. 655

Note.—The Budget for 1948 is on the basis of the estimated budget for 1945, given in Cmd. 6404, p. 209, adjusted for the following factors: (i) the cost of social insurance was raised by £20 millions, owing to the higher cost of old age pensions in 1948 (as compared with 1945) in accordance with the scheme; (ii) the estimates for the cost of the health services were revised in accordance with the estimate given in Cmd. 6502; (iii) owing to the assumption of 3 per cent. unemployment, the cost of social insurance was reduced by £73 millions (i.e. two-thirds of the cost of unemployment benefits), and the cost of children's allowances (on first children) by £10 millions; (iv) all items were increased by 6⅔ per cent. owing to the assumption of a 33 per cent. (instead of 25 per cent.) rise in the price level. The contributions proposed in Cmd. 6404 were reduced to balance the budget, allocating to the Exchequer one-third of the saving in the cost of unemployment and the whole saving on children's allowances. The corresponding Budget for 1938 was brought together for purposes of comparison from published sources, itemised below.

(*a*) Cmd. 6520, Table IV, item 78.

(*b*) *Ibid.*, item 82, plus £13 millions estimated expenditure on workmen's compensation.

(*c*) Includes payments of local authorities on public assistance cash payments and part of health services. See also note (*i*) below. Identical with similar item in Table 14.

(*d*) Residue. Includes £63 millions Exchequer contribution to social insurance. (Identical with item (*c*) in Table 16.)

(*e*) Pensions to widows and orphans, contributory and non-contributory old age pensions. Cmd. 6520, Table II, item 22, *less* war pensions.

(*f*) Unemployment insurance benefits and allowances. Cmd. 6520, Table II, item 23 *less* public assistance.

(*g*) Cmd. 6520, Table IV, item 107.

(*h*) *Ibid.*, Table II, item 24.

(*i*) Cmd. 6404, p. 204.

(*j*) Cmd. 6502, Appendix E. Of this £4 millions was expenditure by the Central Government, and £45 millions by local authorities.

(k) The surplus of unemployment, health and pensions insurance funds. Cmd. 6520, Table IV, item 90.

(l) The contributions were reduced, as compared with the proposals in Cmd. 6404, in order to balance the budget under the assumptions stated above. After estimating the Exchequer contribution as stated in note (m) below, this implied a reduction in the *total* revenue from contributions of 10 per cent. and a reduction in the *per capita* rates of contributions by 16 per cent. (owing to the increase in the numbers of insured, as a result of full employment). Hence, in spite of the higher rates of cash benefits assumed, the required rates of contributions per adult man are 3s. 7d. for insured persons and 2s. 9d. for employers (as compared with 4s. 3d. and 3s. 3d. respectively, proposed in Cmd. 6404).

(m) The Exchequer contribution under the Beveridge Plan (including interest on insurance funds) was estimated at £366 millions in 1945. (Cmd. 6404, p. 209.) Since, of the adjustments stated above, (i) and (ii) offset each other, (iii) implies a reduction of £34 millions, and (iv) an addition of £23 millions, the net result is £355 millions.

Table 16

CENTRAL GOVERNMENT EXPENDITURE IN 1938 AND 1948

(£ millions)

	1938	1948
Interest on the National Debt (a) ..	200	500
Other Consolidated Fund expenditure ..	16	20
Defence Services (b)	379	480
Civil Votes:		
Social Security (c) 152		355
War Pensions (d) 40		100
Grants to local authorities (e) .. 169		125
Other Civil Votes (f) 23		50
Other post-war contingencies (g) .. —		40
	—— 384	—— 670
Cost of tax collection	14	15
Capital expenditures, included in Civil Votes in 1938 (h)	20	—
Total Expenditure	1,013	1,685

Notes.—(a) For bases of estimate, see paragraph 33 (g) above. Interest paid t⁰ public funds is excluded from this item, but included in social security payments.

(b) For 1938, this item includes issues under the Defence Loans on rearmament as well as expenditures on the preparation for war (such as Air Raid Precautions) usually included under the Civil Votes. The 1938 figure is not representative of the pre-war rate of expenditure on defence, which amounted to only £100–£120 millions before rearmament began.

For 1948, the defence expenditure was based on the assumptions stated in paragraph 33 (c) above. The estimate of £480 millions was reached as follows. Pay and maintenance of the Forces, £230 millions (see Table 11). Expenditure on armaments and auxiliary materials, £250 millions. The latter item is more than twice the corresponding normal pre-war rate of expenditure, after allowing for a 33 per cent. rise in prices.

(c) See notes (d) and (m) to Table 15.

(d) See paragraph 35 above.

(e) See corresponding items in Table 14.

(f) Includes cost of civil administration, justice, etc. For 1948, it includes an additional £20 millions on account of the new Education Bill, in addition to the rise in the cost of education due to the 33 per cent. rise in prices. See Cmd. 6458, Appendix.

(g) This item represents an allowance for unforeseen commitments, other than expenditure on capital account.

(h) See paragraph 37 above.

Table 17

THE CONSOLIDATED ACCOUNT OF PUBLIC AUTHORITIES IN 1938 AND 1948

(£ millions)

Revenue	1938	1948	Expenditure	1938	1948
Taxation:					
Central Government	888	(1,655)	Central Government	1,013	1,685
Social Security	122	300	Social Security	320	655
Local Authorities	211	250	Local Authorities	399	415
Total Taxation	1,212	2,205	*Gross Total Expenditure*	1,732	2,755
Income from property	44	70	*Less* Transfers from—		
			Central Government to Social Security	− 152	− 355
Total Revenue	1,265	2,275	Central Government to Local Authorities	− 169	− 125
Deficit	78	—	Local Authorities to Social Security	− 68	—
			Total Transfers	− 389	− 480
Total Revenue and Deficit	**1,343**	**2,275**	**Net Total Expenditure**	**1,343**	**2,275**

Note.—For the individual items except Central Government taxation in 1938, see Cmd. 6520, items 33, 40, 77, 81. For Central Government taxation see Tables 14–16. Central Government taxation in 1948 is derived as a residue being the amount necessary to balance the total budget of public authorities. The difference between the £78 millions deficit in 1938 shown in this table and the £75 millions shown in Table 1 is due to the fact that in Table 1 items are shown at factor cost, while in the present table they are at market prices. The difference between the total taxation of £1,161 millions in 1938 shown in Table 4 and the £1,221 millions shown in the present table is due to (i) general indirect taxes falling on the Government, £32 millions; (ii) subsidies, £15 millions; (iii) workmen's compensation—which was added to public expenditure in Table 15 for purposes of comparability of social security expenditure—£13 millions.

Table 18

YIELD OF CENTRAL GOVERNMENT TAXATION, 1938 AND 1948

(*At the Rates of Taxation in Force in 1938*)

(*£ millions*)

	1938 (Actual)	1938 (Full Employment)	1938 (Full Employment, 1948 prices)	1948
	(1)	(2)	(3)	(4)
Income Tax	333	398	529	620
Surtax	69	83	110	140
N.D.C.	25	36	48	50
Death duties, and stamp duties on the transfer of property	90	95	126	140
Total Direct Taxes	517	612	813	950
Taxes on alcohol, tobacco, matches and entertainment	204	219	291	340
Other specific indirect taxes	94	100	133	150
General indirect taxes	73	81	108	120
Total Indirect Taxes	371	400	532	610
Total Taxation	888	1,012	1,345	1,560
Central Government Income from property	18	18	24	30
Total Revenue	906	1,030	1,369	1,590
Total Expenditure (see Table 16)	1,013	—	—	1,685
Deficit	107	—	—	95
Deficit as percentage of expenditure ..	**10**	**—**	**—**	**6**

Note.—The figures in column (1) based on Cmd. 6520 and other official sources. As regards column (2) the general principle was explained above; the most important individual estimates were that the marginal rate of income tax on *distributed* profits was 20 per cent. and of surtax 10 per cent., and that the average rate of N.D.C. was 4½ per cent. of assessed profits. It was assumed further, that there is no increase (consequent on full employment) in death duty receipts, but stamp duty receipts increase owing to the higher turnover of shares and other capital assets; the yield of specific indirect taxes was related to the estimated change in their consumption; the yield of general indirect taxes to the change in consumption and investment. As regards the adjustment from column (3) to column (4), the increase in incomes shown in Table 13, between the second and the third columns of that table, was assumed to bear income and surtax at the marginal rates given above. Death duties, etc., allow for the expansion of the National Debt. The volume of alcohol and tobacco consumption and entertainments were assumed to be 25 per cent. above the *actual* 1938 level. For other indirect taxes, the assumptions were the same as those stated for column (2) above.

employment in 1938; this estimate is based on the same assumptions as were employed in making the estimate in Table 4, p. 34.

The change in the yield of taxes due to the difference in incomes between the full employment income of 1938 and that of 1948 is shown in the third and fourth columns. The third column shows the change in tax yields due to the change in money values; in accordance with our assumption, this implied an increase of 33 per cent. in the yield of each kind of tax. The fourth column adjusts these figures for that part of the change in tax yields which is due to the change in the real income of each income category, between 1938 and 1948; here the additional taxes payable by each income group were calculated separately, on the assumption that the proportion of marginal income paid in taxation is the same as that assumed for the purposes of the second column, but making certain allowances for the trend in consumption habits.

39. The result of this analysis is that the combined effect of the change in money values, of higher productivity and of full employment is that the tax system of 1938 would yield £1,560 millions in 1948 (instead of the actual £888 millions in 1938) and thus would fall short of the required amount by only £95 millions or 6 per cent. Thus, in spite of the considerably higher post-war expenditure, the 1938 tax system would be consistent with a *smaller* deficit in 1948 than it was in the actual situation in 1938. In order to eliminate the deficit, the average rates of taxes would have to be raised by 6 per cent.—which means an income tax of 5s. 10d. (instead of 5s. 6d.) in the £, if all taxes were raised proportionately.[1]

40. We are now in a position to estimate the total tax burden falling on private incomes by adding together the taxes raised by all public authorities and by deducting subsidies and the general indirect taxes falling on goods and services purchased by public authorities. This is given in Table 19 and shows that the proportion of private incomes paid in taxation (including the higher social insurance contributions under the Social Security Plan) will be 25 per cent., instead of the pre-war 23 per cent. The distribution of this tax burden between the different categories of

---

[1] It should be borne in mind that in this estimate of a standard rate of 5s. 10d. income tax, it was also assumed that the pre-war income tax allowances were fully restored not merely in money but in real terms, i.e. the tax exemption limit was raised to £165, the allowance for married persons to £240, etc.

Table 19

TAXATION OF PRIVATE INCOMES, 1938 AND 1948

(£ millions)

	1938 (Actual)	1938 (Full Employment)	1948
I. Direct Taxes:			
Central Government	517	612	950
Social Security Funds	55	60	176
Total	572	672	1,126
II. Indirect Taxes:			
A. Specific Indirect Taxes:			
Central Government	298	319	490
Local Authorities	141	141	170
Less Subsidies	− 15	− 15	− 20
Net Total	424	445	640
B. General Indirect Taxes:			
Central Government	73	81	120
Local Authorities	70	70	80
Social Security Funds	54	60	124
Less Taxes falling on Public Authorities	− 32	− 32	− 50
Net Total	165	179	274
III. Increase in Central Government Taxation to cover prospective deficit	..	..	95
Total Taxes on Private Incomes	1,161	1,296	2,135
Private Incomes	5,110	5,610	8,450
Taxes as percentage of private incomes	**23**	**23**	**25**

Note.—The derivation of individual items is explained in previous tables, except the yield of social security taxes between the first and the second columns which is in proportion to the rise in employment; the revenue from local rates in the first and the second column is assumed to be the same, in accordance with the assumed behaviour of rents given in Table 2 (while their expansion between the second and the third column is as explained in Table 14). Taxes falling on public authorities for 1938 is derived from Cmd. 6520 (being the difference between item 16 in Table II and item (4) in Table F). For 1948 this item was adjusted to the rise in prices and the expansion of public outlay on goods and services.

income is shown in Table 20 on the assumption that *all* Central Government tax rates were raised by 6 per cent. (as compared with 1938).

Table 20
INCIDENCE OF THE BURDEN OF TAXATION, 1948

	Direct Taxes		Indirect Taxes		All Taxes	
	£Mn.	%	£Mn.	%	£Mn.	%
Rent, distributed profits and interest	700	69	200	18	900	42
Undistributed profits	195	19½	15	1	210	10
Salaries	85	8½	250	22	335	16
Wages and Social Income ..	30	3	660	59	690	32
Total	1,010	100	1,125	100	2,135	100

Note.—For the corresponding estimate for 1938, and 1938 full employment, see Table 4, and for the methods used see notes to Tables 3, 4, 18, and 19. Social insurance contributions are here included in indirect taxation, as in Table 4. It is assumed that the 1938 level of Central Government taxes would be raised by 6 per cent., local rates remain at their 1938 level and social insurance contributions will be as given in note (*l*) to Table 15.

Consumption and Savings

41. We next have to estimate the distribution of available incomes between consumption and savings. The available evidence points to the conclusion that with the long-run rise in incomes, consumption rises more or less proportionately;[1] the disproportionate rise in savings following upon an increase in incomes—which was shown in Table 5, p. 35—is a typically short-run phenomenon. In estimating post-war savings it would be erroneous therefore to apply the same assumptions for the change in incomes over the ten-year interval 1938–48, as were applied for the change from the actual to full employment income in 1938.

The most reasonable hypothesis for estimating savings out of available incomes in 1948 appeared to be to assume that for that part of the rise in real income which is due to long-run factors (i.e. the rise in productivity) savings rise in the same proportion as real income (i.e. in the proportions shown in the "average" column in Table 5); while for that part which is due to the elimination of unemployment, savings increase in a higher proportion (i.e. in the proportions shown in the "marginal" column in Table 5). This assumption implies that in the long run the proportion of income saved varies, not with the amount of real income, but with the level of employment.[2]

[1] Cf. Clark, *National Income and Outlay*, chap. viii.
[2] A similar assumption was made in calculating undistributed profits in para. 36 above.

42. On this assumption, and by taking the distribution of private incomes and taxation as shown in Table 13 and Table 20 above, gross savings come to £905 millions, and net savings (i.e. after deducting death duty, etc., payments) to £765 millions, both calculated at post-war factor cost of production. From the same assumption it follows that consumption in 1948 would amount to £5,550 millions at post-war factor cost, or £4,170 millions at pre-war factor cost, which implies an increase in real consumption of 19 per cent. over the actual 1938 level or 11 per cent. over the hypothetical full employment level in 1938. An increase in real consumption of this order (which implies moreover a rise of 46½ per cent. over the current war-time level) presupposes, of course, that there are no restraints on consumption *other than taxation*; that war-time rationing and scarcities have disappeared and that the consumer has much the same range of choice in spending money as he had before the war. To the extent that these suppositions will not be completely fulfilled by 1948, private savings will be larger, and the expenditure on consumption less, than in this estimate.

The Post-war Balance of Payments

43. In order to estimate the requirements of a post-war full employment policy, we must finally make an assumption about the post-war balance of payments. Our provisional assumption will be that exports (visible and invisible) and foreign income will balance imports, i.e. a zero balance of payments on current account. It may be worth while to set out, however, what this implies.

On the assumption that the importance of imported goods in the British national economy will be the same as before the war— i.e. that there are no measures taken to reduce the proportion either of imports of raw materials, etc., in total production or of imported consumers' goods in total consumption—the total volume of imports can be assumed to expand by 15 per cent. of the increase in real income, that is, by £140 millions (at 1938 prices) or 16 per cent. as compared with the actual level of imports at 1938. At the same time the income from foreign investments, at pre-war prices, will be some £120 millions less.[1] In addition, as we have seen, there was already an adverse balance of

---

[1] Cf. para. 33 (*g*) above.

£55 millions in 1938. Finally, there is the income from "invisible exports" (mainly shipping and insurance) the amount of which cannot be assumed as given—independently of the policies followed about exports and imports—since it varies more or less in proportion with the volume of international trade. Before the war, our invisible exports represented about 10 per cent. of the value of our trade (the sum of exports and imports). After the war, owing to the fall in the proportion of British shipping in world tonnage they might be less.

44. We shall estimate the requirements of an even balance of payments after the war on two suppositions:

(i) On the assumption that the terms of trade will be the same as before the war, but that invisible exports will amount to only 7 per cent. (and not 10 per cent.) of the value of trade, it would require an increase in exports by £325 millions (at pre-war prices), or by 68 per cent. over the 1938 volume, to compensate fully for the various factors specified above. Alternatively, a zero balance of payments might be achieved by a cut of £375 millions[1] or 37 per cent. in imports below the level it would have reached without restriction.[2] Finally, if imports are to be restricted, but only to the 1938 volume, the increase in exports required would be £205 millions, or 43 per cent. over 1938.

(ii) On the more favourable supposition that the terms of trade remain the same and that shipping and insurance will regain their pre-war position (i.e. that they will represent 10 per cent. of the value of trade) the required expansion in exports is 57 per cent.; alternatively, with the volume of exports at the pre-war level, the required restriction of imports (below the hypothetical post-war volume) is 34 per cent.;[3] while the maintenance of the 1938 level of imports would in this case require an expansion of exports by 33 per cent.

44. It may be that none of these policies will be practicable in the early post war years and that the position of equilibrium in the balance of payments will only be achieved gradually. Though the traditional position of Britain was that of a lending country with a

---

[1] The difference between this sum and the required increase in exports (£325 millions) is due to the change in the amount of invisible exports in the two cases.
[2] This implies a cut in imports by 27 per cent. below its actual 1938 amount.
[3] I.e. 23 per cent. below its actual volume in 1938.

favourable balance of payments, there need be no great harm in allowing an adverse balance of, say, £200–£300 millions per annum for a number of years—either by borrowing from abroad, or by liquidating foreign investments still further—provided that the additional resources made available in this way are used to improve the balance of payments position in the future—i.e. either in developing new industries suitable for exports, or industries (such as agriculture) whose product is a substitute for imports. In other words, provided that the Government adopts a long-term plan for the development of industries, the maintenance of an adverse balance over the reconstruction period might be a means of improving (instead of aggravating) the position of the balance of payments in the long run.

Full Employment Policies in 1948

45. We are now in a position to answer the question posed in paragraph 32, what is the rate of investment outlay (public and private) which would assure full employment in 1948? Our hypothesis is that the Government, through a National Investment Board, will so regulate the rate of capital expenditure (by fitting together the investments undertaken by public authorities and by private industry into a common national plan) as to ensure stability and adequacy in the national outlay as a whole. The question which then arises is whether the "required" rate of investment expenditure which emerges from our assumptions is an adequate one, from the general social point of view; and what Governmental policies should be followed if it is not.

46. On the assumptions that Government taxation is just sufficient to cover ordinary expenditure, that the level of exports is sufficient to pay for imports, and that the division of private incomes between consumption and savings is as explained in paragraph 41 above, the rate of net investment consistent with full employment in 1948, as shown in Table 21, is £765 millions—the equivalent of £575 millions in terms of 1938 prices. This is just 25 per cent. greater (in volume) than the actual rate of investment in 1938, which was £460 millions;[1] but it is 13 per cent. lower than

---

[1] £420 millions net private investment (see Table 7) plus £40 millions public capital expenditure, financed in 1938 out of Central and local Government revenue, but excluded from the post-war budgets.

the implied rate of investment expenditure under full employment, and a zero balance of payments, in 1938 which would have
been £660 millions.[1]

Table 21

FULL EMPLOYMENT INCOME AND OUTLAY IN 1948

(*£ millions*)

	1948 Prices	1938 Prices		1948 Prices	1938 Prices
Private Consumption	5,550	4,170	Private Consumption Outlay	5,550	4,170
Private Saving ..	765	575			
Taxation of Private Incomes	2,135	1,605	Public Consumption Outlay	1,135	855
			Balance of Payments	—	—
Private Incomes ..	8,450	6,350	Net Investment Outlay		
Government Income	70	55	(Public and Private)	765	575
Less Transfer Incomes	− 1,070	− 805			
Net National Income	7,450	5,600	Net National Outlay ..	7,450	5,600

Note.—The derivation of all the items in this Table was explained above, with the
exception of "public consumption outlay" (i.e. the expenditure of public authorities
on goods and services on current account) which was derived as follows:

	£ millions
Total Expenditure of Public Authorities (see Table 17)	2,275
Less Transfer Expenditure (see Table 13) ..	− 1,070
Subsidies (Table 19)	− 20
Total Expenditure on goods and services at market prices	1,185
Less General indirect taxes falling on public authorities (Table 19)	− 50
Total Expenditure on goods and services at factor cost	1,135

47. An examination of the requirements of post-war reconstruction in the field of capital expenditure is now being undertaken by various Government departments, and until their results
are published the material for a more detailed analysis will not be

[1] See Table 9, Route I*b*. Out of the total public expenditure of £960 millions,
£200 millions should be regarded as investment expenditure, i.e. the additional
public outlay of £160 millions, plus the £40 millions referred to in the previous
footnote. This, together with the "private investment outlay" of £460 millions,
amounts to £660 millions. The reasons why despite the higher national income,
the corresponding item for 1948 is smaller are: (i) the higher level of public consumption outlay in 1948 (£855 millions at 1938 prices, instead of £760 millions);
(ii) in the calculation of Route I*b* in Table 9 there is implied a budgetary surplus
over public consumption outlay of £100 millions, which augmented the resources
available for investment purposes (as compared with the situation postulated for 1948,
where the surplus is zero) by £73 millions. (The reason for the difference is that in the
calculation of Route I*b* for 1938, the existing rates of taxation were assumed to be
given; in the calculations for the full employment outlay for 1948 in Table 21 the
taxes were determined by the condition that the ordinary budgets should balance.)

available. But without any such examination, it is fairly certain from the considerations mentioned earlier, that if Britain after the war goes in for a vigorous policy of renewing her capital stock—of scrapping obsolete houses and obsolete industrial equipment, and providing for the development of new industries— she would have to spend on capital projects at a far higher rate than in 1938.

In Table 22 an attempt is made to relate the available information about pre-war capital expenditure (given in Table 7) to the requirements of post-war investment under three alternative hypotheses: (i) that the rate of net investment will be as given in Table 21 above (Plan I); (ii) that net investment will be planned at the rate of £750 millions (Plan II); (iii) that net investment will be planned at the rate of £1,000 millions (Plan III); all at 1938 prices. The allocation of the totals among the various categories shown in this Table is largely in the nature of guesswork based on the broad facts about post-war needs, not on the result of a separate examination of the individual categories.

Plan I—apart from allowing for the minimum increase in stocks that can be expected in a normal year—only permits a modest increase in the rate of capital expenditure in industry and in housing. Plan II allows for a rate of expenditure on buildings that would probably be sufficient for the building of 500,000 dwelling houses annually;[1] it also allows a much higher rate of new investment in industrial plant and machinery, public utilities and other fixed capital. Plan III would allow doubling the pre-war volume of *gross* investment in plant and machinery; it also includes an allowance for the British contribution towards the reconstruction of Europe.

48. It is not possible to decide at this stage which of these possibilities comes nearest to fulfilling the requirements of an adequate post-war reconstruction programme; we may, however, discuss their implications for a full employment policy. Plans II and III require that the Government restrict real consumption below the level it would reach with a balanced budget and thereby release resources for investment purposes. This could be done in

---

[1] This is regarded as the necessary rate of building if an adequate number of houses are to be provided, and all slums abolished, in a period of fifteen years.

various ways; the simplest, perhaps, is by creating a surplus in the ordinary budget in the form of a sinking fund, to be covered out of taxation. In making the estimate for post-war Government expenditure in Table 16, we have made no provision for a sinking fund—for the simple reason that the desirable sum to be set aside for this purpose could only be determined after all the relevant factors in the total economic situation were known.

49. It follows from the estimates of taxation, consumption and savings, in paragraphs 40–42 above, that at the full employment

Table 22

ALTERNATIVE FRAMEWORKS FOR THE NATIONAL INVESTMENT PLAN

(*£ millions, at 1938 prices*)

	Actual Net Investment, 1938	Hypothetical Net Investment, 1948		
		Plan I	Plan II	Plan III
Public works (new roads, etc.)	40	40	40	60
Public utilities	60	60	90	100
Buildings	245	300	400	400
Plant and Machinery	20	45	80	140
Other fixed capital	10	30	40	50
Net increase in stocks and goods in process	25	40	40	40
Costs incurred in the transfer of property and investment of savings	60	60	60	60
Contribution to the reconstruction of Europe	—	—	—	150
Total Net Investment	460	575	750	1,000

Note.—For the definitions of the various categories in this Table, see note to Table 7, p. 39. (In case Recommendation 23 of the Beveridge Report were adopted—i.e. industrial assurance made a public service—the item "costs incurred in the transfer of property" should be reduced by £15 millions.)

level of income in 1948 (i) a proportionate increase in *direct* taxes, increasing revenue by £100 millions, would reduce consumption by £62 millions, and savings by £38 millions; (ii) a proportionate increase in the rates of *indirect* taxes, augmenting revenue by £100 millions would reduce consumption by £85 millions, and savings by £15 millions; (iii) a similar proportionate increase in *all* Central Government tax rates would reduce consumption by £71 millions, and savings by £29 millions.

This means that if, in connection with the policy of restricting consumption (in order to maintain a higher rate of investment), all Central Government taxes were increased proportionately, Plan II would involve a sinking fund of £331 millions, and Plan III a sinking fund of £800 millions. As is shown in Table 23, each of these plans is consistent with a higher level of private real consumption than obtained in 1938, and would thus leave the community better off, in terms of current standard of living, than they were before the war. But in the case of Plan III at any rate, the required increase in taxation is so stiff—it implies an income tax of 8s. 8d., instead of 5s. 10d. in the £, if all Central Government taxes were raised proportionately—that it might be preferable, in this case, to secure the required reduction in consumption (at least in part) by other means of control, such as rationing.

50. Table 23 also shows the implications of these plans in case the level of exports is not sufficient to secure an even balance of payments, and an adverse balance of £200 millions is maintained. These are given as Plans I*b*, II*b* and III*b*. The second plan in this case is consistent with a practically unchanged level of taxation, while the first plan would require a *negative* sinking fund of £282 millions—i.e. a 17 per cent. deficit in the current Central Government budget.

Table 23

ALTERNATIVE PLANS FOR FULL EMPLOYMENT OUTLAY
IN 1948

(*£ millions at 1948 prices*)

	Plan I	Plan II	Plan III	Plan I*b*	Plan II*b*	Plan III*b*
Private Consumption Outlay ..	5,550	5,315	4,982	5,750	5,515	5,182
Public Consumption Outlay ..	1,135	1,135	1,135	1,135	1,135	1,135
Balance of Payments	—	—	—	−200	−200	−200
Net investment outlay (public and private)	765	1,000	1,333	765	1,000	1,333
Total Outlay	7,450	7,450	7,450	7,450	7,450	7,450
Sinking Fund	—	331	800	−282	49	518
Percentage increase in rates of taxation as compared with Plan I ..	—	20	49	−17	3	31
Percentage increase in private real consumption as compared with 1938	19	14	7	23	18	11

Note.—It is assumed that the tax revenue for the payment of sinking funds is obtained by a proportionate increase in all taxes raised by the Central Government, and the percentage changes in tax rates relate not to all taxation, but only to taxation raised by the Central Government.

IV. THE LONG-RUN CONSEQUENCES OF CONTINUOUS PUBLIC BORROWING

51. The above calculations were worked out for a particular post-war year, 1948. A plan for a continuous full employment policy would also have to take into account that under conditions of capital accumulation and technical progress, the national income would not remain stationary, but would be steadily rising, with the consequence that the necessary Governmental policies to ensure full employment would also have to be steadily adjusted. Since any addition to incomes could be expected to be only partly devoted to increased consumption and partly to increased savings, a *given* rate of investment outlay would not be adequate to maintain full employment in successive years unless measures were taken to enable the rising production to be fully absorbed in rising consumption. This means that the Government, in order to maintain full employment in conditions of rising productivity, would either have to plan for an expanding rate of investment expenditure over time, or for a gradually diminishing rate of the "sinking fund"—i.e. for a gradual reduction in tax revenue, relatively to any given level of public expenditures.[1] Ultimately, the Government may have to raise the propensity to consume by more radical methods of income redistribution—when it will no longer be possible to afford the degree of inequality of incomes that can be sustained during the period of relatively high investment.

52. It would be beyond the scope of this memorandum to examine the implications of this problem on a full employment policy over a longer period in any detail. The remainder of the paper will be restricted to an examination of one particular aspect of the long-run problem: the effects of a policy of continuous public borrowing under peacetime conditions.

[1] This is, of course, merely a different way of stating the proposition that if as a result of the accumulation of capital there is a steady increase in productive capacity, steps must be taken to ensure that the increase in potential output is matched by a corresponding increase in "purchasing power"—otherwise the increased output will not materialise and unemployment will result. The maintenance of full employment would automatically ensure, of course, that adequate purchasing power is created to absorb the potential output (indeed, the latter is merely a different aspect of the former); but in order to maintain full employment in these circumstances it is not enough to maintain the level of expenditures—they must be steadily increased.

53. If a plan providing for a high rate of investment expenditure were adopted over the reconstruction period, and if the analysis of the various elements of the post-war situation given in the previous section is correct, the Government during the early post-war years would have to provide for surpluses rather than deficits in its "ordinary" budget, i.e. taxation would have to be higher than the level of running expenditures. On the other hand, the Government would have to undertake loan expenditures as part of the national investment budget; the latter might well exceed the "sinking fund" in the ordinary budget so that the net national indebtedness might be growing rather than diminishing, right from the start. Moreover, as time went on and the national real income increased, either the rate of loan expenditure on capital account would have to be raised, or taxation would have to be lowered, relatively to expenditure; in both cases the annual net increase in the public debt would tend to get larger. Further, in the more distant future, when the reconstruction programme will be nearing completion and it will be desirable to reduce the proportion of output devoted to investment, and to raise the proportion of output consumed, remission of taxation might prove the most convenient method of maintaining full employment. Hence, as part of the full employment policy we may have to reckon with a steadily rising public debt in peacetime.

54. Ever since the inception of the British National Debt in 1688, money was borrowed in time of war and gradually repaid during periods of peace; the war borrowings always exceeding the peace repayments (see Table 24). As a result, a strong prejudice grew up against a policy of borrowing in peacetime. But there is, in fact, *less* justification for incurring debt in war than there is in peacetime. Borrowing in time of war does not increase the productive powers of the community and does not sustain employment; also, a great deal of borrowing is concentrated over a relatively brief span of time, so that war-borrowing increases rentier incomes not only absolutely, but as a proportion of the national income.

55. What is the "real burden" of a growing National Debt? Against the popular notions which regard borrowing as a means of "throwing the burden on future generations" and the Debt as a

net loss of real wealth, economists have rightly emphasised that internally held debt does not diminish the total real income of the community; all that the service of the Debt implies is a transfer of income between different members of society; and even this "transfer-burden" can be minimised by an appropriately chosen tax system.

This interpersonal transfer is not, however, the sole relevant aspect of the problem; the existence of the debt would have some economic consequences even if the interpersonal transfer were nil. Let us suppose e.g. that everyone saves during war time (when the borrowing takes place) a constant proportion of his income; so that, when the period of borrowing is over, everyone's interest-income on past savings bears a constant proportion to his other sources of income. If we then assumed that the annual interest charge is paid out of the proceeds of an income tax which is pro-portionate to income, there is no transfer at all in consequence of the Debt. Yet economic incentives have altered; for in the new situation, everyone receives a higher proportion of the same *net* income in the form of a rent (which is independent of current effort) and a lesser proportion as a reward for current effort. Hence the incentive to current effort is diminished.

It is difficult to say how much importance should be attached to this factor, but whatever its importance is, it clearly depends not on the size of the Debt or the annual interest charge, but on on the proportion of the latter to the national income; and it could only become significant when this proportion is large. In Britain, the annual debt burden as a proportion of the national income reached a maximum on two occasions, 1815 and 1924, and in each case amounted to some 7 per cent. of the national income. After the present war, on the assumptions stated above, it will be just under 6 per cent., i.e. £500 millions on £8,450 millions private income.[1]

56. In estimating the effects of a rising National Debt in

---

[1] Between 1924 and 1948 the National Debt on our assumptions will have increased by 300 per cent., the annual interest charge by only 66 per cent., while the national (private) income in money terms by 108 per cent. Thus, despite a Second World War, which—in terms of borrowing—was twice as costly as the first, the burden of the Debt is likely to be smaller after the present war than it was after the last war—a striking consequence of the cheap money policy inaugurated by the Treasury in the 1930's.

peacetime, we must first of all consider the probable growth of the national income. This will be the resultant of the following four factors: (i) the change in productivity per man hour; (ii) the change in the working population; (iii) the change in the length of the working week; (iv) the change in the price level.[1] Let us examine them in turn.

(i) Since the beginning of this century at any rate (and probably over a much longer period, though this cannot, in this country, be established statistically) output per man hour in primary and secondary industry has increased (as the result of technical progress and the accumulation of capital) at the compound rate of 3 per cent. per annum. The national real income per man hour (i.e. including the output of distribution and

Table 24

HISTORY OF THE BRITISH NATIONAL DEBT,
1688 TO 1944
(£ millions)

	Borrowed	Repaid	Debt (at end of period)
War 1688–97 ..	21	—	21
Peace 1697–1701 ..	—	5	16
War 1702–14 ..	39	—	55
Peace 1714–39 ..	—	8	47
War 1739–48 ..	31	—	78
Peace 1748–55 ..	—	3	75
War 1755–63 ..	72	—	147
Peace 1763–75 ..	—	11	136
War 1775–86 ..	121	—	257
Peace 1786–93 ..	—	13	244
War 1793–1815 ..	604	—	848
Peace 1815–53 ..	—	79	769
War 1853–55 ..	39	—	807
Peace 1855–99 ..	—	172	635
War 1899–1902 ..	159	—	794
Peace 1902–14 ..	—	144	650
War 1914–18 ..	7,180	—	7,830
Peace 1919–39 ..	—	33*	7,797*
War 1939– ..	11,796†	—	19,593†

* Excluding the National Defence Loans, 1937–9, which should more properly be allocated to war borrowing. There was a substantial amount of net debt repayment over the period which is concealed in the above figures, since they include the borrowing of the Exchange Equalisation Fund (offset by holdings of gold and foreign exchange) and do not deduct the public debt held by public departments.

† Up to 31 March 1944.

[1] A fifth factor, namely the level of employment relatively to the working population, is here ignored, on the supposition of a full employment policy.

services) has increased at the rate of 1·5 per cent. per annum.[1] There is every reason to expect that this movement will continue in the post-war era; under a full employment policy, it is bound to be even greatly accelerated for three reasons: (i) owing to the higher rate of capital accumulation under full employment; (ii) owing to the extra stimulus given to the introduction of more labour-saving methods of production under a system where the scarcity of labour (and not the scarcity of markets) is the factor limiting the scale of production, and under conditions of approximate stability of population where a much higher proportion of investment expenditure than in the past will be available for purposes of "deepening", i.e. of increasing capital per head; (iii) owing to the fact that with a high demand for labour in industry, the past tendency towards an exorbitant number of people entering the field of distribution might be arrested, in which case the annual increase in productivity, for the system as a whole, would automatically be greater. It seems, therefore, that at a minimum, the rate of increase in productivity under full employment conditions in peacetime could be put at 2 per cent. per annum.

(ii) The future movement of the working population is partly the result of the changes in the age composition of the existing population (due to the past fluctuations in the annual number of births), partly of the movements of fertility and mortality rates in the future. We shall estimate the change in the working population in the period 1945–70 on two assumptions: (a) a minimum estimate, on the assumption that fertility rates will resume their declining trend after the war; (b) a maximum estimate, on the assumption that fertility rates will rise sufficiently to maintain the actual number of births at the average level of the years 1936–40.[2] The first assumption implies a gradual decline in the

---

[1] The difference is due to the fact that the other sections of the economy have not participated in the increase in industrial producitivity, and tended to absorb a rising proportion of the total labour force. Output per man hour in distribution has tended to diminish in the sense that the number of people engaged in distributive services has increased faster than the volume of goods to be distributed.

[2] The estimates were largely derived from the recent League of Nations Report on "The Future Population of Europe and the Soviet Union", by Frank W. Notestein and others of the Office of Population Research of Princeton University. The hypotheses about the trend of mortality rates and of fertility rates in case of assumption (a), are those given in pages 22-36 of the Report.

gross reproduction rate, over the period 1945–70, from 0·8 to under 0·6, the second a gradual rise in the rate from 0·8 to about 1·0.[1]

On the first assumption the population aged 15–64 of the United Kingdom will decline by 2·2 millions, or 6·6 per cent., between 1945 and 1970; on the second assumption, by only 700,000, or 2 per cent. These figures conceal, however, the unfavourable change in the age composition within the group; the numbers in the most productive age group, 20–49, will decline, over the same period, by 14 per cent. in the case of assumption (a) and 10 per cent. in the case of assumption (b). Hence the fall in the *effective* working population (i.e. in terms of units of constant labour power) during the quarter of the century following the war, and assuming that the balance of migration will be zero, might be put at a minimum of 6 per cent. and a maximum of 10 per cent. For the purposes of estimating the movement of the national income up to 1970, we shall assume the maximum figure and put the fall in the *effective* working population at 10 per cent.

Beyond 1970, the different assumptions about fertility will yield, of course, much more divergent results. On the assumption that the gross reproduction rate will fall, in the manner specified above, up to 1970, and thereafter be maintained at that very low level, the working population will fall by about a third every twenty-five years. On the assumption on the other hand that over the next twenty-five years there will be a sufficient increase in fertility to push the *net* reproduction rate to around unity by 1970—a very modest aim to set to social policy; it implies only a 10–15 per cent. rise in fertility over the current war-time level—the population will be eventually stabilised at a level only slightly below that of 1970, with an effective working population of some 12·5 per cent. below that of 1945.

(iii) In the above estimates for the year 1948 it was assumed that working hours in 1948 would be the same as in 1938. It is reasonable to suppose, however, that the trend towards shorter hours will be resumed, in the post-war period, though at a slower

[1] The base of a 0·8 gross reproduction rate for 1945 is founded on the fertility rates of the last three pre-war years, ignoring the war-time jump in fertility. (The *net* reproduction rate was estimated by the Registrar General at 0·9 for 1943.)

rate; and we shall assume that the average hours of work will fall by 10 per cent. every twenty-five years.[1]

(iv) It will be assumed that post-war Governments will pursue a monetary and wage policy which maintains the prices of final commodities constant. This implies that given the share of wages in the total value of output (which in the past showed remarkably little change over long periods), the average rate of money wages will rise in the same proportion as productivity per man hour. A policy of a falling price level, implying constant money wages, quite apart from its other disadvantage of enhancing rentier incomes, would make the task of monetary stabilisation under full employment needlessly difficult; while a policy of a rising price level might be incompatible with the maintenance of stability in the long run.

There is one particular case in which a policy of rising prices would be preferable to that of constant prices. If the supply of goods and services freely provided by the State were to form an increasing proportion of the national real income (i.e. the supply of things which, just because they are not provided through the market, do not enter into the calculation of the price level) the maintenance of a stable relation between the movements of money income and that of real income—which is necessary in order to keep money wages constant in terms of productivity—would require that the price level of marketable goods and services should be allowed to rise.

57. The net result of these assumptions is that, setting off the effects of rising productivity against the fall in the working population, and the reduction of hours, and assuming a monetary policy which maintains a stable relation between money income and real income, the national money income rises over the period 1948–70 at the rate of 1 per cent. per annum, i.e., that it rises on the average by some £90 millions per annum, over the period. This implies that the Government could go on borrowing an amount which adds some £5 millions to the interest charge annually without thereby increasing the interest burden as a proportion of the national income. Assuming that the Government

---

[1] This would bring average hours of work to forty-two per week by about 1970. (In the period 1914–24 average working hours fell by about 10 per cent.; but there was little change in the period 1924–38.)

borrows on the average at 2 per cent., it could borrow an average annual amount of £250 millions without increasing the ratio of the annual interest burden to the national income above the level it will have reached at the end of the war. After 1970, assuming that fertility will have risen sufficiently in the meantime for an approach to a stable population, it could, of course, borrow at a higher rate still—at the rate of some £325 millions per annum. It could moreover borrow at an increasing rate through time, since with an even rate of increase in the national income, the annual increment in income will get steadily larger.[1]

58. The above calculation shows the amounts that could be borrowed annually while maintaining the ratio of the interest on the National Debt to the national income constant. They are not, of course, the true limits of the amounts that could be borrowed while maintaining budgetary equilibrium at a constant level of taxation. With the tax structure postulated in paragraph 40 above, and with the rates of taxation at the level necessary to balance the post-war Central Government budget, 25 per cent. of any increase in the national income could be expected to be paid in Central Government taxation.[2] This means that with an average annual increment of £90 millions in the national income, Central Government tax revenue would expand annually by £22·5 millions, while the annual increase in Central Government expenditure could only be put at £7 millions.[3] Hence after meeting other commitments, a sum of £15·5 millions will be available each year to cover additional interest on the National Debt. This means that —assuming the average rate of interest to be 2 per cent.—the

---

[1] Over the period 1948–70, the national income could not be expected to increase at an even rate through time, because the fall in the effective working population will not proceed at an even rate. Up to about 1960, the working population is likely to remain fairly stable, most of the reduction occurring in the decade 1960–70.

[2] See Tables 13 and 16 above; tax rates were raised by 6 per cent., in accordance with paragraph 40. In case post-war taxation is higher than that (i.e. it allows for the payment of a "sinking fund") the marginal yield of taxation will be more than 25 per cent.

[3] The total annual increase in expenditure over the period 1948–70 being put at £152 millions. This is the net result of the increased cost of retirement pensions under the Beveridge Plan, £196 millions (Cmd. 6404, p. 199) allowing for a 10 per cent. increase in the number of old age pensioners between 1965 and 1970; the net saving in war pensions, £70 millions; the further increase in the cost of education, £60 millions; an allowance for the automatic rise in the yield of death duties, due to the change in age composition (not included in the above estimate of the marginal yield of taxes), £34 millions. This makes no allowance for any saving on other items, such as defence, which in the case of a prolonged period of peace, might be considerable.

National Debt could be allowed to expand at the average rate of no less than £775 millions per annum over the period 1948–70, without having to raise any new taxes for the maintenance of "budgetary equilibrium".

Thus the contention that a policy of increasing the National Debt in peacetime involves a steadily increasing potential burden on the taxpayer is very far from the truth. This could only be the case with a rate of borrowing that is far in excess of anything that might be necessary under peacetime conditions in order to sustain a full employment policy.

59. These estimates are based on the annual growth of the national income that can be expected under any full employment policy. They do not take into account the direct effect which the Government loan expenditure—if wisely invested—would have on the increase in the national income in the future; they hold even if the loan money is spent on objects of current consumption, or on completely useless purposes, such as digging holes and filling them up again. In so far as the loan is spent in ways which directly raise the productive efficiency of the community, we must also allow for the further increase in income and tax revenue resulting from it. On the above assumption of 25 per cent. of any increase in income being paid automatically in taxation, any public investment which increases the future national income by more than 6 per cent. of the loan expenditure will actually make the prospective tax burden relatively *smaller* than it would have been without the loan expenditure; since it will augment the yield of taxation in the future by more than it increases the interest charge.

60. It follows therefore that even if the State policy were guided by purely fiscal considerations—that of reducing the rates of taxation to a minimum—the best course to pursue would still not be to refrain from borrowing, but to undertake public investments which lighten the future tax burden through increasing the national income and thus the yield of given rates of taxation. In the past State investments were only regarded as "self-liquidating" when the prospective money return of the asset created by the investment was by itself sufficient to cover the interest charge. It is now fairly generally recognised however that the price mechanism, even under the most favourable conditions, can

register only some of the gains and losses which result from any particular piece of economic activity; there is a cluster of effects (what the economists call the external economies and dis-economies) which escape the net of price-cost measurement. Thus an investment may be highly remunerative from the social point of view even if its direct return is nil if, in consequence of the investment, the real income of the community is increased. To the extent to which the State, through the tax system, automatically participates in any increase in the incomes of its citizens, such investments may be "remunerative" from the point of view of the State, even though they would not be remunerative when under-taken by private enterprise.

Hence the test of profitability which is decisive in the case of private investments, is not adequate when applied to public investment. This would be true even if the policy of the State were guided by purely fiscal considerations—that is to say, by the object of reducing the burden of taxation to a minimum. It is totally inadequate when the economic policy is governed, as of course it should be, by social considerations—not merely of minimising the tax burden, but of maximising the national income as a whole.

3

EMPLOYMENT POLICIES AND THE PROBLEM OF INTERNATIONAL BALANCE[1]

THE purpose of this paper is to examine the problems that arise in the field of international transactions for any country which desires to maintain its internal level of effective demand and employment by means of domestic measures. No attempt will be made here to analyse the nature of the domestic measures by which a "high and stable" level of employment is maintained. It will be assumed that each country has at its disposal appropriate measures—in the field of fiscal, monetary or investment policies— to attain this objective.

The international problem has two aspects which, though closely inter-related, are best discussed separately: the *structural* and the *cyclical* aspect. The former problem arises in a world where the level of employment and unemployment is stable in all areas, but where some countries desire to maintain a higher coefficient of labour utilisation (i.e. a lower average rate of un- employment) than other countries. The latter, and practically the far more important problem, concerns itself with the balance of payments difficulties that arise whenever any particular country desires to maintain its domestic income and employment in the face of a contraction in incomes and employment in other areas.

I

The purely structural aspect of the problem may be character- ised by the proposition that the lower the level of employment in any one country, given the level of employment in other countries, the lower will be its demand for imports in relation to the world demand for its exports and, therefore, the higher is the rate of exchange at which its international transactions can be brought into equilibrium. A rise in the level of employment in any one

[1] Paper presented to the meeting of the International Economic Association in Monte Carlo, September, 1950. Published in the *Review of Economic Studies*, 1950–1, Vol. XIX, No. 1.

country in relation to others is, therefore, analogous in its effect to a rise in the internal price level in relation to the price levels ruling in other countriès. It should be emphasised that the level of employment and the general level of domestic prices thus constitute two distinct and separate factors in the determination of the equilibrium rate of exchange. A rise in employment, given the price level, will lower the equilibrium rate of exchange in much the same fashion as a rise in the price level, given the level of employment. To the extent that the level of employment and the price level are themselves positively correlated—i.e. that a rise in employment will carry with it a rise in the internal price level on account of rising marginal costs of production or rising money wages, or both—the effects of an increase in employment on the equilibrium rate of exchange will be correspondingly greater.

From the point of view of any particular country, therefore, the international aspects of its own employment-stabilisation policies will be all the more favourable the more its own internal employment policies are synchronised with those of other countries. Given the freedom to vary exchange rates, equilibrium in international transactions is consistent, of course, with varying levels of employment—or, more precisely, with varying relations in the unemployment percentages of different countries. But the higher the level of internal employment in any country in relation to the others, the lower will be the rate of exchange at which—given the relative price and wage levels in the different countries—the balance will be attained; and a lower rate of exchange will normally imply less favourable terms of trade for the country concerned.

If the effects of a relatively high internal level of employment on the (potential) equilibrium rate of exchange, and thus on the terms of trade, are large, the country may be justified in imposing additional import restrictions (in the form of higher tariffs, etc.) in order to reduce its propensity to import and thus render any given volume of imports consistent with a higher level of internal employment. Such import restrictions need not invite retaliation in so far as they merely aim at preventing an expansion of imports that could not be readily financed out of additional exports;

and they should be sharply distinguished from policies which aim at raising the internal level of employment through a reduction in the level of imports below the level of exports—i.e. the policy of "exporting unemployment" through the creation of export surpluses. In the first case, the imposition of restrictions does not effectively reduce the volume of international trade (since the volume of imports of the country imposing restrictions will be no smaller than they would have been in the absence of full employment and without restrictions); nor does it compromise the ability of other countries in maintaining successful employment-stabilisation policies. In the second case, the measures of restriction aim at directly reducing the volume of international trade and render the pursuance of full employment policies in other countries more difficult.

The proposed International Trade Organisation Charter recognises this distinction in making special exceptions for countries "suffering from balance of payments difficulties". It would be desirable, however, if more satisfactory criteria could be evolved for separating cases in which the imposition of import restrictions does not run counter to the economic interests of other countries, from other cases where the imposition of restrictions cannot be justified on such grounds. In particular, it may be desirable to restrict the scope of this provision to such balance of payments difficulties as are caused by the failure of other countries to maintain full employment on some reasonable standard, and to those caused by the policies of import restrictions imposed by other countries which aim at the creation, or maintenance, of balance of payments surpluses, rather than the elimination of deficits.

The problem of maintaining international balance under conditions where each country maintains "high and stable" levels of employment internally is thus, in some important respects, more difficult than was the maintenance of international equilibrium in a world in the past when the levels of employment in the various areas were allowed freely to fluctuate. Under a régime of stable exchanges, such fluctuations represented the major automatic mechanism for restoring balance of payments equilibrium when the balance was, for any reason, disturbed. If a country experienced a fall in the demand for its exports, its internal level of income and employment fell (even without any deliberate deflationary measures introduced in order to re-establish equilibrium) and the consequential fall in imports reduced its balance of payments deficit. Under a system of high and stable levels of employment the adjustment-mechanism represented by such induced employment fluctuations is, by hypothesis, excluded. Similarly, it is difficult to conceive that deliberate variations in the domestic price level for the purposes of maintaining international balance (for the purpose, that is, of compensating for extraneous or structural changes which disturb the pre-existing balance) could be made consistent with the policy of stabilising the internal level of employment.

It follows, therefore, that for the continuing maintenance (as well as the initial attainment) of international equilibrium, exchange rate adjustments would have to be resorted to far more frequently. Past experience has shown, however, that an all too frequent use of exchange rate adjustments (or a régime of freely fluctuating exchange rates) in itself renders the preservation of stable conditions in international transactions far more difficult. Moreover, exchange rate adjustments could also be used—in a manner analogous to import restrictions—for the purpose of "exporting unemployment" rather than for the purpose of restoring the international balance. As pre-war experience has shown, the devaluation of exchange rates introduced by deficit countries in order to meet the problem of an adverse balance may be followed by corresponding devaluations introduced by surplus countries in order to maintain their international competitive position.

Thus while it is difficult to conceive how the balance of international transactions could be continually maintained under a régime of stable levels of employment without the use of exchange rate adjustments, this method could only prove successful if employed judiciously—i.e. if used only in directions that would rectify any existing imbalance in international trade and not in directions that would aggravate it; and if it were used to meet more lasting or structural changes in the underlying demand and supply conditions rather than purely temporary fluctuations.

Certain provisions in the Charter of the International Monetary Fund were originally designed to limit undesirable variations in exchange rates, while allowing at the same time the use of the exchange rate weapon to rectify basic maladjustments. Here again it would be desirable if more satisfactory criteria could be evolved which would secure a greater degree of freedom in exchange rate adjustments, while eliminating the danger of unjustified or disequilibrating variations.

A further problem that emerges in this connection is the pre-servation of domestic price stability. If countries stabilised their levels of employment at the cost of continuing inflation, the preservation of international equilibrium would demand a con-tinuing downward adjustment in exchange rates of the inflation-ary countries. Quite apart from the problems caused by frequent and continuing exchange rate adjustments, mentioned above, experience has shown that it is difficult to carry out such adjust-ments in a manner that would leave the relation between the external value of a currency and its internal purchasing power unchanged. It would, therefore, have a continuing disturbing influence on international trade, either because the exchange rate adjustments of the inflationary countries lagged behind the rise in the internal price level (so that their currencies tended to be continually over-valued), or because, as happened in the major inflations after the First World War, the rise in the internal price level lagged behind the movement in foreign exchange rates (so that the currencies tended to be continually under-valued). It is, therefore, to the interest of any one country that other countries should maintain full employment and internal price stability at the same time, and that they should avoid methods of maintain-ing employment that involve continuing inflation.

II

The cyclical aspect of the problem arises from the fact that, at given rates of exchange, a fall in income and employment in any one country tends to reduce its imports relatively to its exports and thereby generates surpluses in its current balance of payments with corresponding deficits in the balance of payments of the

other countries.[1] From the point of view of other countries, therefore, a fall in employment in any one country creates both a
balance of payments problem—since their exports which, by
hypothesis, were previously sufficient to pay for imports, are now
no longer so—and also an employment problem, since the fall in
exports directly reduces income and employment in the export
industries, with a tendency to further adverse repercussions in the
level of activity of other domestic industries. (The fall in incomes
and employment in the responding countries will also tend to
reduce their imports, thus aggravating the impact of the original
fall in employment on third countries.) These two aspects of the
problem, which may be termed the "liquidity aspect" and the
"employment aspect" may best be analysed separately.

From the point of view of the liquidity aspect, the main problem of countries affected by a recession in employment abroad is
to restore the current balance of international transactions—at
any rate in so far as they are unable, or unwilling, to finance an
adverse balance through the depletion of international reserves or
by borrowing from abroad. In the absence of deliberate measures
to maintain internal employment, the fall in production and
income resulting from the fall in exports will, as already noted,
in itself tend to correct the disequilibrium in the balance of international transactions, as a result of the consequential fall in
imports.

It should be noted, however, that since the fall in income will
normally reduce domestic savings in relation to domestic investment, the "multiplier" effect of the fall in exports will not normally proceed far enough to reduce imports by the full extent of the
fall in exports, but will leave a residual deficit in the balance of
payments on current account. Even in the absence of internal
employment stabilisation policies, therefore, the restoration of
equilibrium in the balance of payments will require the adoption
of deliberate measures by the countries concerned which, in
principle, could take one of the following four forms: (i) internal

---

[1] The terms "surplus" and "deficit" in the balance of payments, here and in the
rest of this paper, refer to *undesigned* surpluses or deficits which are not offset by long-
term capital movements. A fall in employment in any particular country may also
entail a contraction of its net foreign lending, thereby aggravating the balance of
payments problems of other countries. This aspect of the problem will not be separately
considered in this paper.

deflation; (ii) import restrictions; (iii) exchange rate adjustments; (iv) discriminatory exchange or trade restrictions. Only certain of these policies are consistent, of course, with the maintenance of internal employment.

The classic method of dealing with the balance of payments disequilibria induced through a fall in the foreign demand for exports is the method of internal deflation achieved through deliberate credit restriction. According to the classical doctrine the effect of such credit restrictions is to induce a fall in the price level in the deficit country relatively to other countries and thereby rectify the disequilibrium through a change in relative price levels. There is fairly general agreement, however, that the more potent consequence of such credit restrictions is a reduction in home investment, which brings about an additional reduction in the level of incomes and employment, and hence of the imports, of the deficit country.

Under the system of stable exchange rates and general convertibility of currencies any particular country can undoubtedly eliminate its balance of payments deficit by a sufficiently large restriction of credit, provided that the deflationary policy is confined to that country. On the assumption, however, that all countries pursue the same policies, the repercussions of the import reductions achieved by any one country will induce further credit restrictions, and hence import restrictions, by others, and thereby intensify the need for restriction in the former countries. In other words, the attempt to re-establish equilibrium may lead to an indefinite multiplication of deflationary measures in the course of which all countries become engulfed in an ever-deepening depression without a new international equilibrium being attained at any definite point. Unless major countries successfully stand out against this deflationary process through internal expansionary measures and the deliberate toleration of balance of payments deficits, this method may thus defeat its own purpose of re-establishing a general balance in international transactions, apart from being inconsistent with the maintenance of the domestic levels of employment.

During the great depression in the 1930's many countries attempted to soften the impact of these external deflationary pressures through the method of import restrictions and/or exchange devaluation. The advantage of import restrictions as against the method of internal deflation is that the same reduction in imports can be attained without a reduction (or with a much smaller reduction) in the level of internal production and employment. From the point of view of the repercussions of such measures on other countries, however, the policy of non-discriminatory import restrictions has much the same effects as the policy of internal deflation: it will call forth additional balance of payments difficulties, and hence further import restrictions, by third countries. However, assuming that all countries (with the exception of the one initially suffering from a decline in internal employment) are desirous of, and able to, stabilise internal employment, a new equilibrium in international transactions may be attained through a policy of (non-discriminatory) import restrictions, once a similar degree of import reduction is achieved in all countries. It is only attained, however, at the cost of a general reduction (possibly a large reduction) in the volume of international trade, which itself compromises the ability of countries to maintain full employment—partly because the unemployment caused by the reduction in exports may not easily be compensated by increased employment for domestic uses or in domestic industries; partly also because imports cannot be restricted beyond a certain point without causing production to be restricted as well; industrial production cannot be carried on without the importation of essential raw materials. But even if the volume of production and employment is not actually reduced, the economic welfare generated at the given level of economic activity will certainly be less, as a result of the lower degree of international specialisation and exchange.

The third method for dealing with the problem is that of devaluation. A downward adjustment of the exchange rate when adopted by a single country is analogous in its effects to the method of import restriction: it is, in fact, identical with that of the imposition of an *ad valorem* tax on imports of a constant percentage combined with a general export subsidy of the same percentage. From the point of view of the particular country adopting devaluation, its comparative advantage is that exports are stimulated at the same time as imports are restricted, thereby easing the problem of maintaining internal employment. Its comparative disadvantage is that on the side of imports there is no possibility of applying selective restrictions; while as a result of the general export subsidy, there may be a deterioration of the terms of trade.

The great advantage, however, of the method of currency devaluation as against the method of non-discriminating import restrictions is that if more than one country follows this method, its restrictive effects are thereby cancelled in the trading relations between the devaluing countries. Thus if two countries impose a given degree of import restriction (by means of tariffs for example) the effects of these restrictions will be additive and trade will be correspondingly hampered in both directions. If, however, two countries introduce an equivalent degree of currency devaluation, the restrictive effects of either one of these devaluations on the trade between the two countries are thereby automatically cancelled and trade will be carried on between them under the same conditions as before. Provided, therefore, that the method of devaluation is adopted by a number of countries simultaneously, the depressing effects of the method of import restriction (and *a fortiori* of the method of internal deflation) are thereby avoided. In the limiting case, where a depression originates in one particular country, and is followed by equivalent currency devaluations of all other countries, the depression will remain entirely confined to the first country and the international propagation of the deflationary pressure is avoided. Such a universal currency devaluation undertaken by all countries in relation to the particular country suffering from the depression is, in fact, the equivalent of a general trade discrimination introduced by all countries against the depressed country—trade discrimination, which takes the form of a differential *ad valorem* tariff, combined with an *ad valorem* export subsidy, and which is applied by the different countries only in their trading relations with the depressed country.

It is evident from this that the fourth method—i.e. the introduction of discriminatory exchange or trade restrictions against the depressed surplus country—is fundamentally similar in its effects to that of a general exchange devaluation *vis-à-vis* the depressed country. With this method also the international propagation of deflationary influences, inherent in the first two methods, may be effectively prevented. The discrimination in this case takes the form of quantitative restrictions (achieved either through currency allocations or through import quotas) rather than of differential taxes or subsidies. In either case, a sufficient degree of discrimination might be attained to restore a balance in international transactions between the depressed country and other countries without introducing depressive tendencies in the trading relations between the others. With the quantitative method, the equilibrium in the balance of payments will be regained mainly through a reduction in the exports of the depressed country. With the devaluation method, equilibrium will be regained partly through a reduction in the depressed country's exports and partly through a stimulation of its imports. With both methods, the elimination of the surplus in the balance of payments of the depressed country is likely to intensify its own domestic depression. But in neither case is this intensification likely to be any larger than what would occur under convertibility and stable exchanges, as a result of the measures of internal deflation or of (non-discriminatory) import restrictions, adopted by other countries in order to cope with their balance of payments deficits.

The main advantage of the method of devaluation (as against the method of discriminatory exchange and trade restrictions) is that it maintains the volume of international trade between the depressed country and other countries at a higher level, thus improving the degree of international specialisation. In fact, in the absence of trade restrictions of any kind, the rate of exchange which secures equilibrium in the balance of payments consistently with full employment would also ensure the optimal degree of the international division of labour.

The disadvantages of the general devaluation method are: (i) that it is likely to improve the terms of trade of the depressed country with the outside world, thereby rendering the restoration of balance of payments equilibrium more difficult, with a tendency to a further intensification of the depression in the depressed country; (ii) that the efficacy of the method depends on its being universally adopted—i.e. that the devaluation extends to all countries which suffer from balance of payments difficulties, as a result of depression in a third country: in the case of discriminatory exchange control, the country first adopting this policy can, to a certain extent, force its trading partners to apply similar methods of discrimination; (iii) that the efficacy of the general devaluation method depends entirely on the depressed country being willing to maintain its own gold parity exchange rate in the face of a universal devaluation by other countries; if the depressed country also participates in devaluation, the effects of the devaluation on other countries are thereby cancelled—except possibly to the extent to which the current gold production of the other countries (and which may be currently absorbed by the depressed country) now provides finance for a larger volume of imports from the depressed country; (iv) that reliance on exchange devaluation as a method of combating cyclical influences may imply, in practice, an all too frequent use of exchange rate adjustments and thereby introduce an added element of instability in international trade as well as on the level of domestic costs and prices. It was possibly for this last reason that the Charter of the I.M.F. appears definitely to favour the method of discriminatory exchange control (through the provisions of the Scarce Currency Clause) in preference to the method of currency devaluation as a means of dealing with cyclical disturbances in the balance of international transactions.

Thus both the method of general exchange devaluation and the method of discriminatory exchange control are, in principle, capable of preventing the cumulative contraction in world trade that would otherwise follow from a cyclical depression emanating from a major industrial country. It must be emphasised, however, that neither of these methods represents an ideal solution to the problem. In neither case can countries avoid the adverse effects on their own economy resulting from a reduction in the volume of trading with the depressed country; and in the case of general exchange devaluation, they may suffer the additional loss due to the consequential deterioration in their terms of trade with the depressed country. From the point of view of the depressed country, the elimination of the surplus in its balance of payments will always imply an intensification of its own economic depression—although (contrary to a widespread view) this intensification will tend to be of the same order of magnitude, irrespective of whether other countries adopt discriminatory or non-discriminatory methods for restoring the international balance.

For these reasons, a more adequate solution of the problem would presuppose new international arrangements whereby each country would undertake to maintain the normal supply of its own currency to the rest of the world, irrespective of fluctuations in its internal level of activity. This was the basic idea underlying the particular recommendations made in the report on "National and International Measures for Full Employment," which envisaged an undertaking whereby each country would maintain a stable flow of net capital exports, and an obligation to sell its own currency against other currencies if its external disbursements on current account fell below the normal level.

The same objective could, of course, be attained, to a greater or lesser extent, in a number of other ways as well, or through a combination of them (as, for example, international buffer stocks for basic commodities; Government buying of imports with a view to maintaining the value of imports; compensatory public lending by governments, etc.). Such schemes, even if they would not entirely avoid the disturbances of international trade consequent upon a major depression in a major country, would at least ensure that other countries desirous of maintaining full employment could maintain their normal volume of imports and thereby avoid any consequential reduction in their real income. They would also ensure that the deflationary influences within the depressed country proceeded less far than if equilibrium in the current balance of payments had to be re-established through any of the four methods outlined above.

From the point of view of the employment aspect of the problem, it is clear that any country desirous of stabilising its internal employment can, through internal measures, avoid at least the secondary consequences on employment of a fall in exports—i.e. it could offset, by methods of employment stimulation, the adverse effect of a fall in exports on the level of employment in other industries. Normally, it would be able probably to do more than this, through stimulating the domestic consumption of the products of export industries or through finding temporary alternative employment for the unemployed workers in the export industries in the districts in which these industries are located. The degree of success of such policies will depend on the extent to which any particular country's export industries are specialised and the geographic locations of such industries are concentrated. The extent of the problem will obviously depend on how far the economic depression is confined to one country or currency area and how far it is allowed to spread to other countries or areas. The more countries are engulfed by depression, the more difficult it will be for any particular country to maintain its employment through domestic measures.

Primary producing countries experience the effects of a depression not so much in a fall in employment as a fall in prices with consequential deflationary effects in the incomes of primary producers. The necessary compensatory measures here take the form, not so much of employment stimulation, as of domestic price stabilisation by means of guaranteed prices to farmers, subsidies, etc. The ability of primary producers to maintain domestic prices and incomes will clearly depend on the extent to which their foreign exchange receipts, and thus their ability to import, can be maintained as well. The solution of their domestic problem will, therefore, largely depend on the degree to which the depressed countries are willing to maintain the supply of their currencies undiminished.

4

THE LESSONS OF THE BRITISH EXPERIMENT SINCE THE WAR: FULL EMPLOYMENT AND THE WELFARE STATE[1]

THE assumption of a formal obligation to maintain "high and stable levels of employment" (as the famous declaration by the wartime Coalition Government in 1944 put it) was probably the most revolutionary innovation of the century in the sphere of government. It emerged as the result of the joint impact of the Keynesian revolution in economic thought and the Second World War—neither of which could have brought it about by itself in the absence of the other. The appearance of Keynes's new theory of general economic equilibrium in the late 1930's would, no doubt, sooner or later have involved radical changes in public opinion as to what governments can or cannot be expected to do. But without the Second World War it may be supposed that a much longer period would have elapsed before the new ideas crystallised into an attitude towards Governmental responsibilities formally recognised by the responsible political leadership of all colours. The war had created an atmosphere of open-mindedness and readiness for experiment; but this might have petered out in futility (as the similar spirit after the first war, expressed in Lloyd George's famous slogan "a land fit for heroes to live in," petered out) had the new mechanics of thought developed by Keynes not been at hand waiting for application.

In saying this one must not, of course, exaggerate the extent of the psychological change involved. It is not that there was a radical change in public opinion as to what governments *ought* to do; the change concerned far more the question of what governments *can* do. The strict attitude of *laissez faire* which characterised the nineteenth century had been abandoned in Britain long before the Second World War. The idea that the state of well-being and

[1] A paper read at the Centenary Congress of the Société Royale d'Economie Politique de Belgique, Brussels, 1955.

prosperity of the nation should be a prime concern of the Government had not, I believe, been called into question by any Government or Parliamentary party, in England at any rate, since 1906; but the extent to which government could influence the state of economic prosperity was regarded as limited. Mr. Chamberlain (in reply to a Parliamentary question) once said, when he was Chancellor of the Exchequer, that it would be a mistake to assume that governments have it in their power to increase or decrease the general demand for labour and thus regulate the level of employment. They could no more do this than regulate the weather.

It is in this respect that the declaration of the war-time Coalition Government implied a radical change—for here for the first time the Government acknowledged that it was not beyond their competence to see to it that the general demand for labour was sufficient to ensure that everyone genuinely seeking employment would be able to find a job. This, together with the greatly extended scope of publicly provided social services proposed in the Beveridge Report in 1942, laid the foundations of the British New Deal which has come to be known as the Welfare State.

It was the Socialist Government between 1945 and 1951 which translated the policies of the Welfare State into practice. But the Conservative Administration which has been in office since 1951, contrary to the expectations of some people both in Britain and abroad, has continued without any fundamental change the policies adopted by its predecessors, and pursued them with much the same vigour. In the latest declarations of the Government the objective of maintaining full employment has received the same emphasis as it did from the preceding Labour Government. There can be no question, therefore, that the policies of the Welfare State are no mere passing consequence of the spirit of experimentation engendered by the war. They have come to stay.

The purpose of this paper is to review briefly the lessons of this experiment. What were (or are) the main consequences of the deliberate pursuit of full employment? What were (or are) the main instruments of these policies, and how far have they shown themselves adequate in relation to the objectives aimed at?

I. THE CONSEQUENCES OF FULL EMPLOYMENT

On the positive side the maintenance of full employment has brought with it some consequences that were generally expected, others that were, broadly speaking, expected only by the protagonists of full employment, and yet others which were generally unexpected. In the first category we must put the gain in social contentment and the lessening of social tensions in a society where everyone can find a job relatively easily, and where the fear of being deprived of one's livelihood through general economic causes has more or less disappeared.

In the second category we must mention the effects on the real volume of production. Many people feared that in the absence of unemployment production would continually be hampered by bottlenecks and shortages of various kinds (due to the maldistribution of the labour force between industries and occupations) so that on balance the economy would lose in productivity more than it gained through the increase in the volume of work performed. These fears turned out to be greatly exaggerated. Even during the post-war transition to peacetime production loss in output due to shortages and bottlenecks was not nearly as serious as many predicted.

The most important consequence of this policy, however, and the least expected, has been the greatly accelerated growth in productivity from year to year under full employment conditions. It is now widely recognised, as a result of the experience of the years since 1948, that under conditions when the demand for goods and services is increasing adequately to maintain the general shortage of labour, industrial productivity per man may be expected to increase by as much as 4 to 5 per cent. from one year to the next. Between the two world wars, or over the period 1870–1913, the annual rate of growth in industrial productivity was of the order of 2 to 2·5 per cent. There is no need to stress the significance of even small differences in annual compound rates of growth considered over a number of years.

The reason why productivity grows so much faster under full employment conditions is not yet generally understood. One reason for it is that when the general state of the economy is prosperous and the demand for goods of all kinds increases year by year, businesses incur capital expenditure more lavishly; there is more new equipment created year by year, and since new equipment, generally speaking, incorporates all the latest technical developments, the adoption of new techniques proceeds that much faster.

I do not believe, however, that this is the whole explanation. Whilst full employment conditions are associated with a higher rate of capital formation, they also mean that the scrapping of obsolete equipment tends to be delayed (since when demand is high it is profitable to operate relatively high-cost plant); and the one factor would tend to offset the other. Besides, the available statistics (and in Britain we now have far more voluminous and reliable statistics than we used to have before the war) do not support the contention that full employment has meant an unusually large amount of capital investment. The statistics show that whereas industrial production was 55 per cent. higher in the period 1951–3 than in 1938, gross investment in fixed capital (excluding commercial buildings) by companies and nationalised industries was 30 per cent. and net investment 70 per cent. higher in 1951–3 than in 1938.

The main reason for the accelerated rate of increase in productivity is to be sought, in my view, not so much in the level of capital investment as in the beneficial effects of a general scarcity of labour on the adoption of labour-saving innovations of all kinds, some of which involve changes in factory layout, or in organisation, or in design, rather than the installation of more automatic machinery. Where labour is difficult to obtain it becomes the effective bottleneck that limits the growth of profits and turnover of individual businesses. Hence entrepreneurs are led to concentrate on finding ways of saving labour, just as they concentrate on the invention and use of substitute materials when any particular raw material becomes short in supply. The strong incentive provided by the situation to economise labour is the factor mainly responsible for the growth in output in relation to employment.

As against these advantages we must mention on the negative side the steadily creeping monetary inflation which successive post-war Governments have been unable to prevent. The best evidence of this is that in five years between 1948 and 1953 the real gross domestic product (at factor cost) increased by 15 per cent., whereas the money value of the gross domestic product increased by 45 per cent.: and that there was not a single year in that period in which the increase in money income did not exceed by an appreciable percentage the increase in real income. The main cause of this creeping inflation has not been an excessive money supply or an excessive demand for goods of all kinds, but an excessive rate of increase in the general level of money wages. The inflation thus had its origin in money costs and money incomes rather than in a generally excessive demand for goods over supply in real terms.

It would be a mistake to attribute the excessive increase in money wages to the power or the activities of trade unions alone. Money wages increase faster under full employment conditions mainly because there is a more frequent need for adjustment in the relative wages paid to workers of different grades and in different occupations. When there is a great deal of unemployment enough applicants can be found for all kinds of jobs quite irrespective of the relative attractiveness of one kind of job or another. Under full employment, however, it becomes necessary to offer higher wages to attract sufficient workers to the more difficult or less attractive jobs or to industries where demand is expanding relatively fast. Since wages are notoriously rigid in a downward direction, any adjustment in relative wages implies an increase in *average* wages; hence the more frequent the adjustments the faster the aggregate wage bill rises.

The second factor on the negative side consists in the chronic weakness of the balance of payments. Despite the efforts made by successive Governments, Britain has not succeeded in increasing her exports adequately to make her balance of payments safe against periodic shocks originating in changes in prices or in changes in foreign markets. Though large deficits in the balance of payments have only occurred in the crisis years of 1947, 1949 and 1951, it has never been possible to attain that £300–£400 million surplus in the balance of payments on current account which official policy has regarded as the minimum to ensure the international objectives of Britain's economic policy. For the last few years (i.e. since 1951) the volume of exports has risen relatively little and lagged considerably behind the general increase in output:

Exports of goods and services at 1948 prices (£ million):

1948	1949	1950	1951	1952	1953	1954
1·944	2·142	2·471	2·623	2·562	2·524	2·660

Gross Domestic Product at 1948 prices (£ million):

1948	1949	1950	1951	1952	1953	1954
10·074	10·436	10·738	11·182	11·122	11·585	12·083

Thus the volume of exports in 1954 was only slightly above that of 1951, whereas the gross domestic product (in real terms) was 8 per cent. greater. The reason here is to be sought in the problem of ensuring a level of demand high enough to maintain full employment, while at the same time preventing that demand from becoming so large as to drain away for home uses resources which should be devoted to exports.

II. THE MECHANICS OF FULL EMPLOYMENT POLICY

It is in the light of these achievements, and of the difficulties created by the pursuit of full employment policy, that we must now examine the instruments that have been and are being employed for the purpose. These instruments are broadly of two kinds: fiscal policy and monetary policy. Fiscal policy consists essentially in varying the general level of taxation in relation to Government expenditure so as to regulate the purchasing power of the public for goods and services of all kinds. Monetary policy consists in measures of credit expansion and contraction, through the banking system, to regulate the level of business expenditure on investment in fixed capital or in stocks. The main difference between the two policies is that whereas fiscal policy aims at regulating consumers' expenditure directly, monetary policy does so only indirectly, i.e. through affecting the incomes generated as a result of capital expenditure of businesses. Fiscal policy can, of course, also be employed to stimulate or retard business capital expenditure directly, as, for example, through the taxation of business profits and the granting or withdrawal of accelerated depreciation allowances.

The great advantage of the instrument of fiscal policy is that it is capable of adjusting the *pattern* of demand to the pattern of the distribution of resources. Given the distribution of labour and other resources between the capital goods industries and the consumption goods trades, full employment may not be obtainable at all by the instrument of credit control alone since the amount of investment that is necessary to keep the investment goods industries reasonably fully employed may generate an altogether excessive demand for the products of the consumption goods trades. In that situation only a policy of budgetary surpluses can harmonise the proportion of income saved with the proportion of the community's resources devoted to capital investment. Indeed, it was the main characteristic of the policy of the Labour Government in the years 1947–51 to secure by means of large budgetary surpluses a lower relationship between consumption and income (and so a higher relation of investment to output) than corresponded to the public's desire to consume and to save.

Thus the use of the fiscal instrument for the purposes of general economic control meant, under the conditions of post-war Britain, raising more revenue in taxation (and to some extent by different kinds of taxes) than would have been considered appropriate on financial considerations alone. When fiscal policy was first advocated as an instrument of economic control in the 1930's its advocates had generally in mind deliberate deficit budgeting which offended against the prevailing canons of financial orthodoxy. In fact, in the post-war economic situation the pursuit of this policy meant exactly the opposite; in each of the years 1947–51 the Government aimed at achieving not only a large surplus over ordinary expenditure but an overall surplus which more than covered the capital expenditure of public authorities which is normally covered by loans. It frequently escapes notice that in England taxes on expenditure account (now as before the war) for about 40 per cent. of the total revenue, and insurance contributions for a further 10 per cent. The policy of restraining consumption through taxation has in fact depended heavily on increased taxation of articles of mass consumption (such as beer and tobacco) and on durable consumer goods; and not, as is often supposed, mainly on higher progressive taxation of incomes.

Since 1951 the policies adopted by the Conservative Government have meant that more reliance has been placed on instruments of monetary control and less reliance on fiscal policy than before. The level of interest rates has gradually, but more or less steadily, risen, whilst the level of taxation and the excess of Government revenue over expenditure have been successively reduced. This means that in comparison with the years 1948–50 the share of the national income devoted to capital investment has fallen and the share devoted to personal consumption has risen.

The main weakness of the Labour Government's reliance on fiscal policy lay in its inability to control fluctuations of investment in stocks of a speculative character. With regard to long term investment (i.e. capital expenditure on plant and machinery and building of all kinds) the Government had adequate instruments of control, partly through the operation of a licensing system for factories and housing generally, and partly through the fiscal weapon of accelerating or retarding depreciation allowances which had much the same effect as a subsidy on capital expenditure. But there was no analogous instrument for regulating investment in working capital, and it was the latter kind of investment which provided the really unstable element in the economy. While the annual increase in the physical volume of stocks carried averaged about £140 million a year (at 1948 prices) the fluctuation from year to year in real terms was as much as £700 million: as, for example, from minus £200 million in 1950 to plus £500 million in 1951. In comparison, expenditure on fixed capital in real terms was remarkably stable from year to year, showing a small but fairly regular increase. The reason why these large fluctuations in investment in stocks did not (up till 1952 at any rate) cause corresponding variations in domestic employment was that they were largely reflected in corresponding fluctuations in the balance of payments—i.e. in the excess of imports over exports. The balance of payments crises in 1947 and 1951 were partly caused by unfavourable changes in the terms of trade but they were at least equally due to the rise in imports and/or the fall in exports caused by the domestic restocking boom. Thus between 1950 and 1951 the increase in investment in stocks by £816 million (from minus £216 million to plus £600 million) more than accounted for the deterioration in the balance of payments on current account of £782 million (from a balance of plus £440 million in 1950 to minus £342 million in 1951).

These great fluctuations in the amount of investment in working capital were largely caused by changing expectations concerning price movements. In times when world prices are rising, or rather are expected to rise, manufacturers and traders are anxious to hold larger stocks of materials, etc., in relation to turnover than normally; the restocking boom and the balance of payments crisis of 1951 were largely the reflection of the world inflationary trend engendered by the Korean war. The policy of relying on taxation to keep the pressure of demand under control whilst keeping the credit supply elastic meant that the Government had no real weapon at its disposal apart from quantitative import controls (which were tardy in their operation and limited in their effectiveness) for discouraging such speculative fluctuations in business investment: since these are not dependent (over shorter periods at any rate) on the current flow of final demand for goods and services.

The restoration of the equilibrium of the balance of payments in 1952 and subsequent years is generally attributed to the revival of monetary control through the Bank Rate mechanism which was first reintroduced by the Conservative Government in November 1951. It is a matter for argument, however, how important a role monetary measures have actually played in the restoration of equilibrium. The fall in imports in 1952 and 1953 was undoubtedly associated with the reduction in investment in stocks in those years (the value of the physical increase in stocks and work in progress amounted to only £50 million in 1952 and £200 million in 1953, as against £600 million in 1951). The introduction of the new measures of monetary control in early 1952 coincided, however, with a reversal of the trend of world prices so that it is likely that even in the absence of monetary measures traders would have attempted to reduce stocks which were built up to an excessive level in the inflationary expectations of the previous year.

In the current year 1955, the situation has been different. The excessive pressure of demand which developed in the course of 1954 was not due (as far as one can tell from the figures at present available) to any major extent to a restocking boom, and expectations of rising prices have played no great part. The main factor (in my view) was the very sharp increase in demand for durable consumer goods in the course of 1954 which was undoubtedly greatly stimulated by the sharp rise in Stock Exchange values. In this situation tighter credit control can only be effective if it succeeds in inducing a disinvestment in stocks and a reduction in capital expenditure which would compensate for the rise in demand in other parts of the economy. It cannot be said that the measures introduced in February 1955 have yet succeeded in checking the current inflationary trend. Although the liquidity ratio of the commercial banks has fallen (owing to the open market operations of the Bank of England) bank advances have continued to grow at a disturbing rate. There is no sign as yet of any down turn in the volume of business profits; and the Stock Exchange boom has so far continued with an accelerated momentum. The experiments with monetary policy in the first half of 1955 thus rather tend to suggest that when the pressure on the economy results from excessive demand, the ordinary weapons of monetary policy may be ineffective in counteracting the trend, or can only be made effective with considerable delay.[1]

It may be worth describing in some detail how monetary control operates under the British banking mechanism. In Britain, manufacturers and traders do not normally borrow through the issue of short term negotiable instruments but only through the granting of overdraft facilities by the commercial banks. The volume of credit therefore mainly depends on the advances to customers made by the commercial banks. Interest rates charged on these advances are fairly rigid: they were never reduced below 4·5 per cent. under the cheap money era and are not above 5 per

---

[1] The rise in the Bank Rate in February to 4½ per cent. has had an immediate effect on gold reserves since it attracted short-term funds to London. But though the protection of currency reserves is an important immediate objective of monetary policy, it must not be forgotten that the inflow of funds attracted by high interest rates provides merely a breathing space, not a solution of the problem. To judge the efficacy of monetary measures it is necessary to examine their effects on the underlying trends of the economy, and on imports and exports, and not merely on currency reserves.

cent. even at present, despite the fact that the Bank Rate, i.e. the official rediscount rate of the Bank of England, has been raised from 2 per cent. to 4·5 per cent. and money market rates from 0·5 to 3·5 per cent. The commercial banks thus regulate the volume of borrowing not through interest variations but through credit rationing; and stricter credit control depends on inducing the banks to reduce the borrowing limits granted to their regular customers. A rise in the money market rates (which means a rise in the discount rate of short-term Government paper) is important in this connection only in that it enables the banks to earn higher rates of interest on their liquid investments and thus reduces the differential advantage, from a banking point of view, of employing their funds in the form of advances to customers. Up to 1951 the Labour Government attempted to control bank advances merely through asking banks not to extend credit to customers beyond certain limits. Experience has shown that these repeated exhortations proved ineffective. But, for reasons explained above, experience since 1951 has not, in my opinion, fully demonstrated that the means at present employed—i.e. variations in the official Bank Rate and in the money market rates through open market operations—provide a prompt and sensitive instrument for controlling the volume of bank advances. In order to attain this it may become necessary to use additional instruments such as a variable legal minimum reserve ratio which is employed by the Federal Reserve System in the United States.

The experience of the post-war years undoubtedly suggests that exclusive reliance on fiscal policy is inadequate to ensure continued stability in the economy and that there is a great deal to be said for the combined use of the instruments of credit control and of fiscal instruments. But the rehabilitation of monetary policy has led to another danger from a long-run point of view. The experience of recent years tends to show that once Governments become accustomed to think of controlling the economy through the instruments of credit policy, the pressure for tax relief may force their hands and cause them to rely more and more on monetary policy and less and less on fiscal policy. Thus, in the current year when the pressure of demand was becoming excessive and the balance of payments position was again endangered, the use of the fiscal instrument would have dictated an increase in taxation. Instead, the Chancellor of the Exchequer introduced considerable remissions of taxation in his last budget and thus made himself entirely dependent on the restrictive effects of a high Bank Rate for combating inflationary tendencies.

No doubt if the measures adopted are strict and severe enough the Government can in time force the banks to reduce the volume of bank advances and thus cause the firms dependent on bank credit (who make up perhaps one-third of the total) to curtail their expenditure. But the result of this will be that long-term capital investment, and not only speculative investment in stocks, is discouraged, whilst consumption may be further stimulated as a result of tax remissions. In fact, credit control can only be relied on to reduce consumption if it is severe enough to create unemployment—and then it would reduce production even more. The present danger is not so much that the use of credit policy will prove incompatible with the maintenance of full employment, but that it will mean a full employment economy where consumption takes up a steadily growing share and capital investment a diminishing share of current output. In the long run the present full employment policy is threatened more through the inadequacy of capital investment to secure the growth of productive capacity which the increased labour productivity requires than through an inadequacy of effective demand.[1]

The success of the policy may also be threatened by the social stresses to which it may be subjected as a result of the growing inequality of consumption standards. As a result of the lower taxation of business profits the past few years have witnessed a sharp increase in dividend payments which in turn has generated a major Stock Exchange boom and a rise in consumption out of capital gains. The rise in dividends and in share values may have contributed to the recent more insistent demands for wage increases, to the wide-spread strikes, and to the recent faster rate of increase in the money wage level, which in turn may have

[1] Net investment in plant, machinery, industrial buildings and vehicles by companies in the non-nationalised sector fell off markedly in the period 1951–3 as compared with 1948–50: from 202 per cent. of the 1938 level in 1948–50 to 159 per cent. in 1951–3, whilst between the same periods industrial production rose by 10 per cent. Net investment by companies in commercial buildings was negative throughout the years 1948–53.

undesirable repercussions on exports (which have not as yet suffered on account of high domestic costs).

There can be little doubt that, if the pressure of demand can be kept up year after year at a level high enough to maintain the general shortage of labour, the policy must bring large dividends over the years in the form of a higher rate of growth in productivity and real income. But the policy can only be maintained if the tendency to inflation is kept in check, if the balance of payments is safeguarded, and if too frequent strikes of the kind recently experienced on the railways can be avoided. Practical experience has shown that the combination of these objectives requires constant vigilance and a skilful combination of the various instruments of economic policy. Just as the events under the Labour Government showed that the policy cannot be safeguarded by the use of fiscal policy alone, so recent experience under the Conservative Government suggests that it would be equally futile to place the main reliance on monetary policy without deliberately using fiscal measures to regulate effective demand. The main danger is that once governments count on the use of both these methods, political pressures will force them to put increasing reliance on the monetary controls which are relatively harmless and to shrink from using the fiscal measures which are politically unattractive.

Part II

THE CONTROL OF INFLATION

5

A POSITIVE POLICY FOR WAGES AND DIVIDENDS[1]

MORE than nine months have now elapsed since the devaluation of the pound last September, and it would be generally conceded that the effects of devaluation have so far been more favourable than even its protagonists expected. Exports recovered and currency reserves have shown a steady, even spectacular, rise. The terms of trade have deteriorated but by no more than was foreseen. Retail prices have remained remarkably stable, while the rise in wholesale prices has been no greater than could be accounted for by the rise in the sterling costs of imports. Inflationary pressure, so far from growing, has definitely abated. The recovery of exports of Britain and the Sterling Area was no doubt partly caused by the improved economic situation in the United States, and might have occurred even in the absence of devaluation. On the other hand, the effects of the enhanced competitive power of our exports are by no means fully reflected yet in the export figures.

The success of devaluation up to now and in particular the absence of the inflationary consequences that were so widely feared, was undoubtedly due to the policy of restraint on personal incomes—the so-called wage and salary-freeze and the dividend freeze—introduced or reintroduced at the time of devaluation. These were emergency measures, intended to be of temporary duration; and the remarkable manner in which they were hitherto observed, despite their voluntary character, testifies once more to the patriotism and discipline of the public. But it would be both unreasonable and, from a purely economic point of view, also absurd to expect such measures to continue to remain in operation indefinitely. Wages and dividends can only be "frozen" at the levels attained in a particular base period at the cost of a steadily growing loss in economic adaptability and also a growing

[1] Memorandum submitted to the Chancellor of the Exchequer on 21 June 1950.

sense of social injustice. Wage earners could hardly be expected to acquiesce for any length of time in foregoing the prospect of any improvement in relation to others. Similarly, investors could hardly be expected to continue to fulfil their social function of exploiting new profit-making opportunities in a world where risk-bearing is not permitted its gains, but only its losses. It is enough to remember that dividend limitation can only stabilize dividends in an upward, but not in a downward direction, to realize its absurdity as a permanent or even as a semi-permanent measure in an economy mainly run by private enterprise.

On the other hand, it would be foolish to expect that with the passage of time the need for these restraints will gradually pass, so that they can simply be abandoned, after a time, without untoward effects on the economy. The wage and the dividend freeze are not like points-rationing or petrol-rationing which become gradually otiose with the diminished shortage of food or dollars. A more apt analogy is that of a steadily rising pressure of steam in a boiler which will create an explosion all the larger the longer the pressure is confined. The "inflationary potential" (as distinct from the "inflationary pressure") in a situation where full employment continues to be maintained while relative wages are rigidly held to some pre-determined relationship and when dividends form a steadily diminishing percentage of current profits, must grow steadily larger. Yet, if nothing is done, sooner or later either the wage-freeze, or dividend-freeze, or both, are bound to break down. Moreover, the breakdown of either one of these restraints is almost certain to carry with it the breakdown of the other.

The basic shortcoming in the present situation is that the Government applies purely emergency expedients to what is, in essence, a continuing, almost a structural, problem of a full employment economy. So long as full employment is maintained, and labour is generally scarce, the pressure for higher wages, in the absence of restraint, is bound to lead to wage increases out of proportion to the rise in productivity. On the other side, under full employment conditions, such wage increases are bound to lead to price increases of a character that will cause the wage-inflation to become augmented by a profit-inflation, thus carrying further wage increases in their trail. Hence the need for *some* restraint in both wages and profits is not a temporary need in a full employment economy, but a permanent need. The supreme requirement of the moment consists precisely in the recognition of this fact: which means introducing a positive and more permanent policy of flexible restraints in regard to personal incomes, in place of the purely negative and temporary one of freezing incomes at some arbitrary level. If such a policy could be conceived and adopted, the success of a full employment policy in a free society would be assured; and Britain would not only take an important step to assure her own future well-being but, through her example, would also make a major contribution to the stability and prosperity of the Western world.

Is a positive policy of flexible restraints conceivable and practicable? In the opinion of the present writer it undoubtedly is, and the purpose of this paper is to give a brief outline of such a policy, both in regard to wages and salaries, and to dividends.

A Policy for Wages

A policy for wages in a full employment economy has two major aspects. The first consists in ensuring that the rise in the average wage-level over any period is no greater than what is consistent with the maintenance of monetary stability. Broadly, this means that the rate of increase in wages, on the average, must keep in step with the rate of increase in productivity. The second main aspect of wage policy is to ensure that the changes in the wage structure are such as to facilitate, rather than hinder, the necessary structural adjustments in the economy.

This second aspect of wage policy has not so far received the attention it deserves. This is because in an unemployment economy the relative wages between different industries and occupations are comparatively unimportant from the point of view of securing an optimum allocation of resources. When jobs in general are hard to find, the new entrants to industry will necessarily go to the trades where they can find them. Thus between 1929 and 1937 the industries which showed the highest expansion in employment also experienced the largest percentage increases in unemployment, while in industries with declining employment

the unemployment percentage—with one or two exceptions—
also tended to decline. The expanding industries, on the other
hand, were by no means always those offering higher relative
wages. In an unemployment economy relative wages are largely
the outcome of a series of historical accidents and may bear little
relation either to the short-term need for adjustments in the
employment structure or to the long-term need for maintaining
the required distribution of the labour force between different
occupations. Thus the lowest pay was not infrequently found in
the most strenuous and dangerous occupations without thereby
creating a shortage of labour for that type of work.

In a full employment economy, on the other hand, relative
wages must be far more closely geared to the net advantages of
different kinds of work—in other words, to the true supply price
of labour for the different occupations—otherwise the relatively
unattractive occupations will become progressively under-manned,
with the result that the full employment policy will sooner or
later break down. The necessary changes in the wage structure
to achieve that end cannot, of course, be brought about suddenly,
nor could they be planned out in any detail for a long period
ahead. It is important, however, that the wage adjustments which
do take place should at least not be in conflict with this principle,
but should pay due regard to long-term national needs. In many
cases considerations of equity and considerations of the long-run
national interest are in harmony with each other, rather than in
conflict. This applies particularly to some of the under-manned
industries and also to certain crafts inside particular industries
—foundry workers are an example—where for technical reasons
piece-rates cannot be introduced, so that earnings lag greatly
behind those of other workers of similar skill and training whose
incomes have progressively risen with increased productivity. In
cases, however, where wages are already relatively high, and
where labour is not particularly short, the mere willingness of
employers to grant wage increases ought not in itself to provide
sufficient justification for a rise in wages. The essential prerequisite of a successful wage policy lies in the recognition of the
fact that while wages *in general* should increase in proportion to the
rise in productivity *in general*, this does not mean that the changes

in wage-rates in particular industries should be governed by the rise in productivity in those industries. Increases in productivity in particular industries which are not the result of a more intense effort by the workers but of new techniques or more efficient management should, in general, be passed on to the community as a whole in the form of lower prices rather than retained by those in the industry in the form of higher wages and profits. Such price reductions are an essential component of a successful full employment policy: for without them it would be impossible to balance the effects of inevitable price increases in other industries, where wages are relatively low and may have to be raised, even if this entails a rise in prices.

The first step in the creation of a new policy of flexible wage restraints is the establishment of a new machinery for reviewing wage claims from individual industries in the light of the general economic situation. This new Wages Board should preferably consist of representatives of the T.U.C. and the Government. There would be no need for the employers' associations to be formally represented on the Board, since the Board would not (at first at any rate) initiate new wage agreements, but merely review agreements already arrived at between employers and the trade unions in individual industries.

The Board would act on the basis of an annual wage and salary target which would ensure that the net result of the wage and salary increases put into effect in a given year should not exceed, in terms of aggregate annual earnings, the targets laid down for the year. It would be preferable to fix provisional annual targets for a number of years ahead—say for the first three years. The initial target may be put at £200 million a year for wages and £100 million a year for salaries, or roughly 5 per cent. of the existing wage and salary bill. Taking into account the effects of rising piece-rates, a £200 million rise in basic wage rates would probably be associated with a 6–7 per cent. rise in the total wages paid (of a given working population). Although this is higher than the expected increase in productivity (which may be put at 4–5 per cent.) the difference could probably be absorbed without further price increases, if account is taken of the rise in profits in exports resulting from devaluation.

The powers of the Board would consist of recommending the postponement of the putting into force of particular wage increases for a specified period (which may extend, of course, beyond the particular target year). These recommendations would not, of course, have the force of law behind them—any more than is the case with the present wage-freeze. But if the trade union movement could be brought to agree to the establishment of this Board, it could be entrusted also with ensuring that its recommendations are respected.

In deciding upon the period of delay in particular cases, the Board would act on the basis of a list of priorities, agreed upon by the members of the Board, in consulation with the T.U.C. and the Government. In drawing up such a list of priorities, the Board would be guided with due regard to considerations of equity and the national interest. The period of delay initially determined could be reduced subsequently, if the Board felt that the improvement in the economic situation justified a more liberal policy than the one initially adopted.

The unfettered freedom of wage bargaining of individual unions is one of the most cherished rights of the trade union movement; and a policy which, however guardedly, limited this freedom, would certainly have met with outright rejection only a few years ago. Since that time, however, the experience of the post-war period has taught a great deal. The institutions which grew up over the last century were appropriate to an unemployment economy; once the choice between the maintenance of full employment and the preservation of the old methods of wage bargaining is clearly put, and is understood by the workers, there can be little doubt of their answer. The present proposals, moreover, are designed to introduce the minimum of interference with existing machinery for settling wages. The new Wages Board would not "fix" wages, nor would it supersede existing negotiating machinery in any way. It would merely fix the places of individual categories of workers in a queue. Under conditions of full employment, it is almost inevitable that there should be a queue; and given this fact, it also follows that some authority must decide on how the various claims should be ranked.

Whether the trade union movement can be brought to accept

a policy on these lines at the present time, or whether they will only be brought to agreement after further (and perhaps bitter) experience, is perhaps open to doubt. There could be no doubt, however, that it is the duty of the Government to take the initiative in this matter and to put the problem openly and squarely before the public.

A Policy for Dividends

In 1938, of the £560 million paid out by companies in dividends and interest, £250 million consisted of prior charges (debenture interest and preference dividends) and £310 million of the dividends on ordinary shares. The total earnings of ordinary shares, after deduction of tax, amounted to some £396 million in 1938, 56 per cent. of which (or £225 million net) was paid out in dividends. In 1949 £270 million was paid in prior charges and £533 million in ordinary dividends. The earnings of ordinary shares (net of tax) amounted to £778 million of which £293 million was paid (net) in dividends, or 38 per cent. of the total. Ordinary dividends (net of income tax) thus appear to have risen by 30 per cent. between 1938 and 1949, while the after-tax retentions of companies have risen by over 180 per cent. If, with the disappearance of dividend limitation, companies reverted to the pre-war proportions between dividends and earnings, the amount distributed in dividends would rise by some £125 million (net) or a further 42 per cent., while the amount placed to reserve (taking into account the additional profits tax payable) would decline by some £159 million, or about 30 per cent. This would still represent almost twice the amount placed to reserve in 1938 in money terms. In real terms, however—owing to the 130 per cent. increase in the price level of capital goods—it would only amount to some 85 per cent. of the pre-war volume of net corporate saving.

There can be little doubt that a decline in corporate savings, and a rise in dividends of this magnitude would, in the present circumstances, be highly undesirable, both from an economic and a social point of view. There could also be little doubt, on the other hand, that the present form of dividend limitation is untenable as a long run policy. For it penalises the investment of capital in precisely those industries which are subject to large fluctuations of earnings, and where investment in equity capital involves appreciable risks.

While companies, on the average, appear to have distributed just under one-third of the earnings of ordinary shares in dividends in 1949, the policy of limiting dividends to the levels attained in 1947 has already led to a highly anomalous situation as between different companies. Under this policy, the companies in the "safe" trades—such as those manufacturing consumers' goods for the domestic market—which already paid high dividends before the war, and which were in the habit of distributing a high proportion of earnings in dividends, continue to do so, distributing up to 80 or 90 per cent. of the current earnings on ordinary shares. Companies on the other hand which before the war had very low earnings—such as those in the shipping, engineering or textile trades—or which "ploughed back" a high proportion of their earnings, pay dividends out of all relation to current profits —amounting, in many cases, to not more than 10–15 per cent. of the current earnings of ordinary shares. In the case of industries subject to wider fluctuations in demand (such as engineering) the prospect of being allowed to distribute larger dividends in slack times—when their earnings are abnormally low—could hardly compensate for their inability to raise dividends in times when they earn high profits.

While a policy of continued dividend restraint is thus certainly desirable—and is moreover a socially necessary concomitant of a policy of continued wage restraint—any lasting policy with regard to dividends must necessarily permit the rewards of success to be reaped as well as the penalties of failure. It would be futile, for example, to proceed by *relaxing* the existing policy of dividend limitation through the suggestion, for example, that companies could generally raise dividends but by no more than 10 or 15 per cent. over the present level. This would imply a wholly unnecessary concession in a large number of cases, and a totally inadequate one in others. A sound policy of dividend restraint must establish *some connection between dividends and current earnings*, rather than between current dividends and past dividends.

The form of dividend limitation which, from an economic point of view, is least open to objection is the restriction of dividends to some stated percentage of current earnings. Thus supposing that a rise in aggregate dividend payments of, say, 15 per cent. over the current level is considered reasonable—and given the fact that at present on the average 35-38 per cent. of current earnings is distributed—companies could be asked to limit dividends to 35-38 per cent. of the (consolidated) earnings of ordinary shares (after deduction of profits tax). However, a simple rule of this kind would force many companies to reduce dividends substantially over the current level, and would thus encounter strong opposition.

Hence the more feasible procedure would be to choose a "standard percentage" that is below the current average rate of dividend distributions (say 20 or 25 per cent. of the consolidated earnings, after deduction of prior charges and of the profits tax) and to permit those companies whose current dividends are below this standard percentage of earnings to raise dividends up to that level, while continuing the present policy of "freezing" dividends with regard to all other companies whose current dividends are above the standard percentage. In this way a clear principle would be established whereby the right to increase dividends would be linked to the degree of success attained in the business—a principle whose *raison d'être* and mode of operation would be easily understood by the business community. A policy of this kind would no longer bear the stamp of a stop-gap measure of strictly temporary character: especially if, at the outset, it were made clear that given a continued improvement in the economic situation, the "standard percentage" regulating the maximum extent of dividend increases might be raised from time to time. But even without an increase in the standard percentage, the policy would provide a continuing incentive, since companies whose dividends are at or below the standard percentage could reckon on being able to distribute to their shareholders the standard percentage of any future increase in earnings. The "standard percentage" would relate, of course, only to the right to raise dividends; there would be no compulsion on companies to reduce dividends if their earnings fell in subsequent years—any more than is the case with companies whose dividends are initially above the standard percentage.

In this manner, the total amount paid out in dividends could be continually kept under control, without all dividends being actually "frozen." Though approximate estimates of the effects of any given "standard percentage" could only be worked out by the Inland Revenue, it would not be surprising if the effect of a standard percentage of 20 per cent. were found to be of the order of £20 million–£30 million of additional dividend payments (i.e. an increase of 7–10 per cent. in aggregate dividend disbursements) while that of a standard percentage of 25 per cent., £40–£50 million. These increases relate, of course, to the initial year; in subsequent years (given the continuance of the same standard percentage) the increase in disbursements would be very much smaller.

In carrying out such a policy, the same methods of "voluntary" limitation might be relied upon as with the present dividend freeze. Once the reasons for the policy are explained and understood, so that the force of public opinion is behind it, infringements are not likely to be serious.

The practical application of the above principle is capable, of course, of a large number of variations—e.g. as to the manner in which the standard percentage, or earnings, are calculated; and different rules might be introduced for different industries. It is doubtful, however, whether the advantages of any refinements in the rules would compensate for the loss of simplicity. The objection that might be raised against the adoption of any such principle is that it would be "unfair" as between different shareholders, since some companies would be permitted substantial increases in dividends, while others none at all. The simple answer to this is that exactly the same kind of thing would happen if dividend limitation were abolished altogether. The social justification of dividend payments is as the reward for risk-bearing; it is in the essence of this reward that it should be apportioned by the criterion of success, rather than by some criterion of "fairness" or "equity." It may be inevitable, of course, that the announcement of any such policy should lead to substantial shifts in Stock Exchange values, though companies with a high earnings yield normally have a relatively low dividend-yield, so that the rise in the Stock Exchange values of individual shares is not likely to be at all proportionate to the possible increase in dividends under the policy. The last consideration does suggest, however, that the idea of any such change be kept secret until it is definitely announced.

It is, moreover, highly desirable that the new policy both in regard to wages and dividends should be brought before the public simultaneously. While the present dividend limitation has been remarkably well observed by companies up to the present, this is not likely to continue once the present wage-freeze has been replaced by a policy of definite annual wage increases. Any formal abandonment of the policy of dividend limitation, on the other hand, is likely to make it far more difficult to secure working-class support for the new wages policy. This, perhaps, is the most important reason for a modified policy of flexible dividend limitation: it is an essential complement of a successful policy of flexible wage restraints.

ADDENDA

(1) COMMENTS ON CRITICISMS OF THE DIVIDEND LIMITATION PROPOSAL[1]

Three main points were raised in connection with the Dividend Limitation Scheme:

(1) That owing to the differences in the proportion of earnings paid out in dividends in different industries, the operation of the scheme would discriminate between different industries in that it would put some industries in a better position to raise dividends than others.

(2) That anomalies might arise as between firms which have varying proportions of preference share capital to ordinary share capital.

(3) The scheme would permit some firms to make spectacular increases in dividends while others none at all and might, on that account, cause general resentment.

[1] Further memorandum submitted to the Treasury on 23 January 1951.

As far as I understand it, the first and the third points are closely related and it is better therefore to deal with them together. I see little point in this context in comparing the position of different *industries*. The *average* percentage of earnings paid out in dividends in industries is pretty meaningless for purposes of comparison, since within each industry the position of different firms varies far more widely than the differences between averages of different industries. The objection to be raised, therefore, is not that the scheme places different industries in an unequal position, but that it places different *firms* in an unequal position.

And here we come to the fundamental point about the whole scheme. It is based on the recognition of the fact that dividends cannot be kept frozen over any prolonged period without deleterious effects on economic incentives. The purpose of the scheme is to permit increases in dividends for the sake of those incentives, but at the same time to limit the total amount of additional dividends paid to a figure which is reasonable in the light of the current economic situation. Put in other words, the scheme aims at securing the maximum effect from the point of view of incentives of any given additional sum paid out in dividends. Obviously this principle cannot be aligned with ideas of "fairness" or "equity"—it is in direct contradiction to it. If the additional amount which is to be permitted to be paid out in dividends is to be fairly and equitably distributed between the different shareholders, the thing to do would be simply to permit *all* companies to raise their dividends but by not more than 5 or 10 per cent. of the existing level.

A dividend limitation of this latter type might be equitable enough but from the point of view of creating incentives to efficiency, it would be completely useless. In a situation where companies in general already earn far more than they pay out in dividends, the possibility of paying out a little more in dividends provides no added incentive at all to increase earnings. In that case, it may be asked, why should any increase in dividends be permitted at all? If its purpose were simply to allow the shareholders a somewhat higher income (which apparently is all that the Inland Revenue had in mind) it would be simpler to do so by reducing surtax or increasing the allowances on income tax on unearned incomes. The main purpose of my proposals was not to do justice to shareholders, but to buttress industrial efficiency, or to remove existing impediments to efficiency, at the minimum cost to the community both from the point of view of creating additional spending power or increased inequalities of income. This requires that rewards should be apportioned to success; and that the increase in dividends should be concentrated on the conspicuously successful companies rather than be spread wide among the companies at large. It is far better, therefore, that a few companies be permitted spectacular increases in dividends—provided that earnings are high enough to so do— than that a moderate increase in dividends should be permitted to all.

Incidentally this is a principle which I am sure the business community would understand and appreciate. Of all the classes of the community the group of ordinary shareholders are least wedded to the idea of "fair shares." On the contrary, the ordinary shareholder fully expects to make large rewards in case of success to compensate for the losses in case of failure. Otherwise why invest in ordinary share capital at all rather than in gilt-edged bonds?

With regard to the second point, it would be perfectly possible to operate the scheme with reference to the proportion which dividends of all kinds (preferred and ordinary) bear to total profits rather than to the proportion which the dividends on ordinary shares bears to the earnings of ordinary shares. If, for the sake of example, we suppose that the current average percentage of distribution on ordinary shares only is 33 per cent. and it is desired to put the "ceiling" to the scheme at 25 per cent., it would be equally possible to take into account dividends on preference shares and raise the ceiling percentage in a corresponding proportion. Thus, supposing the proportion paid out in both preferred and ordinary dividends in relation to total profits is 45 per cent., the ceiling could be put at 35 per cent. or 40 per cent., instead of 25 per cent. The determination of the ceiling should in each case be related to the total amount of additional dividend payments which in the light of the general economic situation it is regarded as reasonable to permit.

But while it is easy to meet this particular objection, I would still prefer a scheme along the lines proposed in my paper rather than one which allows for preference dividends in the manner indicated. As far as "anomalies" are concerned it is equally easy to construct anomalous cases under the version which allows for preference dividends as under the version which does not. Thus while the original scheme could be said to discriminate against companies which have a low proportion of preference capital to total capital, the latter version may be equally said to discriminate against companies which have a high proportion of preference capital in the total. This latter kind of "anomaly" would be more serious, however, since it would upset current market expectations far more. The incentive effect on any given additional sum of money paid out in dividends is bound to be larger under a more highly geared scheme—i.e. when the ceiling is related to ordinary dividends and the earnings of ordinary shares only—than under the amended version which is less highly geared. On reflection, I do not think that the existence of preference shares should cause any undue difficulty, since the various intermediate categories of shares (such as "preferred ordinary shares") would naturally class themselves into one group or the other according as they would, in ordinary circumstances, automatically participate in any increase in distributions or not.

Anyhow, the Stock Exchange is perfectly capable of making such a division since a "dividend yield" and an "earnings yield" are habitually calculated for each share; while the proposed scheme would merely require a ceiling that is defined as some ratio between these two magnitudes.

As I mentioned before, it would be appropriate to introduce the scheme as a more flexible and therefore suitable version of the earlier dividend freeze which it would replace, but without any pretence at its being a new permanent feature of our economic life. It might be introduced at first as a voluntary scheme, negotiated through the F.B.I., in the same way as the original dividend limitation in 1948, rather than embodying it in statutory form immediately. Whether statutory limitation will be necessary or not will emerge more clearly in the first year or the first six months of its operation and, as I mentioned in my paper, it would be advisable to set the original ceiling rather low since it would in practice be easier to raise it subsequently than to lower it.

(2) COMMENTS ON THE GOVERNMENT'S PROPOSALS[1]

My reactions to the Chancellor's proposals are pretty unfavourable—for much the same reasons as were set out in my paper on dividends a year ago.

You can't have *absolute* dividend limitation as a more or less normal state of affairs in a private enterprise economy, any more than you can abolish the profit motive in a system of private enterprise. This is bound to have the most deleterious effects on efficiency—effects which are none the less serious for being gradual rather than sudden. For one thing, companies will not be able to raise fresh capital, other than loan capital, the amount of which is proportionately limited to their own capital. For a new venture, the prospect of a *maximum* dividend of 7 per cent. in the case of success is of course ridiculously low—this is the yield on the preference shares of well-established companies, with ample margins. For existing firms, 5 per cent. on paid up capital means presumably 5 per cent. on the nominal value of the shares issued; but companies whose reserves are large in relation to nominal capital, cannot issue shares at their nominal price, without seriously prejudicing the rights of existing shareholders. I suppose this difficulty could be overcome by permitting companies to issue bonus shares up to the amount of accumulated reserves. In that case, however, 5 per cent. on paid up capital might well mean a large increase in existing dividends. The operation of this scheme must therefore tend to confine expansion to firms which possess liquid reserves or can build them up out of undistributed profits. This would inevitably strengthen monopolistic tendencies; it would mean also the channelling of investment to those branches of the economy where expansion was so far

---

[1] Written on 27 July 1951. A scheme providing for the statutory limitation of dividends for a three-year period was announced a few days previously.

relatively slow, since in the expanding industries the accumulation of *liquid* reserves would tend to lag behind the expansion of business. A firm which possesses free reserves would have no interest in investing it in another, which needs fresh capital, if it could not benefit by it; hence it would invest it internally, even if the profits prospects were relatively unfavourable. Thus the scheme is bound to misdirect investment, and encourage extravagance of all kinds.

You may say that it is meant for the strictly temporary period of rearmament. But the present troubles with dividends were already largely the consequence of earlier dividend limitations, as a result of which dividends became progressively less related to current earnings. In three years' time the removal of the present limitation would lead to a considerably greater dividend explosion than was experienced in the past two months. Hence the longer this type of "freeze" lasts, the more difficult it will be to get rid of it, without major economic and political instability. And the cost in terms of lower productivity will be realised only gradually, but will be correspondingly lasting. A more or less perpetual dividend freeze (interrupted with brief periods of dividend freedom and corresponding stock market booms) could only be justified if one denied any significance to the profit motive in the running of the economy.

If a drastic scheme of dividend limitation is desired, why not limit *all* dividends to some percentage of *current earnings*? If this were set, at say 33 per cent., the total amount that could be distributed in dividends would be *smaller* than at present. The above objections would not apply to a scheme of this latter kind, or only to a very much lesser extent—since this would still permit the relatively successful to be relatively more highly rewarded, just as much as in the absence of dividend limitation; and it is the relative gain from success, rather than its absolute size, that matters. Also it would be an elastic scheme—it could be relaxed, to a greater or lesser extent, without being abolished. I suppose the objection to that is that it would raise an outcry from those shareholders whose dividends would be cut in consequence. But isn't that a much lesser evil than the rigidity and inefficiency arising from the present scheme? There is really no need to be fair to, or to reduce the risks falling on, ordinary shareholders. Instead of making them all rentiers, it would be a good thing to bring home the fact that dividends represent a fluctuating income, varying with success.

The scheme I proposed a year ago was a compromise between the two ideas—limit dividends to previous levels, but permit increases where earnings are exceptionally high. This was to avoid the purely political objection to a simple link between distributions and earnings. But the present scheme adopts only the "wrong half" of the compromise and rejects the "right half." It goes the whole hog in the direction of "what exists is right"— putting the idea of security and "fair shares" first and taking only the existing state of affairs as the criterion for what is "fair." It is really the Socialist version of Baldwinism. There are other ways of making the Stock Exchange and the capitalists feel uncomfortable—ways which would make the economy less rigid and more competitive, instead of more rigid and effete.

6

MONETARY POLICY, ECONOMIC STABILITY AND GROWTH[1]

1. The present memorandum deals almost exclusively with basic issues concerning the role of monetary and credit policy in the maintenance of stability in prices and incomes, rather than with questions concerning the technique of monetary management. My excuse for putting forth a paper devoted to elementary propositions is the prevalence of confused thinking in this particular field even among eminent authorities. Yet without a basic understanding of the processes through which changes in the amount of money in circulation influence the level of expenditure and the general level of prices, it is impossible to arrive at any sound judgment concerning the merits of particular methods of monetary management.[2]

I. THE MODUS OPERANDI OF MONETARY POLICY

The Supply of Money and the Level of Expenditure

2. It cannot be emphasised too strongly that there is no direct relationship in a modern community between the amount of money in circulation (whatever definition of "money supply" is adopted in this connection) and the amount of money spent on goods and services per unit of time. To proceed from the one to the other it is necessary to postulate that changes in the supply of money leave the frequency with which money changes hands (the so-called "velocity of circulation of money") unaffected, or at least that any consequential change in the velocity of circulation is limited to some predictable fraction of the primary change in the supply of money. There are no valid grounds however for

---

[1] A memorandum submitted to the Committee on the Working of the Monetary System on June 23, 1958.
[2] The present memorandum is restricted to the internal aspects of monetary policy. Its external aspects (questions of the exchange rates, the sterling area system, convertibility, capital movements, etc.) are outside its scope.

any such supposition. The velocity of circulation of money (or what comes to the same thing, the ratio which cash balances bear to the volume of turnover of money payments, per unit of time) is not determined by factors that are independent either of the supply of money or the volume of money payments; it simply reflects the relationship between these two magnitudes. In some communities the velocity of circulation is low, in others it is high, in some it is rising and in others it is falling, without any systematic connection between such differences or movements and the degree of inflationary pressure, the rate of increase in monetary turnover,[1] etc. Such differences can only be explained in terms of historical developments rather than psychological propensities or of institutional factors, while the movements in the ratio can only be accounted for by the varying incidence of the policies pursued by the monetary authorities. In countries where the authorities pursue a restrictive policy, the ratio tends to fall, and *vice versa*. Thus in the U.K. there has been a spectacular rise in the velocity of circulation, particularly since 1955, which fully compensated for the failure of the money supply to expand *pari passu* with the rise in prices and in money incomes. The "money supply" has been kept constant (indeed it has been slightly falling) while the annual percentage rise in the money value of the national product has been as great or greater than in previous years when the money supply was rising. It could not seriously be maintained that this change in the velocity of circulation was in any sense an *independent* phenomenon which happened to coincide in time with the change in monetary policy. It was simply a reflection of this policy: if the supply of money had not

[1] According to the statistics published by the International Monetary Fund, the ratio of the money supply (currency plus deposit money) to the gross national product varied in the latest available year (1957 or 1956) from 54 per cent. in Switzerland, 46 per cent. in Belgium, 38 per cent. in Brazil and 36 per cent. in France to 30 per cent. in the U.S., 27·5 per cent. in the U.K., 18 per cent. in Germany and 13 per cent. in Mexico. In the period since 1951 this ratio fell in some countries, and rose in others, but there was no systematic connection between these movements and the rate of increase in the money value of the G.N.P., or that and the initial magnitude of this ratio. The ratio fell in some relatively "inflationary" countries (e.g. in the U.S. from 37 to 30 per cent., in the U.K. from 36 to 27·5 per cent., in Mexico from 16 to 13 per cent.) as well as in some "non-inflationary" countries (e.g. in Switzerland from 62 to 54 per cent.). It rose in some relatively "non-inflationary" countries (e.g. in Germany from 14 to 18 per cent., in Belgium from 40 to 46 per cent.) as well as in some "inflationary" countries (in France from 31 to 36 per cent. and in Brazil from 35 to 38 per cent.).

been restricted, the increase in the velocity of circulation would not have taken place and it is a matter of doubt, to say the least, whether the course of prices and incomes would have been any different. At any rate the *impact* effect of any change in the money supply is not on the level of payments at all, but on the velocity of circulation.[1]

3. Those who maintain the opposite view (the adherents of the "quantity theory" of money) argue that the social and institutional factors which determine the frequency of recurring payments of various kinds (the frequency of wage and salary payments, the frequency of settlement of business accounts, etc.), together with the uncertainty concerning the exact timing of these payments lead to individuals and businesses having a certain "desired" cash balance in relation to turnover which is substantially independent of the supply of money. It is a mistake to assume, however, that given the normal frequency of various kinds of payments the maintenance of any given *flow* of payments requires some definite quantity of monetary media. Outstanding cash balances invariably contain large amounts held for purely speculative purposes, or out of the "precautionary" motive (i.e. as hedge against unforeseen delays in the inflow of prospective receipts) as well as the so-called "transaction balances" proper, i.e. those arising automatically as the result of differences in the relative time frequency of receipts and out-payments. These latter, in turn, can be reduced considerably through "synchronising" payments and receipts, and through the creation of money substitutes of various kinds. As the experience of Germany and other countries during the great inflations has shown, the economic system in case of need can be "run" on a very small fraction of its normal cash requirements. (In Germany in 1923 money in circulation amounted to less than $\frac{1}{2}$ per cent. of the current level of incomes, expressed at annual rates.) Obviously this cannot be attained without considerable inconvenience; and the resulting rise in the rate of interest paid on short loans is the measure of the extent of this inconvenience. The experience of various countries indicates that when the ratio of cash to turnover is at more normal

---

[1] Failure to recognise this vitiates much of recent thinking on monetary matters. Cf. e.g.the *First Report of the Council on Prices, Productivity and Incomes*, (1958) particularly chap. v.

levels (i.e. in the range of 20–50 per cent. of the annual value of G.N.P.) the "inconvenience" caused by changes in the ratio is not very great—i.e. considerable changes in the money supply in relation to the national income can take place without inducing spectacular changes in interest rates.

The Effect of Changes in Interest Rates on the Level of Expenditure

4. Yet it is through the consequential changes in interest rates that we must look for the effects of changes in the money supply on the demand for goods and services.[1] In theory a rise in interest rates should lead to a postponement of postponable expenditures by both businesses and personal consumers, as well as to some more or less permanent reduction in the rate at which capital expenditures are incurred. Thus a rise in interest rates should cause businesses to reduce the ratio of the stocks of materials and finished goods which they carry in relation to turnover—in much the same manner as their cash payments-turnover ratio—but here the "interest-elasticity" is likely to be much smaller, since economising on physical stocks may involve heavy costs in the form of higher transport charges, losses due to delays in production, etc., and not just "inconvenience."[2] To achieve any substantial reduction in the rate of investment in stocks far greater changes in (short-term) interest rates would have been required than have taken place since 1954.

5. The effect of a rise in interest rates on short-term investment is in any case a temporary one: if the rise in interest rates is successful in inducing traders to reduce their stocks in relation to turnover, it will restrain the pressure of demand as long as this process of adjustment is going on; once the adjustment is completed, the restraining effect of a higher interest rate on the level of expendi-

---

[1] Where the loan market is imperfect (as it is with an oligopolistic banking system) interest rates may not fully reflect the pressure of the demand for loans, owing to the policy of "credit rationing" adopted by the banks. In this case, however, unsatisfied borrowers willing to pay higher rates are likely to turn to other financial institutions willing to cater for their needs. (The mushroom growth of hire-purchase finance houses, for business as well as personal purposes, was a direct consequence of the policy of the "credit squeeze" imposed on the clearing banks after 1955.)

[2] The policy of the "credit squeeze" in the U.K. since February 1955, while it involved a substantial change in the size of cash balances held in relation to turnover, did not cause any contraction in the size of physical stocks in relation to turnover: the (real) rate of investment in stocks, in each of the three years 1955 to 1957 was substantially higher than in the preceding three years.

ture is exhausted. This means that it is hopeless to expect a downward adjustment in stocks induced by credit policy to compensate (more than temporarily) for inflationary pressures emanating from other sectors—from, say, a chronic insufficiency of savings in relation to investment in fixed capital, the budgetary deficit, or the export surplus.[1]

6. The effect of higher interest rates on long-term investment may be more lasting, but here again, only drastic and spectacular changes in interest rates can be counted on to exert a marked effect on capital expenditure. The reasons for this are as follows:

(i) The interest rate relevant to long-term investment is the long-term rate whose movement is sluggish in relation to changes in the short-term rate. (This is on account of the fact that both unusually high and unusually low short-term rates are regarded as temporary by the market; hence a change in the short-term rate normally induces a change in the long-term rate in the same direction but of a considerably smaller magnitude.)

(ii) Such increases in the long-term rate as occur in response to a rise in the short rate are only regarded as temporary since the market assumes that bond prices are depressed on account of the high money rates, and will recover with any reduction in the latter. Hence the rise in the long-term rates will not have the same discouraging effect on capital expenditure as it might have if the current long rates were expected to be permanent, and if it were not open to investors to finance long-term capital expenditure with short-term borrowing on the prospect of being able to borrow over long-term on more advantageous terms later on.[2]

(iii) There is normally a considerable gap between the prospective rate of profit obtainable on direct investment and the market rates of interest on money loans. This gap serves (in Ricardo's words) as "compensation for the [farmers' and manufacturers'] trouble and the risk which they must necessarily encounter in employing their capital productively." However,

---

[1] It is a different matter when the acceleration of stock accumulation or the reverse is the source of instability. This could in principle be compensated for by correctly timed and correctly scaled variations in the terms of short term credit. Cf. paras. 27-30 below.

[2] The very fact that in times of high money market rates the yield of irredeemable bonds may actually stand lower than the bill rates or the bond rates on loans with most maturity is a clear indication that the market expects a fall in the long term rates in the future.

this compensation for risk and trouble is not something rigid, and when the rate of profit exceeds the rate of interest by a considerable percentage (as, for example, when the prospective rate of profit is 15 per cent. and the rate of interest only 5 per cent.), moderate changes in the rate of interest may have no appreciable effect on investment decisions. It must be remembered that in times of rising prices the rate of profit is higher (as will be shown in paragraph 11 below, the annual percentage increase in the price level may be regarded as a flat addition to what would have been the ruling rate of profit with a stable price level) and therefore the gap between the rate of profit and the rate of interest may be abnormally large.[1]

(iv) It must be remembered that in times of full employment, or even of approximately full employment, the capacity of the investment goods industries may exert a far more important limitation on the level of capital expenditure than the cost of borrowing or the availability of particular forms of finance. Thus the rate of building and constructional activity may be confined by the availability of building and constructional labour; expenditure on plant and equipment may be limited by lengthening delivery periods on new contracts.[2] In such situations the range of projects whose execution would be influenced by changes in the cost of borrowing or in the availability of loans might be unusually narrow, and be largely confined to cases where the terms of lending can be regulated by quantitative rules, and where the borrower cannot easily find alternative sources of finance. Such is the case with consumer purchases of durable goods (motor-cars, etc., as well as houses) which can be regulated

[1] The taxation system also operates so as to reduce the sensitivity of investment decisions to changes in interest rates. For what matters from the point of view of the entrepreneurs is the excess of the prospective net rate of profit on investment (net after income tax and profits tax) over the net rate of interest on loans (net of income tax). With a given gross rate of profit the excess of the net rate of profit over the net rate of interest will of course only be reduced (with a rate of income tax of 50 per cent.) by one-half of every percentage point rise in the gross rate of interest.

[2] One of the assumptions of traditional economic theory is that any such limitation would cause a rise in prices and profit margins of capital goods which in turn would reduce the gap between profit rates and interest rates to normal levels. However, when a considerable sector of the economy operates under oligopolistic conditions with "administered" prices, an excess demand can overhang the market for long periods without being eliminated through price inflation. Since a particular investment project consists of a number of complementary expenditures, it is possible moreover that the demand for the products of the competitive sectors is held down by the availability of complementary goods produced by oligopolistic sectors.

by laying down terms (such as a legal minimum of down-payments) for the granting of hire-purchase credit and mortgage finance.[1]

Summary of Above Argument

7. The argument up to this point may be summed up as follows:

(i) Changes in the money supply do not exert any direct influence on the level of monetary demand for goods and services as such, but only through the consequential changes in interest rates which are induced by them. (ii) The magnitude of these consequential changes in interest rates for any given percentage change in the money supply depends on the extent of inconvenience (or, conversely, increased convenience) involved in any corresponding change in the average ratio of cash balances to monetary turnover. Except where this ratio is abnormally small, the elasticity of interest rates with respect to change in the cash balance ratio may only be a moderate one. (iii) Since the regulatory effect of monetary policy essentially resides in the effect of changing interest rates on expenditure, it is more efficacious to concentrate on the regulation of interest rates directly (through open market operations in the money market and/or the gilt-edged market) than indirectly through pressure exerted on the supply of bank credit.[2] (iv) Relatively moderate changes in interest rates may have no certain or predictable effect on either consumer

---

[1] Whether this kind of regulation is the most suitable method of limiting consumer demand is a different question. As against the discouraging effects of either taxation or consumer rationing (by means of building licences, for example) the effects of hire-purchase or mortgage-finance regulations are confined to a particular class of buyers who are dependent on loans for their purchases.

[2] It is erroneous to assume that the quantitive regulation of credit by the clearing banks will have the same effect as a corresponding change in short-term interest rates. This would only be true if the clearing banks were the sole source of short-term credit which of course is by no means the case. Apart from the existence of other types of financial institutions, there is the extension of "trade credit" of varying kinds, of which the involuntary (or at least partially involuntary) credit represented by the debtor's delay in settling account is the extreme example. As a recent analysis of the accounts of 3,000 quoted companies has shown, the *net* amount of trade credit outstanding of the 3,000 companies exceeded by a considerable margin the total amount of their bank credits in 1953; moreover the growth of the *net* trade credit (excess of trade debtors over trade creditors) in the five years prior to 1953 was $2\frac{1}{2}$ times as large as the increase in bank overdrafts and loans. Trade credit received in 1953 by these companies exceeded their bank overdrafts 5 times; trade credit granted $6\frac{1}{2}$ times. (Cf. *Company Income and Finance, 1949-53*, N.I.E.S.R., 1956, Table 5. Unfortunately no figures are yet available to record the effect of the "credit squeeze.")

expenditure or on business expenditure. This is particularly true in times of full employment and inflation when factors other than finance inevitably play an important role in limiting capital expenditures: it may be also important in times of large-scale unemployment and deflation when interest rates are already near their minimum practicable level, and cannot be reduced much further through open market operations.

The Undesirability of Unstable Interest Rates

8. None of this is intended to suggest that increases in interest rates are ultimately ineffective in curbing expenditure. When the prospective rate of profit on new investments is around 15 per cent., a rise in the (irredeemable) gilt-edged rate from 3 to 5 per cent. or even to 6 per cent. might prove ineffective in eliminating an excess pressure of demand. But nobody would suggest that a rise in the yield of Consols to 15 per cent. would not exert a tremendous deflationary impact. Hence provided the authorities are prepared to take sufficiently drastic steps in raising interest rates, it should always be possible to eliminate inflationary tendencies due to an excessive pressure of demand; and if they had sufficient elbow room for lowering interest rates (which may not be the case) they might be equally effective in countering deflationary tendencies through reductions in interest rates. But it is impossible to devise tests which would enable the authorities to judge, in any given situation, how great a change is required; and for reasons advanced above it is useless to look for such tests in the resulting changes of the quantity of money in circulation.

9. There is fair agreement among economists that if monetary and credit policy was to be relied on as the principal instrument of control, changes in interest rates would have to be far more drastic than those recently applied.[1] The reason generally advanced for the reluctance of the authorities to impose more

---

[1] This concerns the effects of changes in the Bank Rate and the money market rates on internal inflationary and deflationary tendencies. Actually, it is a matter of doubt how far changes in the Bank Rate in recent years were prompted by considerations of domestic inflation rather than by the state of the reserves. From the point of view of its external effects there can be little doubt that an increase in the Bank Rate proved an effective device on almost every occasion for bringing to a halt a speculative drain on the pound.

drastic changes in interest rates is the Government's own vulner-
ability to such changes on account of the existence of a massive
short-term Government debt (much of it owed abroad) and the
constant need to refinance a large volume of bonded debt which
matures every year. This must undoubtedly reduce the relative
attractiveness of the Bank Rate instrument as an economic
regulator. I believe however that even if these factors were not
present (on the supposition, for example, that the whole of the
outstanding Government debt were repaid by means of a once for
all capital levy) it would still be impossible to stabilise the level
of demand by means of credit policy alone without highly undesirable consequences in other directions. Reliance on monetary
policy as an effective stabilising device would involve large and
rapid changes in the level of interest rates and, in consequence, a
high degree of instability in bond prices in the capital market.
But the relative stability of bond prices is a highly important
feature of an effectively functioning capital market, and of the
whole credit mechanism in a capitalist economy. If bond prices
were liable to vast and rapid fluctuations, the speculative risks
involved in long-term loans of any kind would be very much
greater than they are now, and the average price which investors
would demand for parting with liquidity would be considerably
higher. The capital market would become far more speculative,
and would function far less efficiently as an instrument for allocating savings—new issues would be more difficult to launch, and
long-run considerations of relative profitability would play a
subordinate role in the allocation of funds. As Keynes said, when
the capital investment of a country "becomes a by-product of the
activities of a casino, the job is likely to be ill-done." In addition,
since average rates of interest are bound to be considerably higher,
the rate of profit required to make investment attractive in the
long run would also have to be higher; to achieve this effect
Government policies would have to aim at stimulating consumption at the same time as they restrained investment. By the force of
circumstances rather than by design, a Government relying on
credit control for combating inflationary tendencies would be
bound to stimulate consumption rather than investment in times
of inadequate demand (for political as well as for technical

reasons) and would thus gradually transform the economy into one of high consumption and low investment—with all its undesirable consequences on the long-run rates of economic growth.[1] Those who argue in favour of credit policy as the main economic stabiliser frequently overlook the fact that the increased instability of interest rates which is a necessary precondition for the effective use of monetary policy as an economic regulator can only be bought at the cost of making the *average* level of long-term interest rates considerably higher than what it would be if interest rates were relatively stable.

The Dangers of a Régime of Stable Prices

10. High rates of interest are not necessarily inconsistent with sustained economic growth *provided the inflationary trend of prices is maintained*. As the examples of various Latin American countries show, when the price level rises by 10 per cent. a year or more, interest rates of 10 or 15 per cent. are perfectly consistent with the high rates of investment required to sustain a 3–5 per cent. annual rate of growth in the real national income. But the objective of those who favour credit restriction as an instrument of economic control is not the maintenance of a steady trend of price inflation, but the attainment of price stability; and when the potential rate of growth is low the latter may only be reconciled with high interest rates (or indeed, with any attainable level of interest rates, high or low) at the cost of economic stagnation.

11. In a steadily growing economy the average rate of profit on investments can, in the first approximation, be taken as being equal to the rate of growth in the money value of the gross national product divided by the proportion of profits saved.[2] Thus if the rate of growth of the money national income is 6 per cent. a year and if the proportion of profits saved (defined as the excess of profits earned over property owners' consumption) is 40 per cent. (or, alternatively, if the national income grows at 7·5 per cent., and the proportion of profits saved is 50 per cent.) the average rate of profit will be 15 per cent. To keep the process of investment going, the rate of profit must exceed the (long-term) interest

[1] Cf. paras. 11-12 below for a further consideration of this point.
[2] For the derivation of this formula, cf. *Economic Journal*, December, 1957, pp. 604-11 and 613-14.

rates by some considerable margin—a margin that is all the greater the higher are the taxes on profits and income. Though nobody knows what the required minimum margin is, at a guess I would put it at 6–10 per cent. gross or 3–5 per cent. net (of taxation), so that a 15 per cent. profit rate is consistent with long-term interest rates of 4–7 per cent. or less. The rate of growth of the money national income is the sum of the rate of growth in production and the rate of growth of prices. Assuming that the 6 per cent. rate of growth in the gross national product in money terms is composed of a 3 per cent. per annum growth in production and a 3 per cent. per annum rise in prices, a régime of complete price-stability would cut the average rate of profit on investment by one-half—i.e. to 7·5 per cent. in the above example. This in turn would only be consistent with continued investment and expansion if the long-term rate of interest were down to 1–2 per cent. If the rate of interest were higher than this, the process of accumulation would be interrupted, and the economy would relapse into a slump. To get it out of the slump it would be necessary to stimulate the propensity to consume—by tax cuts, for example—which would raise the rate of profit and thus restore the incentive to invest. If by such means the proportion of profits saved were reduced to one half—from 40 per cent. to 20 per cent.—the rate of profit would again be 15 per cent., assuming that the level of output, and thus the national income at constant prices, continues to grow at 3 per cent. a year. But the share of savings in income, and thus the share of investment in output, would be only half as high as before, hence the rate of growth of the national product would necessarily become less than it was—with the share of investment in output at one half of its previous level it may be reduced to, say, 2 per cent. a year. This in turn would imply a rate of profit of 10 per cent., possibly necessitating a further stimulus to consumption, a further cut in the investment co-efficient, a further fall in the rate of growth of production, and so on.

12. The moral of this is that it is dangerous for a weakly-progressive economy to aim at a régime of stable prices (let alone at a régime of falling prices!) since when the rate of growth of production is low (on account of a stagnant working population,

a low rate of technical progress, or both) stable prices are only consistent with low rates of profit which may be insufficient to maintain the inducement to invest, unless the latter is stimulated by measures which cut down the ratio of investment to output and thereby reduce still further the rate of growth of production. Thus in the United Kingdom the rate of growth of the "real" gross national product in the period 1950–7 was 3 per cent. a year. Thanks to inflation, the gross national product at current prices grew at a rate of 7·5 per cent. a year. If inflation had been entirely avoided, the average rate of profit on new investment would have been 60 per cent. lower, that is to say, 6 per cent. instead of 15 per cent. (which we assumed for the purpose of this exercise, but which was probably not far off the truth). In Germany on the other hand, in the period 1950–7 the rate of growth of the gross national product at constant prices was 8·5 per cent. and at current prices 11·5 per cent. a year. This explains why Germany was able to combine average rates of profit of 20 per cent. or more with a reasonable stability of prices, and why interest rates on commercial loans could rise to 10–12 per cent. without discouraging investment. Indeed, if German prices had been falling by 1–2 per cent. per annum, instead of rising (owing to a failure of money wages to rise as fast as productivity) the rate of profit would still have been high enough to keep the process of expansion going. In the light of this the objective of stable or falling prices may well be regarded as a luxury which only fast-growing economies can afford.[1] (We shall return to this in paragraphs 23–25 below.)

[1] The *First Report of the Council on Prices, Productivity and Incomes* spent some time in considering the relative merits of rising, stable and falling prices (chap. iv), without any mention of the effect of stable or falling prices on the rate of profit, and the added difficulty in maintaining the incentives to invest at a lower rate of profit. This omission is the more surprising since one of the distinguished members of the Council, Professor Sir Dennis Robertson, was one of the first economists to have perceived this point in his early writings (cf. "The Case for a Gently Rising Price Level" in *Money* (Cambridge, 1922), pp. 122-8). According to Mr. D. H. Robertson (as he then was) a régime of gently rising prices gives a "fillip to production [which] by adding to the flow of goods serves to moderate the very rise in prices which gives it birth" (p. 123), whereas "it is tolerably certain that a price-level continually falling, even for the best of reasons, would prove deficient in those stimuli upon which modern society, whether wisely or not, has hitherto chiefly relied for keeping its members in full employment and getting its work done" (p. 125).

Credit Policy and the Creation of Uncertainty

13. Before we leave the subject of the *modus operandi* of monetary policy we must mention yet another argument in favour of credit policy, as an instrument of economic control. Its advocates would not dispute the undesirable effects of highly fluctuating interest rates; they would argue, however, that the psychological effects of changes in the Bank Rate are far more important than its technical effects; hence the policy could be made effective, even if applied in moderate doses, provided these come "at the right moment" and have the right kind of impact on business psychology. Allied to this is the further argument that frequent use of the Bank Rate mechanism keeps the business world guessing concerning the ultimate intentions of the monetary authorities: and this uncertainty makes businesses responsive to "signals" communicated by the authorities through changes in the Bank Rate, even if, on the basis of a strict calculation of costs and returns, the resulting changes in interest rates would not have affected their conduct. These arguments were frequently used in support of a return to a flexible Bank Rate policy in the early 1950's, but they have been much less prominent recently; and the reason, I believe, is that the expectations that were originally entertained concerning the psychological effects of even moderate changes in the Bank Rate have so demonstrably been proved wrong by subsequent experience. It is fairly generally recognised now that the purely psychological effects of the changes in credit policy which started in February 1955, and which were accompanied by a rising crescendo of warnings and exhortations by the Chancellor of the Exchequer in the course of that year and the following year, were negligible. This does not prove, of course, that the psychological effects of such changes would be equally unimportant on other occasions, but it does show that these effects are completely unpredictable, and hence no reliance can be placed on them.[1]

---

[1] Indeed, it is questionable how far the whole view which regards the deliberate creation of an atmosphere of uncertainty as an effective means of making the economic system amenable to control is a legitimate one. This is a complex question, which cannot be gone into here in detail; but it should be evident that any simple view on this matter is likely to be one-sided. On the one hand, the existence of uncertainty, and the prevalence of a variety of opinion which is associated with it, clearly increases the power of the monetary authorities to determine the rates of interest ruling in the

II. MONETARY POLICY AND THE PROBLEM OF STABILITY

14. It follows from the above reasoning that monetary and credit policy represents, at best, a crude and blunt instrument for controlling inflationary and deflationary tendencies in the economy which should be employed only in circumstances in which, and to the extent to which, no superior instruments of control are available. In order to discover what, if any, these circumstances are it is necessary to review briefly the nature of the various problems confronting the monetary and financial authorities.

(i) Excessive Pressure of Demand

15. First, there is the problem of an excessive pressure of demand for resources of all kinds which must be a reflection of the expenditures on capital account exceeding the planned savings on income account (of individuals, businesses, and public authorities). The manifestations of this are: (a) abnormally long, and lengthening order books in many industries; (b) an acute shortage of labour in the majority of industries;[1] (c) a faster rate of increase of business profits than of wages and salaries; (d) a deteriorating relationship between exports and imports, due to a rising volume of imports, or a falling volume of exports or some combination of both. The remedy must be sought either in a reduction of capital expenditure or in an increase in planned savings; and, from the point of view of the national interest, there is generally a strong presumption in favour of policies which increase savings (i.e. reduce consumption) as against policies which involve a reduction of investments. Unless therefore the excess pressure of demand is due to some sudden spurt, showing manifest instability in the level of business capital expenditures (of which more below), the appropriate instrument of control is to be found not

market through open market operations. On the other hand, the prevalence of uncertainty reduces the extent to which businessmen's decisions are based on neatly balanced calculations of gain or loss, and thus the extent to which such decisions are responsive to changes in interest rates.

[1] In an industrially developed economy such as Britain manufacturing capacity is *normally* more than sufficient for the employment of the available labour force (even without resorting to double shift or treble shift working in the great majority of industries) so that the effective bottleneck limiting production is a shortage of labour, rather than of capacity.

in monetary but in fiscal policy—the more so as the latter is more predictable and immediate in its operation than the former.[1]

(ii) Unbalanced Growth

16. Secondly, as a variant of the former, there is the problem of an excessive pressure of demand in certain key sectors of the economy, due to an unbalanced (or disproportionate) development between the different sectors, which can persist even if the pressure of demand in general is not excessive in relation to available resources. The standard example of this is the failure, in many underdeveloped countries, of the increase in the supply of "wage-goods," particularly of foodstuffs, to match the growth of incomes generated by production. This leads to a constant upward pressure of the price-level of wage-goods, involving periodic upward revisions in money wage-rates which in turn make the rise in costs and prices general throughout the economy and keep up the upward pressure on the prices of wage-goods.

17. This particular combination of a demand-generated inflation of food-prices with a cost-generated inflation of industrial prices is peculiar to underdeveloped countries and is absent in developed countries which either generate food-surpluses (like the United States, Australia, New Zealand or Canada) or else possess the buying power to satisfy their excess food requirements through purchases in the world market (like Britain, Western Germany, Belgium or Switzerland). But a somewhat analogous situation may arise when the growth in the capacity of the export industries of "developed" countries fails to keep pace with the requirements of additional imports which result from the growth of production and incomes in the economy in general. (It is arguable, e.g. that a policy of holding back the expansion of

---

[1] A rise in total taxation relative to public expenditure will always increase total net (planned) savings, though by less than the increase in public savings (since a rise in taxation will be associated with *some* reduction in private savings). The relevant measure of the *change* in public savings is the *change* in the "overall" deficit (or surplus). A change in the "above the line" surplus will make no (immediate) contribution to the relief of inflationary pressure if offset by a simultaneous change in the below-the-line deficit. There are situations, however, in which changes in public capital expenditure reflect opposite changes in private capital expenditure (as, for example, when an industry is nationalised and hence its investment is transferred from the private to the public sector) and in which therefore the change in the surplus on current account gives a better indication of the change in the net income-creating effect of Government operations.

production was forced on Britain in the last few years on balance-of-payments considerations—i.e. on account of the fact that expansion would have raised imports, whilst the capacity of the export industries would not have permitted any corresponding increase in exports.) In such cases overall measures of control, whether through credit policy or fiscal policy, may be inappropriate or insufficient, and the remedy may have to be sought in selective controls of various kinds (as e.g. control over the allocation of investments; the forced expansion of investment in the critical sectors, or food rationing when the driving force behind the inflation is the inadequacy of food supplies, etc.), by means of which the tendencies to disproportionate development can be counteracted or compensated for.

(iii) Wage Inflation

18. Thirdly, there is the case when the driving force behind the inflation is an excessive rate of increase in money wages. To be sure, a continued rise in money wages is invariably involved in every *process* of inflation, since if money wages did not rise, the rise in the price-level could not continue beyond a certain point, whatever the nature of the forces underlying the price rise. But a distinction can be drawn—blurred though it is in a range of border-line cases—between a situation in which the rise in wages *reflects* the forces making for the rise in prices and one in which the rise in wages *causes* the rise in prices to take place—i.e. in which the rise in wages is primary and the rise in prices secondary. In the former category belong the cases (*a*) when the upward revisions in money wages can be shown to be clearly related to a prior rise in the cost of living index, as a result of which real wages fell appreciably below some previously attained level; (*b*) when the rise in wages is mainly the result of the competitive bidding for labour by employers, rather than the demand for higher pay by the workers enforced through collective bargaining. In the second category fall those situations in which the rise in the general level of wages is mainly the outcome of the struggle of wage-earners in different industries and occupations to secure an improvement, or to prevent a deterioration of, their earnings relative to the wages paid in other occupations—in other words,

where the rise in the general wage level is largely a by-product of countervailing pressures acting on the scale of relative wages. In the latter situation the rise in prices is mainly the consequence of the rise in costs (matched by the increase in monetary demand resulting from the rise in incomes) and not of the excessive pressure of demand pulling prices upwards. A wage inflation of the first category is but a particular aspect of the "demand inflation" discussed above, and calls for the same remedies. A wage inflation of the second category, however, is not one that can be expected to be cured by restrictions of demand—not unless the restriction is carried to the point of such heavy unemployment that the wage-earners in any particular industry are unable to hold out for higher wages on account of the competition of unemployed workers.[1]

19. Some economists hold that the wage inflation of the post-war period was mainly the reflection of a demand-inflation—of the competition between employers for scarce labour—and would not have taken place if demand had been damped down to more reasonable levels. They cite as evidence for this the fact that in a number of post-war years the rise in earnings was greater than the rise in wages—which provides some indication that the actual wage rates paid in a number of industries were above the negotiated levels. Even if it is admitted that in times of acute labour shortage wages tend to rise above the negotiated levels, it does not follow that the rise in the negotiated levels themselves would have been avoided or lessened if the pressure of demand had been smaller (and it must be remembered that the rise in the official wage rates accounted for much the greater part of the total increase in wages). Equally it does not follow that if the rise in official wages had been smaller the element of "wage slide" (the excess of actual wages over negotiated wages) would have been substantially greater.

20. Other economists would agree that the wage inflation is of

[1] It is sometimes asserted that with a tight credit policy employers will be unable to grant wage increases or to pass on higher wage costs in higher prices and will therefore offer far greater resistance to demands for higher wages. This is clearly fallacious. Tight credit policy, if sufficiently severe, will force employers to reduce their rate of investment, and possibly even to disinvest. But neither their willingness to grant wage increases, nor their ability to pass on higher costs in the form of higher prices will be *directly* affected by it—any such effect will be indirect, and dependent on a prior reduction in the scale of operations.

the second category rather than of the first. They would maintain, however, that a fairly moderate reduction in the level of economic activity might reduce the pressure for wage increases sufficiently to prevent the rate of increase in wages exceeding the rate of increase in productivity. Assuming that there is a "break-even point"—for wages—at a level of unemployment which is not too large (say, of the order of 2–3 per cent.) it is argued that the loss of production due to a lower level of activity would not be large either; and provided the economy could be kept growing and productivity rising in the same way as under conditions of full employment, the long-run benefits in increased economic and monetary stability would be bound to outweigh the once-for-all cost in terms of lower output.

21. As will be suggested in the following paragraph, there is no evidence to show that a moderate degree of unemployment would suffice to reduce the rate of increase in money wages to levels consistent with cost and price stability. But assuming that this would in fact be the case there is still the question whether it would be possible to run an economy at a consistently moderate level of unemployment; and whether such under-employment equilibrium would be consistent with a satisfactory rate of growth of production year by year. In the first place, there is the question whether an under-employment equilibrium where the general level of production is limited by effective demand, and not by the scarcity of available resources, is at all stable except under conditions in which the level of production is stationary. For when the forces making for economic expansion are powerful enough to cause the level of production to grow from year to year, they will be powerful enough also to cause an expansion of activity which eliminates non-frictional unemployment. Contrariwise, when the restraints on demand are powerful enough to prevent an increase in activity to the full employment level, they will be powerful enough also to put a damper on investment and on the growth of productivity. For these reasons it may not be possible to run a growing economy at half-cock. In the second place, there is the question whether the prospective rate of profit in an economy of stable prices would be attractive enough (relative to the market rate of interest) to keep the process of investment and expansion going.

22. Table I (in the Annex) summarises the experience with regard to money wages, the cost of living, industrial production and productivity over the last six years of twelve mainly industrial countries, arranged in descending order of magnitude of wage inflation. On the evidence of these figures there appears to be little connection between the magnitude of the wage inflation, and changes in the cost of living or apparent changes in productivity; nor does there appear to be any close relationship between the level of unemployment and the rate of increase in money wages. Thus the rate of increase in money wages was approximately the same in the United Kingdom as in Denmark and Austria, though in the former non-agricultural unemployment was most of the time around 1·3 per cent., while in the latter two countries it was around 5 per cent. The fact that ten out of these twelve countries experienced wage increases of around 30–50 per cent. in the six years, or say 5–7 per cent. per annum, rather tends to suggest that there is a certain inherent momentum in the rise of the wage level in an advancing industrial community which is fairly insensitive to changes in living costs or the growth of productivity. Thus Germany (with 48 per cent.) and the United Kingdom (with 43 per cent.) had a fairly similar experience with wage inflation although the rise in the cost of living was 6 per cent. in Germany and 29 per cent. in the United Kingdom, whilst the rise in productivity was 31 per cent. in the former and only 11 per cent. in the latter. The fact that three of the countries near the top of the scale (France, Sweden and Norway) were countries of a very low rate of unemployment, whereas the three countries at the bottom of the scale (Italy, the United States and Belgium) had relatively high rates of unemployment lends some support to the view that wage increases tend to be rather more moderate with unemployment rates of 3–5 per cent. than with unemployment rates of 1–1½ per cent. But even with the latter group, the rise in wages was greater than what would have been consistent with price stability, and there were countries such as Germany, Austria and Denmark which combined high rates of wage inflation with relatively high rates of unemployment.[1]

[1] In the U.K. there were only two years since the war when the percentage of increase in wages was 3 per cent. or less and it is of some significance that these were 1949 and 1950 when Sir Stafford Cripps' policy of wage restraint and dividend

23. The common feature of all these countries has been that they were *expanding economies* during the period under consideration: their investment sufficed for an expansion of productive capacity, and the system operated so as to produce a growth in demand (in real terms) adequate to match the growth in the capacity to produce. The fact that most of them show annual wage increases in excess of 5 per cent. per annum may be no accident therefore: if the argument in paragraphs 11 and 12 above is correct, a 5–6 per cent. annual increase in the money value of the gross national product—which presupposes a similar rate of increase in the total wages bill—is necessary in order to secure a rate of profit on investment high enough to maintain the process of capital accumulation and continued expansion.

24. In the circumstances of Britain in the 1950's annual wage increases of this order were not consistent with the stability of the price-level since the growth in total production was only of the order of 3 per cent. If, however, our reasoning in paragraphs 11 and 12 is correct, it would have been futile to compress the growth in aggregate money incomes to 3 per cent. a year: since at that rate full employment and economic growth might not have been maintained.

25. The basic malaise of the British economy is thus seen to have been the slow rate of growth in productivity and total production. Given this basic limitation, a certain degree of inflation (in my opinion) could not have been avoided—or rather, it could only have been prevented at the cost of jeopardising the modest annual improvement actually attained. The unsatisfactory rate of economic growth since 1951—as Table I shows, the United Kingdom has shown by far the lowest rate of growth of productivity during the period—is variously attributed, by different authorities, to the "overloading" of the British economy, to excessive outlays on defence, on foreign investment or on the social services; to the effects of the "new" monetary policy itself in putting a brake on expansion just as it was gathering momentum;

limitation was in operation (see Table III). Apart from these there was only one year, 1954, when the percentage rise in weekly wages was below 5 per cent., and there were four years, 1951, 1952, 1955 and 1956, when it reached 8 to 9 per cent. In the last two of these years, 1955 and 1956, the rise in wages proceeded at record levels despite the fact that the policy of tight money and credit squeeze were in operation.

and finally, to the low "technical dynamism" of those in charge of British industry, and the lack of compulsion (due to the absence of effective competition, etc.), to introduce technical improvements.

26. My own view would incline towards the latter explanation. No doubt productive investment in Britain has been highly inadequate in relation to her competitors, such as Germany, Japan, France or Italy (the extent of this inadequacy is understated by comparisons of overall percentages of investment since U.K. investment tends to be more concentrated on "unproductive" fields such as housing) but it is difficult to treat this as more than a symptom of the malaise. If British entrepreneurs had been keener on expansion and innovation, the resources for the needed additional investments could no doubt somehow have been found; it was certainly not the lack of financial resources which held them back.[1] In an economy where labour is fully employed, and where the expansion of the working population is small, the level of industrial investment tends to be limited by the speed of adaptation to new techniques—by the rate at which technical change can be absorbed into the economic system. It would go beyond the scope of this paper—and also, I believe, of the Committee's terms of reference—to examine the historical, sociological or institutional factors which make the majority of British businessmen less alert and more sluggish in their reactions than some of their competitors in other countries. But it is here, I feel, rather than in the operation of the monetary and financial system, or in the strength of the competing claims on the national resources, that we must look for the basic cause of our unsatisfactory rate of economic progress.

(iv) Fluctuations of Investment in Stocks

27. Finally, there is the problem of the instability in demand due to fluctuations in investment, particularly investment in stocks. As the official national income estimates show, the varia-

---

[1] The 3,000 quoted companies mentioned in the footnote to para. 7 (which represented over two-thirds of the total paid-up capital of all public companies) held financial assets (cash, marketable securities and tax reserve certificates) of over £1,400 million in 1953, whereas their annual expenditure on fixed assets was only around £450 million.

tion of investment in stocks has been the really unstable element in the British economy since the war. These variations have largely reflected changing expectations concerning price movements and they were largely responsible (in the period 1948–52 at any rate) for the instability in the balance of payments. While the average amount of these investments has been relatively small (in relation to investment in fixed capital) the annual swings have been relatively large; and it can be said that until the re-establishment of a flexible monetary policy at the end of 1951 the Government had no real weapon at its disposal for controlling the rate of investment in stocks which was in any way analogous to the instruments of control of fixed investment, such as the licensing system and accelerated depreciation allowances, not to speak of taxation of various kinds for controlling consumption. Indeed, it is difficult to conceive of a technique for stabilising the rate of investment in stocks other than the institution of buffer stocks or credit policy. The operation of buffer stocks requires international action in most cases. But within limits at any rate it should be possible to stabilise *national* investment in inventories through credit policy. High short-term interest rates, subject to the limitations mentioned in paragraph 4 above, discourage investment in stocks, and vice versa. A sudden restocking boom such as that which followed the outbreak of the war in Korea, is invariably associated with a sudden increase in the demand for bank overdrafts. If through appropriate measures of control such an expansion can be prevented, the rise in inventory investment would undoubtedly be curbed; indeed, with sufficiently stringent measures of financial discouragement, it might be prevented altogether.

28. There are two conclusions to follow from this argument. The first is that the function of credit control should be sought in stabilising investment in stocks (i.e. in offsetting spontaneous tendencies to instability in inventory investment), and not in the control of investment in fixed capital or the control of consumption which can far more appropriately be secured by other instruments. Hence, it is the regulation of short-term interest rates which is important, and not the variation in bond yields—since manufacturers and traders are unlikely to borrow on long term for increasing their investment in liquid assets, though they sometimes

operate the other way round. Secondly, while the quantitative control of bank credit may prevent, or at least hinder, increased investment in stocks by that part of the business community which is dependent on bank credit, it will not have the same discouraging effect on carrying stocks as a general increase in short-term interest rates.[1] This is partly because as we have seen (paragraph 7, note 1) the limitation of advances by the clearing banks may lead to increased trade-credit or increased lending by other financial institutions; partly also because putting pressure on one sector of the trading community—i.e. the one dependent on bank overdrafts—cannot be as effective as an inducement extended to all. I am a little dubious therefore of the various suggestions—i.e. the reintroduction of Treasury Deposit Receipts or a variable minimum liquidity ratio—for operating credit policy "on the cheap," so to speak, which aim at making credit control effective without invoking the variation of short-term borrowing or lending rates.

29. This is not to suggest that varying the short-term interest rate is a sensitive or dependable instrument. In times when price expectations are very volatile (and this in turn can only ensue from past experience of instability) the changes in interest rates required to compensate for the changing inducements to hold stocks may have to be pretty severe. The actual change in the amount of investment of both fixed and circulating capital in the ten years 1948–57 is shown in Table II. This shows that in the quinquennium 1948–52 variations in stock investment were appreciably greater than in the quinquennium 1953–7. The greater stability of short-term investment in the latter period might at first be regarded as an achievement of credit policy; however, as Table III shows, world prices were remarkably stable in the period 1953–7 whereas they were highly unstable in the period 1948–52. The incentives to instability which existed in the former period were thus absent in the latter and it is therefore not possible to say how much credit is to be given to the new credit policy—

[1] If the loan markets were perfect an increase in the severity of credit rationing by the clearing banks would automatically induce a general rise in short-term interest rates. Owing to imperfections in the market, however, the two are by no means equivalent to one another and it is quite possible that the former policy should discourage potential borrowers without discouraging inventory investment by potential lenders.

how the new policy would have coped with the kind of situation which emerged in 1951 and 1952 and which has not recurred in later years.

30. The best guarantee against vast political fluctuations of investment in stocks is an international buffer stock scheme which would confine fluctuations in world commodity prices within moderate limits. Failing this monetary policy can and should be used to moderate these fluctuations though one cannot feel entirely confident of the promptness and efficacy with which it can be made to operate.

ANNEX

Table I

WAGES, PRICES, PRODUCTION AND PRODUCTIVITY IN SELECTED
COUNTRIES IN 1957

(*1951 = 100*)

Country	Wages	Cost of Living	Industrial Production	Productivity[1]	Percentage of non-agric. unemployment 1957[2]
Japan	169	121	231	174	2·5
France	158	118	145	145	0·7
Sweden	149	124	117	117	1·2
Norway	148	124	134	128	1·3
Germany	148	106	172	131	3·4
Austria	144	126	151	132	5·1
United Kingdom	143	129	118	111	1·3
Denmark	142	118	115	115	4·8
Netherlands	138	115	138	131	1·4
Italy	138	113	155	142	11·1[3]
U.S.A.	130	108	119	121	4·3
Belgium	130	107	119	118	3·5

[1] Ratio of Percentage Change in Manufacturing Production to Percentage Change in Manufacturing Employment.

[2] Unemployment outside agriculture as percentage of wage and salary earners outside agriculture.

[3] Percentage of occupied labour force outside agriculture.

Source: I.M.F. International Financial Statistics, June 1958.

E.C.E. Economic Survey for Europe in 1957, chap. II, table 6.

U.N. Monthly Bulletin of Statistics.

Table II

CHANGES IN FIXED CAPITAL FORMATION AND IN PHYSICAL INCREASE IN STOCKS AS COMPARED WITH PRECEDING YEAR, UNITED KINGDOM, 1948–57

(*£ million*)

	1948	1949	1950	1951	1952	1953	1954	1955	1956	1957
At 1948 prices Fixed capital formation										
Private (est.)	−70	50	40	−60	−30	80	160	160	80	80
Public (est.)	190	90	40	70	60	100	−10	−40	10	40
Total	120	140	80	10	30	180	150	120	90	120
Physical increase in stocks										
Private (est.)	−230	−170	−60	330	−350	80	90	130	−130	(100)
Public (est.)	50	60	−190	260	−40	10	−150	60	60	(20)
Total	−180	−110	−250	590	−390	90	−60	190	−70	(120)
At current £'s Fixed capital formation										
Private	−	55	60	20	50	110	205	275	190	170
Public	230	95	60	170	170	140	−20	15	85	100
Total	230	150	120	190	220	250	185	290	275	270
Physical increase in stocks										
Private	−190	−170	−60	480	−575	175	140	185	−165	145
Public	35	60	−215	305	50	−100	−215	90	90	30
Total	−155	−110	−275	785	−525	75	−75	275	−75	175
Balance of Trade	390	100	80	−570	670	−120	40	−210	320	−10

Estimates in brackets are provisional

Source: C.S.O.

Table III

PERCENTAGE CHANGES IN PRICES COMPARED WITH PREVIOUS YEAR
IN THE UNITED KINGDOM

	1948	*1949*	*1950*	*1951*	*1952*	*1953*	*1954*	*1955*	*1956*	*1957*
Board of Trade Wholesale Prices ..	14	5	14	22	3	—	I	3	3	I
U.N. World Exports (sterling prices)	8	3	22	19	−3	−5	−I	—	2	3
Imports—goods and services	8	2	16	28	−5	−8	—	5	−I	2
Wage Rates (weekly) ..	5	3	2	8	8	5	4	8	9	5
Retail Prices (C.S.O.) ..	8	3	3	9	9	3	2	5	5	4

Sources: Annual Abstract of Statistics.
U.N. Bulletin of Statistics.

7

THE RADCLIFFE REPORT[1]

WITH the return of a Conservative Administration in 1951, Britain reactivated monetary policy as an instrument of economic control after a lapse of twelve years. At first, the relatively mild measures adopted in November 1951 and in the early months of 1952 seemed to justify the high hopes of the protagonists—the inflationary trends of the Korean boom year were rapidly reversed; there was considerable destocking, and Britain's balance of payments on current account improved sharply. In fact, as is now recognised, these were repercussions of the changing trend of world prices after the short speculative boom engendered by the Korean war and had little if anything to do with the monetary measures adopted by Britain. The turn of events, however, had certainly enhanced the belief in the efficacy of a "flexible" monetary policy, and when there was a renewed threat of domestic inflation and of a balance of payments crisis in February 1955, much sharper restrictionist measures were taken. But on this occasion the hoped-for consequences did not materialise. Despite the pressure on liquidity, bank advances continued to rise, inducing a whole series of further measures of quantitative and qualitative credit restriction, including an unprecedented request by the Chancellor of the Exchequer to the clearing banks (in July 1955) "for a positive and significant reduction in advances over the next few months." None the less, the level of demand and the pressure on domestic resources continued to rise even after the volume of bank advances was last stabilised. By the time the Suez crisis supervened (in September 1956), opinion was fairly general that there was something wrong with the way monetary controls operate, and that if any reliance were to be placed on monetary measures in future, there had to be a thoroughgoing review of the mode of operation of financial institutions and of the controls exercised by the Bank of England. Hence the appointment,

---

[1] Originally published in the *Review of Economics and Statistics*, Cambridge, Mass., February, 1960.

in May 1957, of a Committee "to inquire into the working of the monetary and credit system and to make recommendations" under the chairmanship of Lord Radcliffe.[1] The Committee (the first of its kind since the Macmillan Committee reported in 1931) sat for two years, questioned over 200 witnesses, received some 150 special memoranda, and finally issued a unanimous report of some 340 pages.[2]

The really remarkable feature of this Report is that it manages to maintain complete unanimity (without a single note of reservation by any of its members!) whilst putting forward views that are far from the traditional or the orthodox. The Report contains a detailed review of the history of monetary measures since 1951 and an exhaustive analysis of the nature of British financial institutions which brings to light many important and interesting features not hitherto known, as well as a number of statistical compilations concerning the assets and liabilities of various types of institutions that were not previously available. But for American readers, and for students of monetary theory generally, the sixty pages devoted to "the influence of monetary measures" which deal with the fundamental issues will undoubtedly provide the main interest of the Report.

It is not an easy task to summarise the Committee's views without danger of misrepresentation—partly because some of its conclusions are expressed in rather guarded terms and partly because the conclusions stated in some of the paragraphs are contradicted (or, at least, seemingly contradicted) in others; thus, it is not possible to distil a consistent set of principles without a certain amount of interpretation. The reasons for this are to be sought, not in any lack of expository talent in the Committee, but in their desire for unanimity, which could only be secured at the cost of vagueness at critical points and the omission of important links in the chain of argument. From the point of view of the usefulness of the Committee's work for future policy, it would undoubtedly have been better to abandon the search for unanimity

---

[1] The other members of the Committee included two economists (Professors A. K. Cairncross and R. S. Sayers), two bankers, two trade unionists, and two businessmen.
[2] *Report of the Committee on the Working of the Monetary System*, London, H.M.S.O., Cmd. 827. The meetings of the Committee were held in private, but its hearings (as well as all the memoranda submitted to it) are to be published in three volumes.

and to set forth the divergent views, where divergences existed, in a clear and systematic manner. (In the report of Lord Radcliffe's previous commission of inquiry, the Royal Commission on Taxation, the haziness associated with unanimity was fortunately avoided.)

Subject to this element of uncertainty inherent in the Report's peculiar manner of exposition, the Committee's views on the main issues of monetary policy may be summed up as follows.[1]

1. The purpose of monetary action is to regulate the total demand for goods and services, but this cannot be achieved by controlling the "quantity of money," meaning by "money" (in the British context) notes and bank deposits. The Committee rejects the view (a doctrine which "in its extreme form . . . is perhaps not widely held in this country") that if only the central bank keeps a tight control on the supply of money and "either keeps it fixed or allows it to increase only with the growing needs of a growing economy, all will be well." The Committee would not go so far as to say that "the supply of money is an unimportant quantity" but they "view it as only part of the wider structure of liquidity in the economy" (388-9).

2. The "haziness of the connection" between the supply of money and the level of total demand "lies in the impossibility of limiting the velocity of circulation" (523). "We have not made more use of this concept because we cannot find any reason for supposing, or any experience in monetary history indicating, that there is any limit to the velocity of circulation; it is a statistical concept that tells us nothing directly of the motivation that influences the level of total demand" (391).

3. "An analysis of liquidity, on the other hand, directs attention to the behaviour and decisions that do directly influence the level of demand" (391). The meaning of the notion of the "overall liquidity position" is nowhere explicitly defined, but it is clear from the argument in several places that it is meant to include easily realisable financial assets—deposits in the savings banks, shares in building societies, bonds of relatively short maturity, etc.—as well as the "methods, moods and resources of financial

---

[1] Numbers in parentheses refer to the paragraph numbers in the Report.

institutions and other firms which are prepared (on terms) to finance other people's spending" (389 and 392).

4. The Committee rejects the view that central banking policy could be made more effective by substituting "for the traditional control of the supply of money a complex of controls over an indefinitely wide range of financial institutions." This would be "unwelcome . . . not mainly because of its administrative burdens, but because the further growth of new financial institutions would allow the situation continually to slip from under the grip of the authorities." However, the overall liquidity position can be controlled by action taken by the central bank to manipulate "the entire structure of interest rates" (as distinct from action "confined to the short-end of the market") because "a movement of interest rates implies significant changes in the capital values of many assets held by financial institutions; a rise in rates makes some less willing to lend because capital values have fallen, and others because their own interest rate structure is sticky. A fall in rates, on the other hand, strengthens balance sheets and encourages lenders to seek new business" (393 and 394).

5. It is for this reason that the Committee "follow Professor Kahn . . . in insisting upon the structure of interest rates, rather than some notion of the 'supply of money,' as the centrepiece of monetary action" (395). They do so not because they have any sanguine expectation concerning the incentive effect of changes in interest rates upon the willingness to invest or to save. They are sceptical of the effects of changes of interest rates upon the incentives to save (450); and they have not been able to find that the credit squeeze (of 1955–8) had "any marked effects on holding of stocks of commodities" (460), whilst as regards long-term investment, the evidence suggested that any effect was "not on projects already in train but on capital projects in their earliest planning stages—implying an effect on spending not immediately but many months later" (460).[1] None the less, the manipulation of interest rates, extending over the whole range of the financial

---

[1] A more substantial, though purely temporary, effect was secured through hire-purchase controls (the increase in minimum down payments), a form of regulation which the Committee dislikes owing to its important "directional" effect—in concentrating the impact of the change of demand upon a relatively narrow range of industries.

market, should have some effect by creating a "diffused difficulty of borrowing" (472) through its effect on the liquidity position of financial institutions of all kinds.[1]

6. Accordingly, the main function of central bank policy should be not just the setting of the Bank Rate (which has a largely "symbolic" significance, 441) or open-market operations in the short end of the market, but the management of the National Debt, which they regard as the "fundamental domestic task of the central bank." "It is not open to the monetary authorities to be neutral in their handling of this task. They must have, and must consciously exercise, a positive policy about interest rates, long as well as short, and about the relationship between them" (982). In a separate chapter on debt management the Committee reveal, however, that in connection with the large and continuous refinancing operations of the Treasury handled by the Bank of England, the monetary authorities do already exert a much more powerful direct influence on the long-term bond market than is commonly realised. Their plea, one presumes, is therefore for a more conscious and deliberate attitude in setting long-term interest rates at levels thought desirable on general economic considerations.

7. The implication of this major conclusion is greatly weakened, however (if not altogether destroyed), by the Committee's repeated insistence that they do not regard a policy of deliberate variation in the level of long-term interest rates as at all desirable. "An argument for more effective use of the interest rate weapon is an argument for widely fluctuating rates, not just for movement in one direction. If the wide fluctuation could usefully be confined to short rates, the case might be strong. But we have found that stocks of commodities are extremely insensitive to interest rates, and in any case they are often financed with long-term capital, and could be much more widely so if firms found this much cheaper. It is at fixed capital that the rate of interest must strike if it is to have any direct impact, and for this purpose

---

[1] This is in apparent contradiction to their conclusion regarding the policy of the credit squeeze in the latter half of the 1950's (which had substantial effects on long-term interest rates as well as short, apart from the quantitative control of bank credit) that "the obstructions to particular channels of finance had *no* effect on the pressure of total demand, but have made for much inefficiency in financial organisation" (469; italics supplied).

the longer rates are relevant . . . we have therefore to consider whether it would be advisable to contemplate much larger swings than hitherto in long-term rates of interest. . . . This course appears to us as probably impracticable and certainly so disadvantageous as to warrant our ruling it out as a general line of policy. . . . There is no doubt that at present deliberate manipulation of long interest rates in sharp degree would be distrusted as an artificial juggling with markets . . . a stronger and more universal objection to widely fluctuating rates of interest [is that] the intricate and highly developed network of financial institutions bases some of its strength on the existence of a large body of highly marketable Government bonds whose market values are assumed to have a considerable measure of stability. . . . Their capital and reserve strength would be regarded as gravely weakened if they did not usually hold large blocks of bonds of reasonably stable value. One of the sources of strength in the nineteenth-century development of British financial institutions was undoubtedly the existence of an absolutely secure National Debt; some of this advantage would be thrown away if the market values of bonds were subject to very sharp variations. For these reasons we reject any suggestion that the rate of interest weapon should be made more effective by being used much more violently than hitherto" (488–91). But if this is so, what remains of their contention that monetary policy is only effective through its effect on the liquidity (i.e. the "reserve strength") of financial institutions; and that *therefore* manipulation of the structure of interest rates must be "the centrepiece of monetary action"? And how is it to be reconciled with their claim (514) that the "one positive recommendation" they are able to make is that the authorities "could make a more deliberate use of interest rates"? If the "consciously exercised positive policy" of the central bank in the bond market is not to be understood as deliberately inducing variations in bond prices, but as stabilising them, this is the equivalent of saying that monetary action should play a purely passive role in the regulation of the economy, at any rate in relation to short-term variations in the pressure of demand.[1]

---

[1] In a later passage, the Committee clarify somewhat the contradiction between their insistence on continuous and deliberate intervention in the long-term market and their rejection of a policy of fluctuating long-term rates by saying that "the

8. This last conclusion—that monetary policy should play a purely passive role in the (short-term) regulation of the economy—is nowhere explicitly put, though the Report contains plenty of passages indicating that something like this was at the back of the Committee's mind. Their whole review of the monetary policy of the late 1950's amounts to a severe condemnation, partly because of its ineffectiveness, partly because of its jerkiness, and partly because of its "directional effects," in concentrating its impact on particular industries or firms, which is undesirable from the point of view of the economy.[1] "We are driven to the conclusion that the more conventional instruments have failed to keep the system in smooth balance. . . . It is far removed from the smooth and widespread adjustment sometimes claimed as the virtue of monetary action; this is no gentle hand on the steering wheel that keeps a well-driven car in its right place on the road" (472). And, as for the future, "we envisage the use of monetary measures as not in ordinary times playing other than a subordinate part in guiding the development of the economy" (511). "We do not find any solution to the problem of influencing total demand in more violent manipulation of interest rates; we find control of the supply of money to be no more than an important facet of debt management; we cannot recommend any substantial change of the rules under which banks operate; we do not regard the capital issues control as useful in ordinary times; and we believe that there are narrow limits to the usefulness of hire-purchase controls . . . when all has been said on the possibility of monetary action and its likely efficacy, our conclusion is that monetary

authorities should think of rates of interest—and particularly long rates—as relevant to the domestic economic situation. The authorities should not aim at complete stability of rates, but should take a view as to what the long-term economic situation demands and be prepared by all means in their power to influence markets in the required direction" (498). But they do not explain, or even discuss, the question of how the "authorities" or anybody else can take a clear view of what kind of interest structure "the long-term economic situation demands." If the authorities succeeded in overcoming the inflationary trend, long-term interest rates should be set low to encourage capital development and growth. Given the continuance of inflation they should be kept relatively high to avoid undue pressure on resources. But there is no way in which monetary policy can simultaneously be operated so as to overcome inflationary or deflationary tendencies and to promote long-term stability on the assumption that they have been overcome already.

[1] Thus hire-purchase restrictions induce instability in the group of industries producing durable consumer goods (468); credit restrictions in general invariably discriminate against the fastest-growing firms which are alone dependent on outside sources of finance for their expansion (481).

measures cannot alone be relied upon to keep in nice balance an
economy subject to major strains from both without and within.
Monetary measures can help, but that is all" (514). The Committee is sceptical also of the effect of monetary measures on
international capital movements and thus on the balance of
payments position on which the Macmillan Report laid such
stress (439–41) and looks to an enlargement of international
reserves through a reconstituted International Monetary Fund as
a solution to short-period balance of payment crises (675–8).

9. If monetary measures are not to be relied upon to maintain
economic and financial stability, what is? The alternatives are
direct controls (such as building licences, consumer rationing, etc.)
or fiscal measures, but the Committee refuses to enter into the
question how far these should be employed in preference to, or in
combination with, monetary measures. "Our terms of reference do
not permit us to evaluate the advantages and disadvantages of
direct controls and fiscal measures or to consider the extent to
which they might be used to supplement or substitute for monetary action" (515). Nevertheless the few paragraphs devoted to
fiscal policy indicate that, in their view, fiscal measures, though
effective in their impact, may lack the degree of flexibility required to deal with short-period fluctuations (517). On the other
hand monetary measures are slow in their impact—in fact "the
less objectionable they are in other respects the slower they are to
achieve their effects" (519).

And here the matter rests. The Committee makes few concrete
recommendations—the most notable among them is for more
research and statistical information, to be organised and published
by the Bank of England, and for better continuous co-ordination
between the Treasury and the Bank of England, through a
newly set-up high-level committee. And they give their (reluct-
ant) blessing to the use of various "emergency measures" in
"emergencies" (such as a quantitative ceiling on bank advances
and/or variable minimum reserve requirements; control over new
capital issues and over hire-purchase credit) though the use of
several of these controls in the recent "emergencies" was severely
criticised in the Report for inappropriateness or inefficiency.

But on the major issue of how to prevent "emergencies" and

how to keep the economy on an even keel, the Report has nothing, or almost nothing, to say. In their self-denying ordinance of holding strictly to their terms of reference (which, incidentally, on any reasonable interpretation, would have permitted a far more comprehensive inquiry into the problem of economic and financial stability), they have refrained from expressing a view, not only on the relative merits of various instruments of economic control, but on the real nature of the problem which necessitates the use of controls, whether of the monetary, fiscal, or any other kind. The British economy, like other Western economies, has suffered since the war from two major instabilities. The first consists in the chronic tendency of money incomes (both wages and profits) to increase at a faster rate than production, thus causing a continued upward drift in money costs and prices. The second consists in fairly violent short-term swings in the pressure of domestic demand, associated with corresponding swings in imports and in the balance of payments (as well as of domestic production and employment) which, in the case of Britain, can clearly be ascribed to swings in inventory accumulation caused (one presumes) by the volatility of expectations concerning short-period trends in commodity prices.

As to the first, the Committee completely abstains from any view or analysis, despite the fact that it is the problem of chronic inflation which most agitates the public mind. There is no reference to the question of whether this chronic inflationary trend is predominantly demand-induced or cost-induced; if the former, what causes the chronic tendency to excess demand; if the latter, how could the rise in money incomes be restrained, and how far are either monetary or fiscal measures appropriate instruments for dealing with this problem?

As to the second, the Committee has plenty to say but nothing to recommend. If monetary measures are incapable of preventing or offsetting the swings caused by fluctuating rates of inventory accumulation, are we to assume that these are inevitable? The classical theory of the Bank Rate and of money-market operations regarded these instruments as the ideal weapon for stabilising the demand for holding stocks despite varying inducements, or even for inducing compensatory variations in stockholding in response to instabilities emanating from other parts of the system. The Committee is emphatic in holding that variations in the Bank Rate and in short-term interest rates generally, even when accompanied by other measures of credit restriction, are ineffectual in preventing a bout of inventory accumulation or decumulation. If that is so, monetary policy loses most of its *raison d'être*, for it is not a suitable instrument for controlling short-period variations in long-term investment; nor is it clear why long-term investment needs to be controlled in this way since, in recent British experience, it was only on rare occasions that the fluctuations in long-term capital outlay provided the primary source of instability. And if monetary measures do not provide an appropriate weapon, is there nothing else which can be put in their place?

Finally, whilst the Committee's rejection of the orthodox view concerning the relation between the money supply and the level of demand is greatly to be welcomed, their views would have commanded far greater attention had they been set out with more explicit reference to basic economic theory. The quantity theory of money which held the stage for so long is still the most commonly accepted hypothesis on the relationship between money and prices among the great majority of the world's bankers and a disconcerting number of its economists. To them, at least, the Committee owed a more thoroughgoing explanation why it rejected certain basic propositions which previous authorities (including the Committee's own predecessor, the Macmillan Committee) held so sacrosanct. The key to the Committee's views is to be found in their statements concerning the velocity of circulation of money. The basis of the quantity theory, and of the whole "monetary" approach to economic policy which follows from it, is the belief that there is some "normal" velocity, firmly grounded in long-standing habits and conventions, which brings it about that changes in the *quantity* of money in circulation enforce corresponding variations in the *flow* of monetary expenditure. The Committee, on the other hand, believes that the velocity of money is a "purely statistical concept" of no causal significance, which varies automatically with changes in the quantity of money in relation to total expenditure—how else to interpret their statement

that "it is impossible to limit the velocity of circulation"? I
believe that they are fundamentally correct in the view that the
hypothesis of any independently given velocity, grounded on
things like the frequency of various kinds of payments—i.e. that
wages are paid weekly, salaries monthly, business accounts quarterly, etc.—is a mirage, and that velocity can be speeded up or
slowed down to an almost indefinite extent without any alteration
in the habitual frequency of various types of money payment.
Moreover this speeding-up process follows automatically from
even a slight delay in the settlement of accounts, which may be
caused by a shortage of cash in any part of the system—in other
words, the very "illiquidity" caused by a reduced money supply
tends to communicate itself throughout the system and, in its
spread, to cause the daily average of cash balances to be reduced
in relation to the flow of in- and out-payments (which of course is
the same thing as saying that it causes the velocity to rise). But
since this is the point at which a major break occurs with traditional thinking, the reasons *why* the old-established views on
velocity (and hence on the critical role of money supply) are
wrong, and what follows from it, should have been set out systematically and in detail.

In the same way the emphasis on the "whole liquidity position"
in contrast to the "money supply" (and on the control of bank
advances as distinct from bank deposits) must be puzzling to all
those who believe that non-monetary financial institutions are
merely channels in the investment of funds, incapable of "creating" money or credit in the manner of the clearing banks whose
deposits alone provide media of payment. The Committee's whole
position is in contrast to this view, and is evidently based on the
assumption (nowhere properly explained) that financial institutions, whether or not they provide direct media of payment, do
invariably create "liquidity"—since it is the peculiarity of all such
institutions that their liabilities are considered as "liquid assets"
by the lenders (i.e. their depositors) whilst their assets are not
treated as liquid liabilities (or negative liquid assets) by their
borrowers. Hence the growth of non-monetary financial institutions, by providing new substitutes for deposits with the clearing
banks, has much the same effect as a spontaneous reduction in the

desire to hold "money." (The main point about "money substitutes" is surely that they provide a substitute for holding cash,
irrespective of whether such substitutes are customarily used as
means of payment.) But if this is so, there is no significant difference
between the case for controlling the activities of the clearing
banks and that for controlling those of the so-called "non-
monetary" financial institutions: indirect control through the
"structure of interest rates" is neither more nor less powerful (or
adequate) in the one case than in the other.

8

ECONOMIC GROWTH AND THE PROBLEM OF INFLATION[1]

I

It is a commonplace to say that the theoretical speculation of each generation of economists centres around the particular problems which are in the forefront of public interest. If problems of unemployment and economic stagnation were the main objects of speculation in the 1930's, it is only natural that interest should be focussed on economic growth and inflation in the 1950's. For the post-war age has become development-conscious and productivity-conscious to a degree that was unknown to earlier generations; also, the trend of rising prices has assumed an extent and a duration, in most of the advanced economies of the West, not previously encountered under peacetime conditions.

Yet while the centre of critical interest shifts with the general background, there is also a strong underlying continuity in the development of economic theory—the insight gained in the investigation of one set of problems in one particular decade is not lost sight of; it serves as the basis for the investigation of the new set of problems of the succeeding decade. There is, moreover, a certain natural rhythm in the development of knowledge: as the conclusions reached at an earlier period are gone over afresh, and reinterpreted in the light of new experience, they invariably bring to light fresh implications that were hidden at the time of their original discovery and which open new avenues for thought. In the course of this process the tools—the particular techniques of thought—are retained and sometimes improved upon, while some of the basic assumptions of the theories which originally employed them are discarded. A particular instance of this, of which I shall say more presently, is the application of the Keynesian techniques of analysis to full-employment situations. The

[1] Two public lectures delivered at the London School of Economics and Political Science on 6 and 13 February 1959 and originally published in *Economica*, August and November, 1959.

existence of an under-employment equilibrium, where effective demand, and not the scarcity of available resources, governed the general level of production, was of the very essence of the Keynesian economic theory as originally put forward. Yet the key to some of the post-war theories of economic growth is the application of the same principle—the principle of effective demand—to full-employment situations in which, according to their author (who, however, was himself not very consistent in this), these principles were not thought to have any application at all.[1]

I believe I am right in saying that until recently it would have been incorrect to speak of a *theory* of economic growth. Apart from a few exceptions, of which the late Professor Schumpeter was an outstanding example, economists of the neo-classical school were predominantly concerned with problems of market equilibrium—with the pricing process, and not with the problems of growth; and the techniques developed by this theory were ill adapted for dealing with capital accumulation and growth as a *continuing* process. The most advanced part of the Walrasian general equilibrium theory—the theory of capital, as developed by Wicksell—was really concerned with the implications of a state of long-period stationary equilibrium; and in so far as this theory was intended to be applied to problems of growth and accumulation, it was through the device of comparative statics—by a comparison of *two* states of stationary equilibrium, one of which possessed a larger amount of capital than the other. Beyond a few vague generalisations such as that progress involved a continued increase in the stock of capital in relation to income and a falling rate of profit, these theories had precious little to say about a growing economy; and if these generalisations were themselves contradicted by experience, the contradiction was attributed to the influence of residual features which were outside the scope of the theory—to the "non-economic" variables, such as changes in "knowledge."

With Keynesian "macro-economics" a way was cleared to a new approach to a theory of growth but, apart from the rather isolated attempt of Harrod, most Keynesian economics for the first ten or fifteen years after the publication of the *General*

[1] Cf. e.g. *General Theory*, p. 112.

Theory were more concerned with the explanation of cyclical fluctuations than with economic growth. These trade cycle models were sometimes made to revolve around a rising long-term trend, and thus earned the title "dynamic," but these trends were tagged on to the cycle models and not themselves explained—nor was it ever properly considered whether the existence of a rising trend is compatible with the unhindered operation of the multiplier-accelerator mechanism on which the cycle models are based.

My own ideas in this field owe a great deal to the pioneering essay of Sir Roy Harrod more perhaps for the stimulus it provided to fresh thinking, than for its assumptions or conclusions; and this, I believe, holds good for several other people who have worked in this field, such as Mrs. Robinson and Professor Champernowne.

My first lecture is devoted to three major aspects in which this new approach to the problems of growth and accumulation radically departs from earlier theories, both Keynesian and pre-Keynesian. My second lecture will draw certain conclusions that follow from this analysis with regard to the causes and consequences of inflation.

(i) The first of my three aspects concerns a generalisation of the Keynesian theory of income generation so as to cover both under-employment and full-employment situations.

(ii) The second concerns the relation of technical progress and capital accumulation.

(iii) The third concerns the relation of the rate of economic growth to the profitability of investment.

I am conscious that these three aspects do not suffice by any means to give a comprehensive account of the new growth theory, but they are necessary and I hope sufficient to support the propositions about inflation which I shall consider in the second part.

I. THE THEORY OF INCOME GENERATION AND FULL EMPLOYMENT

Keynes's theory of income generation—which can be summed up by saying that expenditure decisions determine incomes, and not the other way round or, what comes to the same thing, that it is investment which determines savings, and not savings which determine investment—was the really novel feature of his *General Theory*, which revolutionised our thinking far more, in my view, than other features, such as his theory of interest. Yet I always had the uneasy feeling that, as originally put forward, it attempted to prove too much; if the general level of production is really determined by effective demand, irrespective of the available resources, the equilibrium level of employment could be anywhere—in *any* relationship that is, to the supply of labour. Yet in the history of advanced capitalist societies periods of severe unemployment were exceptional and not the rule; apart from periods of acute depression, unemployment did not appear to exceed a few per cent. on the average since the second half of the nineteenth century.[1] (In the forty years, 1881–1920, in the U.K. it averaged less than 5 per cent., including both boom and depression years.) As the actual level of employment averaged 95 per cent. of the full employment level, this is unlikely to have been a mere coincidence; it strongly suggests that forces must have been at work which operated on the relationship between effective demand and supply, or between the propensity to invest and to save, in such a way as to yield an equilibrium level of employment that was fairly close to, if not equal to, the full-employment level.

To some people this would provide a justification for preferring the classical theory to the Keynesian, and for arguing that the money and capital markets did, after all, behave in such a way as to adjust the level of investment to savings and thereby generate sufficient investment to absorb the savings forthcoming at full-employment levels of income. I myself would regard this explanation as inherently implausible, and I might adduce, if called upon to do so, various bits of evidence for the view that it was the Keynesian and not the classical mechanism of income generation which was operative in the advanced centres of capitalism for periods extending long before the First World War. But I think there is a perfectly good "Keynesian" explanation for the prevalence of full-employment or near-full-employment conditions— and it is to be found in the fact that in a competitive society (I ought to say a *fairly* competitive society—I do *not* mean perfect

---

[1] This was not so, of course, in "underdeveloped" countries whose unemployment, however, was of a different kind—not a reflection of an insufficiency of effective demand.

competition) variations in the strength of demand cause variations in the level of prices in relation to costs; these variations in turn have a powerful influence on the community's propensity to save or to consume, and thereby adjust the level of effective demand so as to make it coincide with the available supply, as determined by the resources available. Keynes, in postulating that the *propensity to save* is given independently of the level of investment, and thus of the strength of effective demand, has implicitly assumed something which I am sure he would have denied if put explicitly—that is, that the level of prices in relation to costs, or in other words, the relation of profits to income, has no effect on the community's propensity to save. Yet it is a well-known fact that the proportion of profits saved is very much greater than the proportion of savings out of wages, salaries or rentier income; the one is about ten times as large as the other. It is around 50 per cent. whereas savings out of contractual incomes are more like 5 per cent. (The reason for this is not merely or mainly that residual incomes are so much more uncertain and fluctuating than contractual incomes: it is that in the case of business profits, the long-term prospects of the enterprise are closely linked with the accumulation of internal savings; even though in the short period, business capital expenditures are not directly influenced by variations in *current* savings.) Hence a relatively high level of investment, by causing effective demand to be high, also causes profits to be high: and these profits themselves provide the savings for the finance of this investment. When effective demand is relatively low, profits are relatively low, and thus the propensity to consume relatively high. Hence the Keynesian determinants, the propensities to invest and to save, and the theory of the multiplier, are more likely to operate so as to determine, not the level of employment, but the distribution of income between profits and wages at full employment. The very fact that prices rise or fall under the influence of demand creates an automatic tendency towards full employment, at any rate within certain boundaries.[1]

[1] This proposition bears only a purely superficial resemblance to the celebrated "Pigou effect" of which Professor Patinkin and others have recently written, and which relies on an adjustment in the propensity to save via the reduction of both money costs and money prices and the consequent rise in the real value of money balances. I do not believe in the "Pigou effect," which is irrelevant to a world where money wages are not highly flexible in a downward direction; but it is curious that

To illustrate the nature of this equilibrium, and the conditions under which the forces analysed by Keynes lead to full-employment, rather than unemployment, equilibrium, I should like to make use of the time-honoured device of the "representative firm." This is assumed to behave like a small-scale replica of the economy as a whole—that is to say, it is assumed that variations in the output of this firm reflect equivalent variations in the aggregate volume of production.

I shall begin by drawing the short-period cost curves of this firm—average and marginal prime cost—in a perfectly orthodox manner as found in the textbooks (Fig. 1). But we must remember that our *prime costs consist of wage-costs only* (since raw material costs cancel out for the economy as a whole), and I assume money wages to be given.

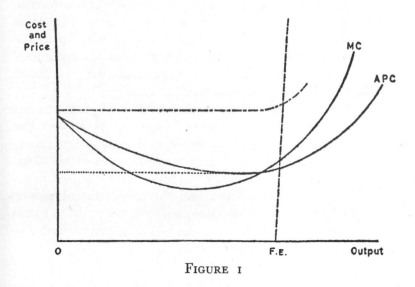

FIGURE 1

I should like, however, to introduce three amendments to this picture. The first is that we can ignore the falling portion of the *APC* curve and assume that average prime and marginal costs are constant, as shown in the dotted line in Fig. 1, up to a certain scale

the many economists who have written about the "Pigou effect" have not hit upon the fact that a fall in prices *relatively to costs* is bound to reduce the propensity to save far more powerfully than one which reduces both prices and costs in the same proportion.

of production where they begin to rise on account of the more intensive use of capacity, or the need to resort to inferior capacity.

The second is that employment rather than physical capacity is the effective bottleneck setting a limit to production for the economy as a whole—i.e. it is assumed that the available capacity is more than sufficient to employ the available labour force. Hence the limit of production to our firm, which employs a constant fraction of the total labour force, is full employment (as shown by the dashed line in Fig. 1), which may itself be stretched somewhat through the use of over-time and the drawing-in of people like married women on the fringe of the labour force.

The third is that whatever the state of demand, our firm, for fear of spoiling the market, will not reduce prices, relative to costs, below a certain point. There is thus a *minimum margin of profit* which we can call the degree of monopoly or market imperfection, or whatever we like, remembering that it does not necessarily *set* the price, it merely sets a rock-bottom to prices. (In Fig. 1, the dot-and-dash line indicates the minimum price at the given level of prime cost per unit of output; the excess of this over the dotted line indicates the minimum margin of profit.)

With these amendments, the short-period supply curve to the firm, S–S, will be determined by the "degree of monopoly" line and the full-employment line, as shown by Fig. 2.

Keynes's "effective demand" curve (D–D), should be represented by a vertical straight line, when investment is regarded as a constant independent of output, and the proportion of income saved treated as a constant invariant with regard to the relationship of prices and costs. The equation of this curve according to the well known multiplier formula is

$$D = \frac{1}{s} I \quad \dots\dots\dots\dots\dots\dots\dots (1)$$

where $s = \frac{S}{Y}$, the (linear) fraction of income saved, and I represents the level of investment. The intersection of the D–D curve with the S–S curve indicates the equilibrium level of output or employment.

If we assume, however, that s is not a constant but a variable

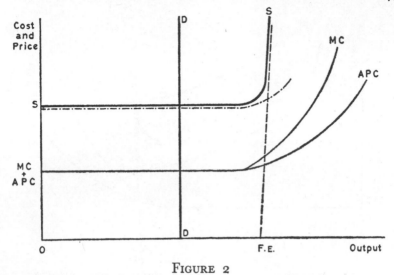

FIGURE 2

depending on the level of prices in relation to costs, we are replacing the above equation (1) with the following equation:

$$D = \frac{1}{(a-\beta)\dfrac{P}{Y} + \beta} I \dots\dots\dots\dots\dots(2)$$

where $\dfrac{P}{Y}$ represents the margin of profit as a proportion of the selling price (or the share of profits in income) and a the proportion of profit saved and β the proportion of other income saved.

Equation (2) yields a *forward-falling* demand curve (in place of a vertical curve) much like the Marshallian demand curve, since the lower the price in relation to prime costs, the greater the effective demand generated by the given level of investment. As shown in Fig. 3, this can yield either a full-employment or an under-employment equilibrium, depending on whether the demand curve cuts the supply curve in the horizontal section of the latter (as shown by D–D, with the point of intersection P) or in the vertical section (as shown by D'–D', with the point of P').

However, we must now also allow for the fact that not *all* investment is independent of output. Some of it is "autonomous" but the rest is "induced," the latter only coming into operation when

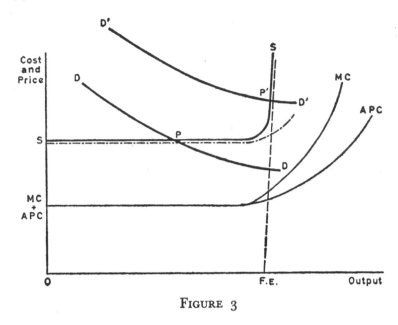

FIGURE 3

the degree of utilisation of capacity permits a normal rate of profit being derived; in other words, when receipts cover average *total* costs (including "normal" profits). Allowing for this, our equation (2) becomes

$$D = \frac{1}{(a - \beta)\dfrac{P}{\Upsilon} + \beta}(A + I') \quad \ldots\ldots\ldots (3)$$

where A denotes "autonomous" investment (i.e. investment that is independent of the current level of activity) and I' "induced" investment which will vary with the level of output and the degree of utilisation of capacity.

In Fig. 4, the curve ATC indicates average total costs (including "normal" profits) and the point N (where the curve ATC intersects the $S-S$ curve) the level of production which yields a "normal" profit on the existing capital equipment. Beyond N, any further increase in production will "induce" investment in the shape of additions to productive capacity, and it is reasonable to suppose that the increase in investment associated with an increase

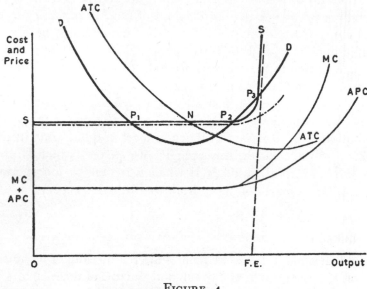

FIGURE 4

in output will exceed the increase in savings, for any *given* distribution of income. Hence equation (3) will yield a U-shaped demand curve; the curve will be falling up to N (when induced investment is zero) and will slope upwards to the right of N (when induced investment is positive). As shown in Fig. 4, this will yield multiple positions of equilibrium, P_1, P_2 and P_3, of which only P_1 and P_3 are stable positions whereas P_2 is unstable (since at P_2 where the demand curve cuts the supply curve from below, a small displacement in either direction will set up cumulative forces away from P_2 until either P_1 or P_3 is reached).

It follows that an under-employment equilibrium is only *stable* under slump conditions when induced investment is zero.[1]

It also follows that it is impossible to conceive of a *moving* equilibrium of growth to be an under-employment equilibrium. Such an equilibrium is necessarily one where productive capacity is growing, and where, therefore, induced investment is positive,

---

[1] It is possible to assume, of course, that the shape and position of the demand curve at P_1 is not determined by "autonomous investment" but by a negative constant in the savings function—i.e. that savings become zero at some positive level of income.

and hence the $D - D$ curve slopes upwards and not downwards. It therefore postulates the equilibrium of the P_3-type and not of the P_1-type. In that situation, the profit margin must be above the minimum level, and the distribution of income will tend to be such as to generate the same proportion of income saved as the proportion of investment in output.

It only remains to add that all this is perfectly consistent with Marshallian orthodoxy—looking at it as a *short-period* theory of distribution. For all it says is that the level of quasi-rents in the economy will depend on the strength of demand, which is precisely what Marshall said. It is when we come to long-period analysis that we part company from the orthodox theory.

2. TECHNICAL PROGRESS AND CAPITAL ACCUMULATION

This brings me to the next point—the relationship of technical progress and the growth of capital, and the role of these factors in determining both the rate of growth of productivity and the propensity to invest.

Since the very beginnings of human society, man's ability to exploit the powers of nature to his own advantage meant on the one hand a continued increase in the density of population in a given natural environment and, on the other hand, a continued increase in the amount of material aids (of man-made instruments) used per unit of labour. This latter assertion is more difficult to substantiate than the former since there is no reliable measure of the *quantity* of instruments per worker, when the character of these instruments is itself continually altering. However, I shall beg all questions connected with the measurement of the quantity of capital—which has given rise to so many headaches, both in theory and as a matter of statistical measurement—and assert that whether we measure capital in terms of values deflated by some price index, or in terms of weight of steel and other materials embodied, or in terms of animal or mechanical power, or in terms of any other reasonable index that we may choose, we should get substantially the same answer—that as productivity rose, the amount of capital per head rose with it, and if we compared different societies at different stages of development, we should find a very close correlation between the value of output per head and the value of capital per head. As far as statistics can tell, there is very little difference in the capital/output ratio between rich and poor countries—they are not significant in relation to the very *large* differences either in terms of output per head or in terms of capital per head.

The main point is that technical change and capital accumulation go hand in hand, and it is not really possible to isolate the effect of increased knowledge or ability or know-how from the effect of the accumulation of capital. The rate at which a society accumulates capital depends on the rate at which it adopts improvements in productive techniques; in the absence of such improvements, and abstracting from the growth of population, the process of accumulation would be rapidly brought to an end. Nor is it possible to distinguish, in general, the technical change which is the result of some brand new discovery from that which merely represents an improvement in know-how—in the ability to use and to exploit knowledge which has already existed, in some shape or another, in the minds of some people. Further, just as technical progress causes accumulation, the process of accumulation stimulates the growth of knowledge and of know-how.

Hence it is useless to analyse the effects of capital accumulation in terms of a production function which assumes a given *state* of knowledge, and then assume that this function continually shifts upwards with the progress of knowledge (see Fig. 5).[1] Since the accumulation of capital necessarily takes time, and both accumulation and the progress of knowledge are continuing processes *through* time, all that we can say is that there will be some historical relationship between output per head and capital per head which embodies the effect of both technical progress and accumulation (such as, e.g. that indicated by the dashed line in Fig. 5). This relationship will not generally conform to the usual assumptions about diminishing productivity; doubling capital per man may well involve doubling or more than doubling output per man, thus giving a marginal productivity to capital that need be no smaller than its average productivity, or may even be greater.

[1] In Fig. 5, the amount of capital (per head) is measured horizontally, output vertically, and the curves $f_t(K)$, $f_{t+1}(K)$, etc.. denote the production functions at dates t, $t+1$, etc.

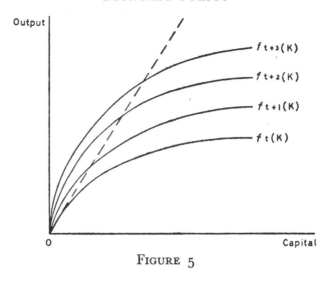

FIGURE 5

In other words, to obtain the linear-and-homogeneous production function required by the theory we must include "technical
knowledge" as one of the variables, and treat it as a factor of
production in an analogous manner to labour and capital (or
land). But this is illegitimate, since technical knowledge is not a
quantifiable thing; it cannot be bought or sold, and cannot have
its marginal contribution imputed to it, any more than is the case
with other unappropriated scarce agents of production.[1] This
means, however, that in terms of labour and capital alone, the
"production function" will not be homogeneous and linear, and
the "marginal productivities" of capital and labour cannot serve
as the basis of the determination of factor prices (or even be
isolated!) since their sum will more than exhaust the total
product.

Whether, with the accumulation of capital, the rise in output-
per-head will be more or less than proportionate to the rise in
capital-per-head will depend, not on technical factors alone, but
on the *speed* with which capital is accumulated relative to the

[1] As is well-known, any function whatsoever in *n* variables may be regarded as a
subset of a larger function in more than *n* variables which is homogeneous of the
first order. But as Samuelson points out, it is not legitimate to treat as variables of
the "production function" anything other than such inputs as are quantitatively
measurable economic goods or services (*Foundations of Economic Analysis*, p. 84).

capacity to innovate, and to absorb changes in productive techniques. Whatever the rate of progress of knowledge, any particular society has only a limited capacity to absorb technical change in a given period. Hence it is more sensible to take as given, not the relationship between capital stock and output—the idea underlying the notion of a production function—but the relationship between the rate of accumulation and the rate of change of output. This latter relationship expresses the "technical dynamism" of the economy, since the more "dynamic" are the people in control of production (the entrepreneurs), the readier they are to change techniques and to introduce innovations, the faster will productivity increase and the faster will capital be accumulated.

It is the shape and position of this "technical progress function" which will exhibit features of diminishing returns. If we plot percentage growth rates of output per head $\left(\dfrac{\dot{Y}}{Y} \right)$ along Oy and percentage growth rates of capital per head $\left(\dfrac{\dot{K}}{K} \right)$ along Ox, the curve will cut the y axis positively (since a certain rate of improvement would take place even if capital per head remained unchanged) but it will be convex upwards, and reach a maximum at a certain point—there is always a maximum beyond which a further increase in the rate of accumulation will not enhance further the *rate* of growth of output (Fig. 6). This means that the increase in capital (per head) will yield increasing or diminishing returns in terms of output according as the rate of accumulation is relatively small or large. If the rate of accumulation is less than OP, output will increase faster than capital, and vice versa.

Given its "technical dynamism," a capitalist economy, after a certain period of adaptation, will tend to settle down to a rate of economic growth and accumulation where the growth rate of capital is the same as the growth rate of output, since at this point the profitability of investment (the rate of profit on capital) will be neither rising nor falling. The historical constancy of the capital/output ratio, of the share of profit in income and the rate of profit on capital in advanced capitalist economies, is thus explicable in terms of forces which tend to bring these two

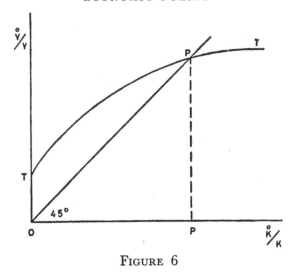

FIGURE 6

growth rates (of capital and of output) into equality with one another.

On this analysis, it is the technical dynamism of an economy, as shown by the height or position of our technical progress curve, which is responsible both for making the rate of accumulation of capital and the rate of growth of production in the economy relatively small or relatively large. It explains why there is no long-run tendency to a *falling* rate of profit, or for a continued increase in capital in relation to output, either in slow-growing or in fast-growing economies. In economies whose technical dynamism is low, both the rate of accumulation and the growth of production will be relatively low, but in either case, growth can go on at a steady rate, without any necessary tendency to diminishing returns and thus to a gradual approach to a stationary state.

This view—that it is the technical dynamism of society which determines the rate of growth of both capital and output of the economy as a whole—is not meant to deny that any particular entrepreneur installing new capacity may not have a wide choice of techniques at his disposal, and that he will not make his choice on economic criteria in selecting that technique which promises to yield the highest rate of profit. But it does mean that the optimum technique will primarily depend on the cheapness and dearness of labour in terms of commodities in general and thus in terms of the various labour-saving instruments of production, and not on the prevailing rate of interest. In other words, the general level of the productivity of labour in the economy, which reflects the general state of accumulation *already* attained—since this determines the level of wages in terms of commodities—will ensure that in any particular industry the techniques adopted will be neither more labour-saving (and capital-using) nor less labour-saving than is appropriate to the particular stage of development of the economy as a whole. An entrepreneur, charged with, let us say, the construction of a hydro-electric dam, will employ very different techniques in India where labour is cheap than in America where it is dear. But there is no reason why there should be any difference in the prospective rate of profit earned on these techniques; if there is, the difference may be in either direction. There is no functional relationship between the price of labour in terms of commodities (which depends on output-per-head and capital-per-head) and the prevailing rate of profit on investments (which, as we shall see presently, depends on other factors).[1]

3. THE RATE OF GROWTH AND THE PROFITABILITY OF INVESTMENT

Our analysis so far amounts to a denial that anything that may be termed the marginal productivity of capital or of labour has any role to play in determining the distribution of incomes or the ruling rate of profit. We have provided an alternative explanation for the determination of distributive shares, but we have said nothing so far as to the factors which determine the *rate* of return on capital. Is there nothing in the notion of a productivity-rate of interest, determined by *real* forces, and which governs the demand schedule for investable funds, as distinct from the monetary and psychological factors which govern the supply schedule?

[1] The assertion that the existence of a functional relationship between the chosen technique (or rather the chosen amount of capital per head) and the price of labour relative to the prices of capital goods also carries with it a unique relationship between the chosen amount of capital-per-head and the ruling rate of profit is based of course on the postulate of a linear and homogeneous production function, and is not valid otherwise.

The answer is that there is, and its existence in no way depends on the validity of the notion of marginal productivity, although it is not necessarily inconsistent with the latter notion. It is to be found in the dependence of the rate of profit on the rate of growth. I myself discovered this connection some twenty-three years ago,[1] when I was working on the theory of capital, on marginal productivity lines, and examined the case of an economy where all goods are capital goods—like a slave state, where labour is owned, and can be accumulated, in much the same way as material instruments. I found that the rate of interest in such a society is nothing else but the percentage excess of the goods produced over a period over the goods consumed in its production—in other words, it reflects the *net* productivity of the whole system. It is equal to society's maximum potential rate of growth: the rate of growth that would materialise if the whole of the net product were devoted to further accumulation.

The same result was shown by von Neumann, in his famous model of general equilibrium.[2] Neumann's model does not necessarily require a "slave state," but only the assumption (made by Ricardo and his school), that the supply of labour is indefinitely expansible at a constant real wage.

I think these results can be generalised and shown to apply to any steadily growing economy where the proportion of output devoted to investment, and the distributive shares are constant— where, in other words, wages and profits form a constant proportion of output. The second of these requirements is implied in the first when the propensities to save out of profits and wages are assumed to be given.

The derivation of this is quite simple. In a state of full-employment equilibrium, using the same denotation as before, it follows from equation (2)

$$\frac{P}{Y} = \frac{1}{a-\beta} \frac{I}{Y} - \frac{\beta}{a-\beta} \quad \dots\dots\dots\dots (2a)$$

In a steadily growing economy the ratio of investment to output depends on the rate of growth and the capital/output ratio.

[1] Cf. *Econometrica*, July 1937, pp. 228-30.
[2] *Review of Economic Studies*, Vol. XIII (1), 1945-6, p. 1. (Originally read at a mathematical seminar of Princeton University in 1932 and published in German in 1938.)

Hence denoting the rate of growth by G, and the capital/output ratio by K/Y:

$$\frac{I}{Y} = G\frac{K}{Y} \quad \dots \dots \dots \dots \dots \dots \dots (4)$$

But the rate of profit on capital, P/K, is by definition

$$\frac{P}{K} \equiv \frac{P}{Y}\frac{Y}{K}$$

$$\therefore \frac{P}{K} = \frac{G}{a-\beta} - \frac{\beta\frac{Y}{K}}{a-\beta} \quad \dots \dots \dots \dots (5)$$

When $\beta \rightarrow 0$ (i.e. savings out of non-profit income are negligible or else balanced by non-business investment)

$$\frac{P}{K} = \frac{G}{a} \quad \dots \dots \dots \dots \dots \dots \dots (5a)$$

In commonsense terms this means that the rate of profit depends on the rate of growth of the economy and the proportion of profits saved. In a steadily growing economy with constant distributive shares, the rate of growth of production will be the same as the rate of growth of profits. It can be shown moreover that equation (4) has a more general application if G is taken to mean the rate of growth of *profits* (whether or not the latter equals the rate of growth of output). For the rate of profit on investment can be defined as the marginal rate of profit on capital for the economy as a whole, i.e. the increase in profits (ΔP) over the increase in capital (ΔK). When business investment is entirely financed out of profits

$$\Delta K = aP$$

Hence
$$\frac{\Delta P}{\Delta K} = \frac{\Delta P}{aP} = \frac{\frac{\Delta P}{P}}{a} \quad \dots \dots \dots \dots \dots (5b)$$

The important result which emerges from this is that the marginal efficiency of capital depends on how *fast* an economy is growing (or rather, on how fast profits are growing), and not on how richly or how poorly it is endowed with capital in relation to labour. This explains why the profit that can be earned by investing capital in advanced economies well endowed with capital is often greater than the profit that can be earned by investing in under-developed countries where capital is scarce in relation to labour.

I shall examine the implications of this on the problem of maintaining steady growth in the second lecture.

II

We concluded the previous lecture by suggesting that the rate of return on capital in a growing economy will be a function of the rate of growth of incomes, and of the propensities to save out of profits and out of non-profit incomes. Now, if we neglect non-profit savings (consisting of both personal savings and government savings) on the ground that they are largely balanced by non-business loan expenditure, the rate of return reduces to the simple formula: the rate of growth of profits divided by the proportion of profits saved. (In a steadily growing economy, however, distributive shares will be constant over time, and the rate of growth of profits will be the same as the rate of growth of the national income.)

4. THE SUPPLY PRICE OF RISK CAPITAL

This formula focusses attention on the factors which govern the rate of profit, actual or expected, on capital invested in business ventures—it thus governs the demand function for investment or, as Keynes put it, the marginal efficiency of capital. In order that investment should take place, it is necessary that this rate of return should be equal to, or higher than, the supply price of risk capital. According to Ricardo, capital accumulation will only continue when the rate of profit is high enough "to afford [the farmers and manufacturers] an adequate compensation for their trouble, and the risk which they must necessarily encounter in employing their capital productively."[1]

This particular statement of Ricardo's is really an early statement—perhaps the earliest statement—of what has since come to

[1] *Principles*, in Ricardo, *Works*, Sraffa ed., p. 122.

be known as the "liquidity preference theory." For let us note that the factors "risk and trouble" set a minimum price, not to the supply of savings, but merely to the productive employment of wealth as against other forms of holding wealth which do *not* involve "risk and trouble." These are essentially similar therefore to the illiquidity risk on which Keynes concentrated attention, and which causes the yield of long-term bonds to stand higher than the *normal* (or expected) level of the short-term rate of interest. Indeed, by focussing attention on the liquidity premium which the holding of *money* commands as against the holding of gilt-edged bonds, Keynes inadvertently diverted attention from the fact that gilt-edged securities themselves possess considerable advantages from the point of view of liquidity, both in relation to less marketable securities and even more in relation to investment in real assets such as factories or houses. The additional yield of, say, house property in relation to gilt-edged is a reflection, not mainly of the uncertainty concerning the future level of rents, but of the easy marketability of gilt-edged in relation to house property, which makes it possible for the investor to consider gilt-edged holdings as a form of reserve that can be readily "switched" into other forms as and when profitable investment opportunities present themselves; this easy marketability is certainly absent in investment in real property (or plant and equipment). Moreover, the premium which gilt-edged securities command as against direct investment in fixed assets may be quantitatively far more important than the liquidity premium which money and short-term paper commands in relation to gilt-edged securities. According to the calculations of Professor Phelps Brown, the rate of return on capital in Britain in the second half of the nineteenth century (in 1870–1914) was steady around the level of 10 per cent. (on industrial capital alone it was 15 per cent.) at the time when the yield of Consols moved around $3-3\frac{1}{2}$ per cent.[1] On this calculation the premium on investments in financial assets of prime security as against the "productive employment of wealth" amounted to at least 6–7 per cent. No doubt this compensation covers other elements beside the illiquidity risk in a narrow sense—

[1] Cf. E. H. Phelps Brown and B. Weber, "Accumulation, Productivity and Distribution in the British Economy, 1870-1938," *Economic Journal*, June 1953, p. 286.

all of which were summed up by Ricardo under "risk and trouble." But the illiquidity risk—that is, the risk of not being able to withdraw from a commitment, once entered into, should the owner wish to change the disposition of his assets subsequently—is undoubtedly an important element in itself, as is indicated by the fact that businesses do not normally expect the same kind of return on investments in working capital (which are regarded as part of the "liquid assets" of the business) as on investments in fixed assets.

The necessary margin by which the expected return on any particular investment project must exceed the "pure" long-term rate of interest in order to qualify for adoption is influenced also by the level of taxation of profits in the form of income tax as well as profits tax, though more so by the latter than the former. Though nobody knows what this minimum margin is at the present time, at a guess I would put it at 10 per cent. gross or 5 per cent. net of taxation, which would make the necessary minimum rate of return come to 15 per cent. when the pure long-term rate of interest is around 5 per cent.

The fact that the rate of interest cannot be reduced to zero, or rather to below some mimimum which is necessarily higher than zero, sets a certain minimum limit to the supply price of risk capital, which is in itself fairly high. Thus if the differential is assumed to be 10 per cent. and the minimum pure long-term rate of interest, below which it cannot be brought by any amount of monetary liquidity, is 2 per cent., the minimum rate of profit necessary to secure the inducement for continued investment is 12 per cent. This in turn is only consistent with the continued accumulation of capital when the rate of growth of income exceeds a certain minimum—a minimum which cannot be calculated precisely (since the savings parameters in our equation can only be guessed within limits) but which is likely to be between one-half and one-third of this rate, that is to say, between 4 and 6 per cent. per annum.

5. MONEY GROWTH AND REAL GROWTH

It is here, in my opinion, that the question of rising or falling prices assumes critical importance. For the determinant of the *money* rate of return is the rate of growth of income in *money* terms, which will exceed or fall short of the *real* rate of growth according as prices are rising or falling. If this is correct, a régime of completely *stable* prices is only consistent with a steadily growing economy when the real rate of growth in the national income is fairly high—when it exceeds 4–6 per cent. per annum. *A fortiori*, a policy of stable incomes and falling prices—which so many economists, starting from the Swedish economist Davidson at the turn of the century, have regarded as a kind of ideal—is not consistent with growth at all: not unless the population increased so rapidly that *aggregate* incomes grew at the required minimum rate, despite the fact that incomes *per head* were constant.

Thus in this country since 1946 the gross national product in money terms grew at a compound rate of $7\frac{1}{2}$ per cent. per annum, while the real rate of growth was just under 3 per cent. The annual rise in output prices was thus around $4\frac{1}{2}$ per cent. and the pure long-term rate of interest rose gradually from a low of $2\frac{1}{2}$ per cent. to around 5 per cent. Taking the average rate of profit at $2\frac{3}{4}$ times the rate of growth, the *money* rate of profit comes to 20 per cent. But the *real* rate of profit on this assumption comes to only just above 8 per cent., which would not have sufficed, on our hypothesis of a 10 per cent. minimum margin, to give adequate inducements, unless the rate of interest was *minus* 2 per cent. This is precisely what the inflation had done; it reduced the *real* rate of interest to negative levels throughout most of the period, and to around zero during the recent period of relatively high interest rates.

It follows that price stability is only consistent with steady growth when the rate of growth of productivity and/or of the working population is sufficiently large to give a relatively high rate of growth to the total national product. In a weakly growing economy, price stability will mean stagnation unless the propensity to consume is raised sufficiently to offset the effect of a lower rate of growth of profits through a higher share of profits in total income. Thus if the savings propensities were halved, the share of profit in income would be doubled at any given ratio of investment to output, and the rate of profit on capital would be doubled at any given rate of growth of income. (But the requirement of combining a régime of stable prices with a high and growing share of profits in the national income makes the policy objective of avoiding any excessive increase in money wages the more Utopian.)

If the rate of profit is insufficient for *steady* growth, this does not mean that the system will relapse into permanent stagnation— if it did, the past history of capitalist economies could not have exhibited the trend rate of growth which it has shown. But what it does mean is that the process of accumulation and growth is periodically interrupted: periods of accumulation tend to get telescoped into a certain proportion of the years; progress proceeds by fits and starts, and not at a steady rate. Given a sufficiently high rate of growth of productivity (and/or of the working population), or given an adequate supplement to the real rate of growth in the guise of inflation, there is no reason why "booms" should not be perpetual. There is no reason, in other words, to regard the trade cycle as inevitable, provided that money incomes can be kept rising at a rate that is both adequate and steady.

Hence a slow and steady rate of inflation provides a most powerful aid to the attainment of a steady rate of economic progress. One of the few economists of our generation who seems clearly to have perceived this point, in his early writings, is Professor Sir Dennis Robertson who originated the idea, and who coined the phrase, of the policy of the "gently rising price-level." He was well aware, as shown by his book, *Money*, that a progressive rise in the price-level "so long as it is not so blatant as to generate social disorder or sap the foundations of contract . . . stimulates the production of goods: by benefiting the pockets of the controllers of industry stimulates also their energies and activities: . . . and this fillip to production, by adding to the flow of goods, serves to moderate the very rise in prices which gives it birth." Hence "so long as the control of production is in the hands of a minority, rewarded by means of a fluctuating profit, it is not impossible that a gently rising price-level will in fact produce the best attainable results, not only for them but for the community as a whole. And it is tolerably certain that a price-level continually falling, even for the best of reasons, would prove deficient in those stimuli upon which modern society, whether wisely or not, has hitherto chiefly relied for keeping its members in full employment and getting its work done."[1] On the other hand, Keynes, who had such a remarkable intuition in this field, was curiously blind to the implications of continually rising money wages for the inducement to invest. He believed that with the progressive accumulation of capital there would be a gradual slowing-down in economic progress leading to a fall in the marginal efficiency of capital which in turn would lead to an ultimate Day of Judgment (as Professor Pigou called it) when the rate of interest fell to the absolute minimum governed by liquidity preference and when further accumulation and progress necessarily came to an end. He certainly failed to perceive that the simple expedient of allowing money wages to rise faster than productivity—which to us, these days, seems such an easy thing to do—is enough to lay this particular ghost indefinitely. If the *money* rate of interest cannot be brought down below a certain floor, the *real* rate of interest certainly can *crash* through it—indeed, it may be difficult to prevent it from falling too far! Granted the fact that in the last resort we can always have recourse to a little inflation there is really no reason why an unfavourable constellation between Liquidity Preference and the Marginal Efficiency of Capital should bring capitalism to its ultimate doom.

Having said all this, I do not wish to leave you with the impression that the inflation of the post-war era was the best in the best of all possible worlds. While it is highly probable that *some* inflation in the circumstances was necessary to provide adequate stimuli to continued growth, the actual extent of the inflation does appear to have been greater than that required for the purpose. This is shown by the fact that rising investment levels (both absolutely and as a proportion of the national income) were combined with a fairly sharply rising trend in the money rates of interest since 1948—a clear indication that the money rate of profit exceeded the rate of interest by more than the required minimum.

As I mentioned before, the actual rate of growth of money incomes, both wages and profits, was around 7½ per cent. a year.

[1] *Money*, 1922, pp. 122-5.

It seems probable,, though one cannot of course be certain, that much the same levels of employment, real investment and rates of productivity growth would have been attained if the rate of increase of money wages and money profits had been only around 4–5 per cent. a year. On the other hand I would be worried about a policy which restricted the rate of increase in money wages to the 2–2½ per cent. which corresponded to the rate of growth of real output per man: not that the prospects of attaining any such objective are sufficiently great to give one much cause for anxiety. (In the majority of industrialised countries in the post-war era, and not only in Britain, annual wage increases averaged 5–8 per cent. a year.) But a target for annual wage increases of 4–5 per cent. a year does not seem to me beyond the bounds of possibility; nor does it seem to me beyond reach so to improve the technical dynamism of the British economy as to raise the rate of growth of productivity to somewhere near that figure. In other words, the objective of price stability could be attained, and could only be attained consistently with economic growth, by a combination of measures that would on the one hand reduce the rate of wage inflation, and on the other hand raise the rate of growth of productivity so that the two rates would ultimately converge in the middle, so to speak.

In the remaining part of this lecture I should like to go in more detail into these two critical aspects of the problem—the rate of increase in money wages and the rate of growth of labour productivity.

6. CAUSES OF WAGE INCREASES

Amid the welter of conflicting views on inflation it is reassuring to find a fair unanimity among economists on the key role of the rate of increase in money wages in the inflationary process. Without a continued rise in money wages inflation could not go on as a *process* in time—since whatever forces were present in the economy making for a rise in prices, they could only have caused a once-for-all rise in prices which would in itself have served to eliminate the excess demand that gave rise to it. It is the rise in wages which governs the *increase* in monetary demand, and thus the rate of increase in incomes in general. It is generally agreed also that the rate of increase in money wages has little if any influence on the *share* of wages in the national product: when money wages rise at a faster rate, money profits will also rise at a faster rate; there is no reason to suppose that wages over any period of time stand higher in relation to profits over that period than they would have stood with a lower rate of increase in money wages.

It is when we come to analyse the factors which determine the increase in money wages that there is a conflict of opinion between those who believe that it is governed by the pull of excess demand in the labour market—by the competitive bidding of employers for labour, each offering jobs a little above the prevailing level of rates in order to attract labour from other employers—and those who believe that it is mainly the outcome of collective wage negotiations and reflects the pressure for wage increases from the side of the unions. On the former view the role of collective wage negotiations is mainly to put an official stamp, so to speak, to the wage increases that would have come about in any case, under the pressure of market forces; while on the latter view, competitive bidding for labour by employers accounts for a small part of the annual rise in wages, represented by *some* of the excess in the rise in actual earnings over the increase in negotiated levels. (In Britain this excess averaged 1 per cent. a year since 1948, while the rise in negotiated wages averaged 6 per cent. annually. Assuming that one-half of this excess was due to the wage-drift caused by competitive bidding, the other half reflecting the effect of overtime and piece-rates, the "demand-pull" element, on this latter view, accounted for only about one-twelfth of the rise in wages that had taken place.)

The demand-pull theory assumes a degree of perfection in the labour market which is unrealistic. It relies on the assumption that when production is limited by labour shortages it pays an individual employer to offer higher wages if thereby he can attract labour from other employers and thus increase his own output. But whether it does so or not depends on whether it is possible for him to offer higher rates to newcomers without increasing at the same time the wages of his existing workers; and on the number of additional men the employer wishes to engage in relation to his existing labour force. A large establishment clearly could not discriminate in favour of new employees without a serious deterioration of labour relations; added to which is the fact that the elasticity of supply of labour to a large employer may not be very large. Hence it is only in cases where the individual employer hires only a single employee or a few employees (as, for example, in domestic service) that a shortage of labour is likely to exert an upward pressure on the wage level from the side of demand.

Recently Professor Phillips has published some interesting calculations[1] showing that there was a strong negative correlation in the 1861–1913 period (and to some extent also in the post World War II period) between the rate of increase in money wages on the one hand and the level of unemployment *and* the rate of change of unemployment on the other hand. I think he has established the existence of these relationships; but I do not believe that they support the particular inference which he draws from them (even for the pre-1913 period)—i.e. the inference that the rise in wages reflects mainly the competitive bidding for labour by employers, with "employers bidding more vigorously for the services of labour in periods of *increasing* demand than in a year during which the average percentage of unemployment was the same but the demand for labour was not increasing."[2] I think his figures are perfectly compatible with the alternative theory— indeed, I am prepared to argue that they provide a better support for that theory than for his own.

On this alternative theory the rise in money wages depends on the *bargaining strength* of labour; and bargaining strength, in turn, is closely related to the prosperity of industry, which determines both the eagerness of labour unions to demand higher wages and the willingness and ability of employers to grant them. It is when investment is high that profits are high, and it is in periods of rising total production and rising productivity that profits are rising. Such periods in turn are periods of low unemployment, and also periods of falling unemployment. If instead of relating wage increases to unemployment and the rate of change of unemploy-

---

[1] A. W. Phillips, "The Relation Between Unemployment and the Rate of Change of Money Wage Rates in the United Kingdom, 1861-1957," *Economica*, November 1958.
[2] *Ibid.*, p. 283.

ment, Professor Phillips had related them to the increase in production, or to the increase in profits of the previous year, I am
confident that he would have found an even better correlation—
for *all* his periods, inter-war and post-war, as well as pre-war,
excepting perhaps those years when Sir Stafford Cripps was
Chancellor and a policy of voluntary restraint by the labour unions
was in operation.

Prosperity, and rising prosperity, determine the bargaining
strength of labour, simply because in most cases—with the exception perhaps of some large monopolies or oligopolies—neither
employers nor unions take into account the rise in prices and
profits that would *result* from wage increases, so that the scope for
wage increases is limited by what can be granted out of the profits
earned at the *existing* level of prices. No doubt wage increases
lead to a rise in prices as well as costs, but in most cases this process is an indirect one, operating through the subsequent rise in
the level of demand; it is not something that is taken for granted,
and brought into the calculation beforehand. (If this were not so,
there would be no reason why employers should resist demands
for increased wages—indeed, they ought to welcome them.) In
practice, the general rate of increase in the wage level is largely
determined by the rate of increase in wages in leading industries,
and it is the *already attained* increase in profits of these industries,
whether resulting from a previous increase in demand or from a
rise in productivity, which governs the increase in negotiated
wages. Added to this is the fact that the employers' eagerness to
come to a settlement is closely related to the prevailing state of
business activity. In times of low order books, the prospect of a
strike, involving a shut-down of the works for a certain period,
does not frighten the employers; in certain circumstances they
might even welcome it if it enables them to lower costs by tele-
scoping operations into a shorter period. It is in times of high business activity that strike action is both costly and embarrassing to
the employers. It is these factors, and not the competition of
unemployed labour as such, which often make the bargaining
strength of labour weak in times of relatively high unemployment.

There is thus a complicated interaction, in a growing economy,

between the rise in profits and the rise in wages. The rise in production leads to a rise in profits as such; this in turn leads to a
rise in wages which, by increasing demand further, causes a faster
rate of increase in profits. It is therefore more correct to speak of a
profit-wage spiral than of a price-wage spiral: for the rise in
wages is prompted by the rise in profits, irrespective of whether
the rise in profits was accompanied by any (or by a corresponding)
rise in prices. As Professor Phillips concludes, there is no evidence
that the rise in the cost of living is normally a significant factor in
determining the rate of increase in wages. The cost-pull or the
wage-pull is not motivated by the rise in the cost of living: it is
motivated by the rise in profits which governs the employers'
ability to grant wage increases; and though this process is consistent with a shortage of labour for its operation, it does not by
any means presuppose such a shortage.[1]

As against this, the demand-pull theory favoured by Professor
Phillips is up against a host of difficulties. For one thing, it cannot
explain why, in the Crippsian period, 1949–50, the rise in both
wages and earnings should have been so moderate (the rise in
wages averaged less than 3 per cent. in these two years) when
unemployment was no greater than in the surrounding years. If
the rise in wages is primarily motivated by the competitive bidding
for labour by employers, an appeal for voluntary wage restraint
to the unions would merely increase the gap between the rise in
negotiated wages and the rise in earnings; it would not slow
down the latter. Secondly, the demand-pull theory cannot explain
why periods of rising production and profits should cause a rapid
rise in wages, even in times of high unemployment—as for
example, in 1936 and 1937, when wages rose at comparable rates
to the post-war years, despite the fact that unemployment
averaged 11–13 per cent. of insured workers. Finally, the demand-
pull theory can hardly explain why the rate of wage inflation
in countries like Germany should have exceeded that of Britain,
despite the fact that, owing to the rapid rise in the working
population, a period of exceptional production growth was associated with the persistence of considerable unemployment.

[1] This is best shown in not-fully-developed economies like Italy, where wages in the
industrial sector habitually rise at least as fast as in the "full-employment" economies,
despite a great superfluity of labour.

7. PRICE STABILITY AND UNEMPLOYMENT

I have dwelt on Professor Phillips' views at some length, simply because a misguided diagnosis of the causes of wage inflations can play such a vital role in policy decisions which are of the utmost importance to the economy. Professor Phillips' conclusion from his investigation is that, assuming an increase in productivity of 2 per cent. a year, "if aggregate demand was kept at a value which would maintain a stable level of product prices, the associated level of unemployment would be a little under 2½ per cent. If, as is sometimes recommended, demand were kept at a value which would maintain stable wage rates the associated level of unemployment would be about 5½ per cent."[1] The clear implication of this is that it is possible through the regulation of effective demand to combine steady growth with stable prices, or even with stable incomes and falling prices, provided only that unemployment is maintained at some "required level" which is by no means unreasonably large.

There are a number of things, in my opinion, which are fatally wrong with this conclusion. In the first place, for reasons analysed in my previous lecture, an under-employment equilibrium when the level of production is limited by demand, and not by production bottlenecks, is only stable when the level of production is stationary over time, so that there is no *growth* in output giving rise to induced investment. If effective demand is kept at a high enough level, and at a growing level, to induce a steady growth in capacity year by year, forces are inevitably generated which will push the economy to the point of maximum production in the short run: at any lesser level of output, as we have seen, the demand curve will cut the supply curve the wrong way round, and equilibrium will be unstable. For this reason it may not be possible to run a growing economy at half-cock, i.e. to keep it steady at a less-than-full-employment level of activity.

But even if by a combination of superb skill and cunning and the sureness of touch of a tight-rope dancer, the Treasury and the Bank of England succeeded in keeping the economy in a moving state of unstable equilibrium—succeeded, in other words, in

[1] *Economica*, November 1958, p. 299.

maintaining a steadily growing real demand for goods and services, whilst never allowing the economy to run up against the bottle-neck of full employment—it is a fallacy to believe that the mere fact that unemployment is not allowed to fall below some critical level will suffice to keep down the rise in wages and profits to some prescribed level. For the very fact that production is growing will mean that profits are growing; it is the growth in profits which causes wages to rise and thereby steps up the rate of growth of profits and also of wages. It is not enough, therefore, to create unemployment in order to stop a wage inflation. Since in a capital-ist economy rising production is closely interlinked with rising profits—it is impossible to have the one without the other—a policy of "damping down demand" can only succeed in stopping the inflationary spiral if it also brings to a halt the process of growth. A 5, or even 10, per cent. rate of unemployment is per-fectly compatible with a profit-wage spiral so long as growth goes on; and recent history is strewn with attempts to bring monetary depreciation to a halt by measures which brought the growth of production to a halt, whether or not they succeeded in halting the rise in prices.

Fortunately there is no real, inescapable dilemma here. All that is necessary is to recognise that the proper way of dealing with inflation is to damp down, or restrain, the rate of increase in money wages *as such*, instead of damping down the demand for goods and services. If the increase in wages is slowed down, the growth of monetary demand will be automatically damped down too, and so will the rise in profits. Measures restricting the cost-push inflation coming from the side of the unions, unlike measures restricting the demand for goods, do not necessarily interfere with the real rate of growth of the economy.

A democratic community, unlike totalitarian countries, cannot stop wages from rising by the mere fiat of the governmental authority, whether through freezing wages, compulsory arbitra-tion, the imposition of a central authority with vetoing powers, or the like. But within our existing institutional framework it is possible to develop arrangements which would tend to slow down the growth of wages and profits without the use of compulsory powers. The most promising line of approach seems to me the introduction, on American lines, of a system of "wage-contracts" concluded for a definite period, say, for two years or longer. If by this means the period elapsing between the renegotiation of wages could be lengthened, the annual rate of increase in wages would be reduced, simply because the rate of growth of profits would be slowed down if wages were held steady for longer periods. If wages were negotiated afresh after, say, the lapse of every *two* years, the biennial round of wage increases would be bound to be less than twice the annual round. It is with some such arrangement that the rise in wages could be brought down to the 4–5 per cent. annual rate which I mentioned earlier as a reasonable target.

8. RATE OF GROWTH OF PRODUCTIVITY

More intriguing is the question whether, and by what means, the rate of growth of output per head could be stepped up so as to make this "safe" level of wage and profit inflation of 4–5 per cent. a year consistent with stable prices. (A faster rate of economic growth would of course be a good thing in itself quite apart from the objective of avoiding inflation!) On this issue, most people pessimistically assume that the rate at which productivity is growing over time is just one of the facts of nature. Yet the rate of growth of productivity shows wide variations between different countries and periods: it could hardly be regarded as a law of nature that the annual growth of productivity should be 2 per cent. in Britain, $3\frac{1}{2}$ per cent. in America, 6 per cent. in Germany, Italy or France, and 10 per cent. in Japan, as was the case in the 1950's (not to mention the fancy figures that drift across the Iron Curtain). These differences in the rates of growth of production were of course strongly correlated with the ratio of gross investment to the gross national product; fast-growing economies invariably invest a higher proportion of their current product than slow-growing economies. A higher ratio of investment to output is therefore an essential precondition for stepping up the rate of growth of the economy.

Yet it would be a mistake to believe, I think, that we could double the rate of growth merely by doubling the share of investment in output. If this were true, investment would have tended to expand on its own, so to speak, through the operation of market forces. As I argued in the previous lecture, the technical dynamism of an economy, its capacity to absorb or assimilate technical change, sets a limit to the *useful* rate of investment; and there are several instances (e.g. Norway) to show that a government-directed expansion of the investment coefficient may merely lead to a sharp rise in the capital-output ratio with only a moderate effect on the rate of growth of productivity.

The factors which determine the growth of productivity partly depend on the improvement of design of newly installed plant and equipment, and partly on the rate of disappearance of obsolete equipment which sets a limit to the extent to which new equipment can be usefully absorbed by the economy. These factors are interconnected: since the faster the rate of improvement in productivity on newly installed equipment, the faster the decline of prices relative to wages (the faster, in other words, the rise in *real* as distinct from *money* wages), which in turn determines the rate at which ancient equipment disappears from the production process, and the greater, therefore, the scope for the introduction of new equipment. Further, a higher rate of increase in *real* wages not only increases the rate of turnover of equipment, but it tends to enhance the rate of improvement of design on new equipment, since it gives stronger incentives for making the new equipment *more* labour-saving. It is for this reason that the rate of growth of productivity appears to be positively correlated with the rate of growth of working population, for when the employed population is increasing, the rate of absorption of new equipment is relatively high (the average age of equipment is falling); this in turn accelerates obsolescence, and hence makes room for a still higher rate of absorption of new equipment at the same time as it enhances the rate of improvement of design. The low rate of growth of productivity in Britain may thus have something to do with the near-stationariness of her industrial working population: this makes for a low rate of absorption of new equipment, a slow rate of growth in real wages, hence a low rate of obsolescence and weak incentives for design-improvement.

If this view is correct, a great deal could be done by measures designed to accelerate the rate of scrapping of obsolete equipment and the consequent release of labour which would make room for a higher rate of absorption of new equipment. This may be stimulated by the revival of price-competition, tending to eliminate inefficient firms and inefficient plant; it could also be stimulated by special tax measures, complementing accelerated depreciation allowances at one end by obsolescence taxes at the other end —by some kind of negative depreciation allowance on the employment of over-age plant, if this were feasible.

There is no time to probe more deeply into such problems. All I have been able to do here is to indicate some of the reasons for the belief that there is no real justification for having a fatalistic attitude concerning the rate of economic growth that could be attained in the British economy, given the proper diagnosis and given a purposive direction.

Part III

THE PROBLEM OF TAX REFORM

9

THE REFORM OF PERSONAL TAXATION[1]

SYSTEMS of taxation can be judged from various viewpoints or criteria. We know that taxation is necessary—it is a necessary evil—but we want to get as good a system for collecting any given sum of revenue as we can. What we mean by "a good system" depends on what sort of considerations we have in mind. It is usual to judge any question concerned with taxation, or the tax system as a whole, from three different considerations to which a fourth may be added. The first of these is equity; the second is expediency (by which is meant the economic effects of taxation); and the third is administration—how efficiently any particular tax or set of taxes can be administered. It has often been said that however equitable a system of taxation is on paper, it cannot be regarded as fair or just if, owing to administrative shortcomings, the intentions of the law cannot be carried out in practice.

My fourth consideration is also concerned with economics. It is, however, rather different from the traditional aspects of the economic effects of taxation—it is concerned with taxation as an instrument of economic control. This is a new aspect which the writers on public finance in the nineteenth century, and even in the early decades of this century, never considered systematically. The idea of using the fiscal instrument for general economic ends is something that is comparatively recent. But, if you accept the view that this is one of the important objectives of taxation, then it ought to be considered on its own, since it involves rather different considerations from the others.

From the point of view of equity, the question is how fair is the distribution of taxation as between different individuals and social groups. From the point of view of the economic effects of taxation what one is asking is how much distortion the imposition of taxation causes to normal or ordinary behaviour. The importance of "economic effects" depends on the magnitude of such distortions.

[1] An address given at a meeting of the London and District Society of Chartered Accountants on 29 October 1957 and printed in *The Accountant*, 12 April 1958.

The distortions can be on the side of man's activities as a consumer, or on the side of his activities as a producer. I would regard the latter as far more important than the former. It is evident that when you impose heavy taxation on some commodities and not on others, you tempt people to rearrange the pattern of their expenditure so as to minimise the liability to tax. This rearrangement is a distortion of behaviour which arises incidentally, not on account of the imposition of taxation as such, but because of the particular forms of taxation adopted.

In the same way, personal taxation can cause distortions of behaviour of various kinds, and here again these are so well known that I do not need to labour the point; it can make people work less than they would have worked or make them take fewer risks. More important, it can also make them spend more and save less than they would have spent and saved if the same money had been taken from them by some means other than those of personal income tax.

From the point of view of economic control, what we are asking is how efficiently any particular system can translate into practice the political objectives of the Government. For example, the Government wishes to fight inflation and to restrain spending. It can do so by monetary policy or by fiscal policy—through raising taxation. My colleagues are very much divided as to the relative appropriateness or efficacy of these two kinds of instruments of control. But all economists agree that taxation does serve as an alternative instrument of control to credit policy. As soon as you admit that, however, the question arises, "Are all taxes equally good in this regard, or are some forms of taxes better than others?"

Finally, there is the question of administration. Direct taxes, graduated and differentiated according to personal circumstances, as you all know from experience, are not easy taxes to administer. If it were simply a question of collecting money, I think most of us would agree that it would be better to do without income tax and such-like, and collect all the money that the Government needs by a tax on sales, on turnover, etc.

The sole justification for having elaborate taxes levied on persons rather than on objects or transactions is that a progressive income tax or a progressive estate duty is a tax on the individual, directly related to his ability to pay. Income merely serves as the base of personal taxation because it is chosen as a yardstick or as a measure, on the basis of which the State wishes to tax the individual. But any graduated tax—whether it is related to a man's total capital, total property, total expenditure, or total income—is a tax on persons and not on objects. Such taxes are necessary in order to secure equity or fairness in the distribution of the burden of taxation, and are not really necessary for any other purpose. This is their main justification. They are the only kind of taxes imposed in accordance with the taxpayer's ability to pay.

On this occasion I should like to discuss the reform of taxation mainly from the point of view of equity and fairness. The first question we ought to clarify is: "What, if anything, do these terms mean?" It is not possible to give any very precise definition to notions such as "taxable capacity" or "ability to pay." But that does not mean that these notions themselves are of questionable validity. They very clearly mean something, even though if one wants to quantify them with precision one always comes up against difficulties.

Measurement of Ability

Similar difficulties are met in defining precisely the ability of individuals—I mean not the ability to pay, but general ability. The notion of ability clearly has a meaning for us. None of us would question that some people are abler than others, and yet, if you try to measure ability by any sort of test—and social psychologists and educationalists have been constantly busy in devising tests of ability, such as intelligence tests, and various systems of examination or selection—you may find that there is no single test that is really satisfactory for measuring the ordinary everyday sense of the term "ability." We find, as for example in the new methods of selection adopted by the Army in the last war, that if you want the best system of selection, you must not rely on any one test, but a combination of them. One is less likely to go wrong if one selects a number of tests, and awards points, so to speak, for each particular test, as e.g. an intelligence test, an ordinary sort of education test, an endurance test, etc., and co-ordinates the results. The nature of the tests varies with the problem in hand. I think it is generally accepted that if you want to measure ability you cannot do so by devising one ideal test, because the one ideal test that measures ability does not exist.

Ability to Pay

Exactly the same, in my view, is the case when you are concerned with the particular kind of ability, namely, the ability to pay taxes, or taxable capacity. It is clear that different individuals' taxable capacities differ and we should aim at a system which distributes the burden of taxation in a manner that is as close as possible to this concept of ability to pay, or taxable capacity.

There is an important and fairly widespread confusion here that I would like to clear up. A system of taxation which distributes the burden of taxation in accordance with a man's "economic power" or "spending power" is not the same thing, or not necessarily, as an egalitarian system of taxation. An egalitarian system of taxation is one which uses the taxation instrument as a means of obtaining a higher degree of social or economic equality.

But the question whether a particular system of taxation is fair or unfair does not depend primarily on whether it has the right sort of progression, whether there is adequate differentiation in the tax burden between people who are differently situated. It depends on whether there is reasonable equality of treatment between people who are similarly situated. That is the real test of fairness. A fair tax system aims at ensuring that those people who have the same taxable capacity, or the same ability to pay, should pay the same amount in tax. In other words, the major problem of a fair system of taxation is that people with the same "spending power" should pay the same taxes. The question of how much people with a high taxable capacity should pay as against people with low capacities is a secondary question and far less important, in my view, in judging the equity and fairness of the system.

Indeed, "fairness" is not really the right term with regard to the second aspect. The extent to which the system produces economic equality as compared with the degree of economic equality that would prevail without it is a question of the sense of social justice of the community. It depends on the purely political question of how much inequality society wishes to tolerate. It is an outcome of opposing interests in the country, of various political groups and pressure groups, and so on. It is a thoroughly political question.

Equity and Fairness

But I am contending that the question of equity and fairness is not a political question. It is possible to approach this problem in an impartial way. For obvious reasons, it is very difficult to get perfect agreement on these things, so that different individuals, who may be of different political persuasion and be differently situated economically, may yet agree to consider the same tests or the same combination of tests as appropriate for judging this relative ability to pay, though they may never agree on how the tax burden should vary in relation to their ability.

Using the terms equity and fairness in this sense, I have not the slightest doubt that the present system of taxation in this country is absurdly inequitable. Not that I regard it as worse than that of other countries; there are just one or two countries whose system of taxation is better than ours, but not many. It is inequitable to a degree that is unknown and unsuspected by the general public and is only realised by experts. I only came to realise it gradually when, through the work I was doing on the Royal Commission on Taxation, I had an opportunity to examine the system far more closely than I would have done in my individual capacity as a taxpayer. By the words "absurdly inequitable" I mean that the tax burden on some people is very heavy and on other people it is very light, according to chance differences that ought to have nothing whatever to do with the allocation of the burden of taxation.

We penalise our public servants to the highest degree. The fact that our public servants take it lying down and do not make too much fuss about it ought not to blind us to the fact that, pound for pound of taxable capacity, a high civil servant or a judge is enormously more heavily taxed than, say, a stockbroker; and between these extremes there are people who work in industry in responsible positions who are in a sort of intermediate category. You find very much the same inequities again among the people who derive their income from property. To an audience of accountants I think I need not go into detail.

Sources of Inequities

Among the sources of inequity in our taxation system are the difference in treatment of money coming from the trust funds and non-trust funds, the treatment of capital gains, differences between Schedule D and Schedule E, and the fact that business expenses, apart from the difference between Schedules D and E, can be associated with some kinds of office and not with others. All these are sources of inequity. But our system is not merely inequitable. It is inequitable in such a way that on most rankings of the social importance or merit of the functions different people perform in society there is an inverse relationship between the way people are treated for tax purposes and their social rank. If some inhabitant from Mars were to come and judge how important the various functions performed by different individuals are in society, solely from the lightness or heaviness with which the tax system hits them, he would think that professional speculators performed the most valuable services to the community, and the high officials of the Civil Service, or of the Judiciary, etc., performed the least beneficial services. If the social value of the services performed by an individual were quantifiable, one might almost argue that there is a clear negative correlation between the social worth of the services performed in earning a particular income, and the tax liability to which it gives rise.

It is true that an efficient system presupposes relatively moderate rates of taxation. It is easy to say that all these evils grew up in our tax system over the last thirty to fifty years—our tax system in the late nineteenth century was not what it is now. Then it was a more reasonable system from my present point of view. These evils developed because the State chose to levy taxes at such heavy rates or, at least, very heavy top rates or marginal rates. An efficient system cannot be run when the rates go up, as they did until recently, to 95 per cent. of the marginal portion of the income. You could not expect a society to function if this 95 per cent. was genuinely intended to apply and was genuinely carried out.

Loopholes in the System

But we are confronted with the vicious circle of a deteriorating tax system, where the rates of taxation go up and up and the loopholes become larger and larger, so that the State is charging all the time more and more on less and less. Every year new loopholes are opened. It is true that some loopholes are closed by successive Finance Acts but, taken by and large, the loopholes that are closed in the tax system by special anti-avoidance provisions are small in importance compared with the loopholes that are newly opened through fresh concessions presented in response to pressure of vested interests.

Such concessions have little real justification and they inevitably lead to further anomalies because, once one group of the community is given some concession then, by the force of analogy, you must extend a similar concession to other groups. So the game goes on. In fact, at present some taxes, notably estate duties and surtax, are not in the nature of compulsory levies so much as of voluntary contributions.

This was never better illustrated than when a few months ago a rich man died leaving behind a taxable estate of £9 million. There was a front-page headline in a daily newspaper, "Mr. So-and-so left £9 million for the love of Britain," the implication being that purely out of love of his country, he avoided all the steps that any prudent man in his position would have taken to avoid these enormous liabilities on his estate.

Case for a Voluntary System

I ought to add that I think there is something to be said for a voluntary system of levies, from more than one point of view. Thinking mainly of the degree of consent or toleration on behalf of the community towards a particular system of taxation, the voluntary or loophole-ridden system is as good as you can get, because those who are particularly upset about the taxes they are called upon to pay have some outlet and do not have to pay so much, whereas other people, who do not feel so strongly about it, can go on paying more. The law creates a safety valve which prevents the infuriated minority from becoming thoroughly recalcitrant members of the community.

I think there might be even more to be said for a system that is openly voluntary. It is a mistake to think that you must have compulsory levies in order to collect money for taxation. Think of the way hospitals were financed before the war. If we abolished all surtax tomorrow and simply told every rich man who was liable to this tax: "You assess yourself and send us a cheque for what you think is fair for you to pay," I am not sure whether the amount collected would not exceed the amount that is actually collected under the present system. There must be many people who, faced with the necessity of having to ask themselves in all conscience how much they ought to contribute to their country, would assess themselves far more heavily than they are now assessed at after they have taken advantage of all the loopholes and avoidance devices which the law allows. Not that one should object to people making use of avoidance devices, if they are legal. It is up to the law to close them. The trouble is, as I have already said, that the tendency is in rather the opposite direction, towards the opening up of fresh avenues for tax avoidance.

There is a great deal of nonsense talked about the burden of taxation in this country being so tremendously heavy. On paper it is frightfully heavy but, in fact, if you compare the percentage of the gross national product paid in income taxation in this country with that of, say, the United States, we find that the percentage is higher in America, despite higher exemptions and allowances and more moderate top rates, and despite the fact that the American system is almost as loophole-ridden as ours.

It would obviously be far better, not only from the point of view of equity and fairness but from that of the economic effects of taxation and administration, to collect any given sum of money by means of an efficient system at moderate rates, than by means of an inefficient loophole-ridden system at high rates. But there is this difference—that with an efficient system with moderate rates you put yourself—and when I say "you" I mean the wealthy minority, or the social *élite* of the community who pay these taxes—at the mercy of the political majority in a way which is not the case with an inefficient system with high rates. For in the former case, even if the tax rates are moderate to start with, there is always the risk of their going up subsequently, whereas with an inefficient system, the extent of the tax squeeze is limited to the amount taken when the rates approach the ceiling.

Income and Property

I must not spend too much of my time on these general considerations because you want to know what my actual views are on what can and ought to be done. I have already said that I do not believe in reliance on any single criterion or yardstick as a measure of ability to pay, because no single yardstick can do full justice as between individuals in different situations. In this country we place almost an exclusive reliance on income—we are the original inventors of income tax—although what we mean by "income" is a very arbitrary thing and is the result of a long period of legislation and judicial interpretation which has not improved the concept from the point of view of equity. Even if we had an ideal measure of taxable income, I would still maintain that income is an inadequate measure of taxable capacity taken in isolation because it ignores the taxable capacity that resides in property as such. So long as property and income varied in proportion to one another, it would not make any difference whether taxes were levied on income or on property, because the relative burden would be the same.

But one cannot assume this to be so either as between property owners and non-property owners, or as between different property owners. The taxable income resulting from property shows the widest variations. In some cases the capital is in forms which yield very little taxable income, and in other cases it is in a form which yields a great deal of taxable income. So, in the case of two individuals with differing relationships between property and income, one cannot say that a fair distribution of the burden can be ensured by taxing their income alone, nor could one say that of a tax on property alone.

Perhaps this can be made clearer by an example. Assume two men, both of them with a taxable income of £5,000 a year, but one of them has a property of £50,000 and the other a property of £100,000. Obviously one cannot say that these two people have the same taxable capacity—because clearly a man with a £100,000 property is much better off than a man with a £50,000 property and the same income, though not as well off as the man who has double the income as well as double the property. Hence property is no more adequate than income as the *sole* criterion of taxable capacity.

A Scheme with Five Taxes

To introduce yet another consideration, I think that the level of spending in the sense of one's living standard is a test of taxable capacity. The extent to which a man spends a great deal in relation to his taxable income or property is an indication that he gets more out of his income and capital; he uses more of the community's resources for his own ends than another man with the same income and property. For that reason I think that he ought to be taxed more heavily than another man whose spending is smaller, although his property and income, etc., are the same.

It is on the basis of such considerations that I put forward a scheme[1] to the Government of India according to which a man should be assessed not just to one tax but to five different taxes, each levied at correspondingly moderate rates, and all on the basis of a single return.

The five taxes comprise in addition to income tax in the way we understand it here: a tax on realised capital gains; an annual tax on property (of the type which already exists in some fourteen countries, though not in England or America); a tax on total personal expenditure; and finally a general gift tax payable by the recipients of gifts to replace the existing system of death duties.

The idea behind this last tax is that there is no particular justification for taxing property at death, except that of administrative convenience—a dead man is less able to squeal than a live one. Death duty is a periodic levy on property falling on the person or persons who inherit a man's estate. The legal notion

[1] *Indian Tax Reform*, Ministry of Finance, Government of India, New Delhi, 1956.

that the estate duty is a tax on the deceased is really nonsensical—
though it may have had rather more justification in the old
days when people saved specially during their lifetime to cover
death duty liabilities on their decease. If the incidence of the
estate duty is really on the legatee and not on the testator,
the sensible thing is to recognize this and to impose a tax on the
recipient.

However, it ought to be a tax on all gratuitous transfers,
which means a tax on gifts *inter vivos* as well as on everything
received by way of inheritance and bequest. It should be levied
not according to the size of the estate or the wealth of the donor,
but by reference to the size of the gift and the wealth of the
recipient. I do not think one needs to argue the case for this
principle at great length. The point of progressive death duties is
to counteract the tendency towards the concentration of property
in fewer hands. But if that is the underlying principle the rate of
progression of the levy ought to vary with the size of the individual
bequest, and not with the size of the estate.

The annual property tax, levied on an individual's total estate,
was to start at the rate of $\frac{1}{2}$ per cent. per annum and to rise gradually to a maximum rate of $1\frac{1}{2}$ per cent., and was to replace
differentiation by means of earned income relief. The personal
expenditure tax was in lieu of surtax. Both ordinary income
and capital gains were to be taxed at the same rate, and it was
proposed that the highest marginal rate of income tax should be
no more than 45 per cent.

Administration of the System

It only remains for me to say something on the way I think a
tax system of this kind should be administered. I think this ought
to be much easier to explain to an audience of accountants than
to other audiences, because what I in fact suggested as an annual
return for the purpose of assessing an individual for all these taxes,
was much the same kind of statement as a balance sheet and a
profit and loss account relating to an individual's *personal account*
(rather than to his business affairs). In fact, I am sure that
many accountants in private practice are already called upon to
prepare annual accounts for their clients showing their capital

position at the beginning of the year and their capital position at the end of the year, giving a record of all capital transactions, income receipts, and withdrawals with the whole thing checking in much the same way as, on sound accountancy principles, a balance sheet and a profit and loss account ought to check.

I suggested in India a single comprehensive tax return drawn up on analogous principles, on the basis of which the taxpayer can be simultaneously assessed to all five taxes. It was to consist of a statement of wealth and assets at the beginning of the year and a statement of assets at the end of the year; a statement of receipts from gifts, and the outlay on gifts; a statement regarding the receipts from the sale of assets and the purchase of assets; and a statement of the borrowing and lending account, where all loans made were entered or repayments of past loans and all borrowings, etc., and also all other cash receipts and payments. From this return taxable income, capital gains, capital value, net savings and gifts can all be computed. The personal expenditure of the individual can be computed as the difference between income and net savings. At the same time this computation would have to be fortified by a sworn statement by the taxpayer to the effect that to the best of his knowledge and belief the balance agreed with his gross personal expenditure during the year. (I cannot go into details as to how chargeable expenditure was to be defined—it is not of course the same thing as gross personal expenditure but is derived from the latter after a number of adjustments and deductions.)

Experience in India

In the special circumstances of India, there appears to be a large amount of straightforward tax evasion; something which I do not believe exists in this country, though none of us knows for certain because it is the nature of tax evasion that it is not made public. However, there is a strong suspicion, at least, that in India it is very widespread and I suggested, as one way of checking it, a control system by means of code numbers and tax slips. (Something of this kind already exists in Sweden, I believe.) These tax slips are nothing else but certified vouchers given by the recipient of cash whoever he may be (the borrower in the case of a loan, the lender in the case of a debt repayment, a seller of capital assets of all kinds, etc.), and were to be statutory for particular classes of payment, broadly of capital transactions.

I suggested that every potential taxpayer should have a code number for tax purposes, and the system of code numbers was to be similar to the national registration numbers of the last war— the successive numbers or letters indicating the tax district, the tax office and finally the number of the file of the taxpayer in the particular tax office. The code numbers both of the person who received the cash and the person who handed over the cash were to be stated on the voucher. The voucher was to be handed over by the recipient of cash to the other party in three copies which were to be stamped at the tax office. It would be in the taxpayers' interest to have these vouchers thus certified in order to claim exemption from liability particularly in connection with the expenditure tax—i.e. to show that so much of the money to be accounted for was laid out in transactions, such as the purchase of capital assets which do not attract tax. Two of the copies were to be routed to the various files through the system of code numbers. Production of tax vouchers would be necessary to certify exempt outlays, whereas the tax office would have an accumulating file of vouchers to check the correctness of the taxpayer's own return as regards receipts. Some such system of control would do a great deal to check tax evasion in a country like India but I would not wish to say that it is an essential part of the efficient administration of these taxes (either of a capital gains tax, an expenditure tax or an annual property tax) in Britain.

I have no information at the moment how far these recommendations concerning the method of administration of these taxes, as distinct from their imposition, are to be followed. The Indian Government has adopted the capital gains tax, the annual capital tax and the expenditure tax; and the Finance Minister has also announced in Parliament that he will introduce a gift tax in the next Budget. I would be chary, however, in claiming too much credit for all these reforms because the actual taxes adopted (both as to scope and definition, as well as to the schedule of rates) are so very different from what I originally recommended.

10

TAX REFORM IN INDIA[1]

AN effective system of progressive direct taxation is vital to the survival of democratic institutions in India. The need for this arises not merely on financial grounds—to raise adequate resources for purposes of accelerated economic development—but in order to bring about the degree of social cohesion and co-operation that is essential for the successful functioning of a democratic system. In a community where there is such a wide gap between the position of a privileged minority of well-to-do and the vast majority who live in dire poverty, social cohesion can only be achieved if economic inequality is effectively lessened and the tendency towards increasing concentration of wealth is effectively counter-acted. This can only be done through the instrument of taxation. It is in any case inevitable that heavy burdens should be laid on the broad masses of the population, if India is to attain a satis-factory rate of development in the coming decades. It will not be possible to carry through this programme successfully with the con-sent and co-operation of the people if the privileged minority of the well-to-do are not made to bear a fair share of this burden. More-over in matters of taxation, as in the administration of the law, it is not enough that justice should be done—it must also be seen to be done. If owing to defects in the tax law, or in their administra-tion, highly progressive taxes on wealth or income have no visible effect on the prevailing economic inequality, or in the standards of living of the rich, the mere enactment of advanced tax legisla-tion will prove fruitless.

A Fair Start

In the last few years India has made a fair start towards creating an effective system of progressive taxation with the introduction of the new taxes on capital gains, on wealth, on personal expendi-

[1] Substance of an address given to the Informal Consultative Committee of the Parliament in New Delhi on 16 December 1958. Published in *The Economic Weekly Annual*, January 1959.

ture, and on gifts. It has thus laid the basis for a system which may serve as a model to other democracies, both developed and under-developed. But it is no use blinking at the fact that the reforms so far introduced are, at best, a beginning; that the legislation of some of the new taxes is seriously defective whilst the measures for their effective administration have not yet been provided; and that other and equally important reforms in the field of business and company taxation have not been tackled at all. Unless some of the recent legislation is amended in important respects, and unless it is supplemented by legislation in other fields and by far-reaching reforms in the administrative field, there is a serious risk that this noble attempt at creating an egalitarian democracy will end in failure.

Whether the political or social urges which led to the recent reforms continue to prevail or not, I am convinced that the Indian tax system should not be frozen at the point which it has now reached. If an effective tax structure is to be created, reform will have to be carried a great deal further; if on the other hand political forces were to become dominant which would effectively bar this development, there would be little point in preserving such a complicated system of taxation.

Among the new taxes the expenditure tax and the gift tax are so heavily riddled with loopholes and exemptions that they bear only a superficial resemblance to the taxes whose introduction I originally recommended. Though the new capital gains tax represents a considerable advance on the form in which it was originally enacted in India, it still suffers from serious shortcomings which undermine the basic purpose of personal income taxation of securing equality of treatment between different tax payers. The wealth tax alone was enacted in a form that is comparatively free from loopholes, though this too contains features that could justifiably be criticised.

Defects of the Indian Expenditure-tax Act

The most serious defect of the Expenditure-tax Act is that it ties the liability to this tax to a minimum income limit which opens the door to endless manipulations and is bound to make the tax largely ineffective in practice. Expenditure represents an alternative base to income for measuring spending power or ability to pay. The difference is only that an income tax taxes savings and exempts dis-savings, whereas an expenditure tax exempts savings and brings dis-savings into charge. There is much to be said (for administrative and other reasons) for making use of both principles of taxation, and levying some of the taxation on an income base, and some on an expenditure base. But it is essential, in this case, that the liability to the one should not be made dependent on the extent of the liability to the other. By making the liability to the expenditure tax dependent on the size of income, a concession is made to savings without making a corresponding charge on dis-saving.

This is far more serious than it may appear at first sight since it is always open to any taxpayer to make his income smaller than it could be (even though he may not always be in the position to make it larger). This provision thus makes it possible for a tax-payer to telescope his income into particular years in which his spendings are kept low, and to telescope his spending into those years in which his income is kept low enough to entitle him to exemption from the expenditure tax. It is therefore bound to have a highly destructive effect—one is almost tempted to say that this particular provision alone makes the tax little more than a show-piece.

In addition, the Expenditure-tax Act contains a long series of exemptions of various kinds—such as expenditure on marriages, on medical expenses, election expenses, the purchase of cottage industry products, etc.—which have no counterpart in the income tax laws and which will make it very difficult to administer effectively. I do not wish to argue the moral or economic justification for exempting any particular form of personal expenditure from taxation—any one of these exemptions may have something to be said for it, either on grounds of fairness or expediency. But it is surely inequitable to exempt particular categories of personal outlay from expenditure taxation if these are not also exempted from income taxation.

For the great majority of people income provides the sole source of expenditure; their ability to spend is confined by income taxation just as effectively as by expenditure taxation. If it is not justified to reduce a man's liability to income-tax on account of his having exceptional expenses to bear on account of illness, or marriage, for example, why is it justified to reduce his liability to expenditure tax? Why should people whose source of spending is capital as well as income be more leniently treated than people whose only source of spending is the income which they earn? And (bearing in mind the high exemption limit to expenditure tax and the low exemption limit to income tax) why should the necessitous expenditures of large spenders be so carefully looked after when the necessitous expenditures of small and moderate spenders are not? From the point of view of equality of treatment whatever concessions are made on grounds of necessitous expenditure for the one tax ought to have their counterpart in the other tax.

Gift Tax Equally Defective

Analogous criticisms can be made against the Gift-tax Act, which in its final legislative form is only a pale shadow of what it was originally intended to be. The purpose of a gift tax, like that of the estate duty, is to restrict the freedom of individuals to pass on their property rights to others. As the American economist Henry Simons once said, the whole of private property, and the income derived from it, is a gift from the community. It is only by the will of the community that particular individuals can enjoy the privileges of ownership protected by law and administration; and the constantly evolving property laws define the actual nature of the rights which these privileges confer. Inheritance taxes are, in effect, a form of limitation on the privileges conferred by ownership: they allow an individual (subject to various limits circumscribed by law) the unfettered enjoyment of his own property, but they do not allow him to pass on his property unhindered to the next generation. But if this limitation is held to be justified, on what basis can one differentiate between *inter vivos* gifts and gifts by deed of will?

There is a long list of exemptions in the present Gift-tax Act which has no counterpart in the Estate-duty Act; and the provisions of that Act are so framed as to make it possible for an owner through the mere process of spreading the gifts over time to reduce the incidence of the gift tax to a small fraction of that of the estate duty, or even to avoid the tax altogether. As is well known, it was the introduction of the estate duty which led to the wholesale passing on of property by means of *inter vivos* gifts so as to avoid that duty—hence the need for a gift tax. But the present tax, by failing to integrate gifts over successive years for tax purposes, and by giving a series of exemptions to gifts of particular kinds (including a large annual exemption) entirely fails in this purpose.

These loopholes in the expenditure and the gift tax legislation are bound to reduce the yield of these taxes to a small fraction of what they should have been—which in turn is bound to create agitation for their complete removal. Opponents of these taxes are certain to ask, if such complicated taxes yield so little, what is the point of having them at all?—ignoring the fact that the low yield will be the very consequence of the loopholes and exemptions on the introduction of which they insisted. In the absence of loopholes, the gift tax and the estate duty taken together at the current rate schedule, could be expected to yield some 20–30 crores of rupees annually. As it is, the combined yield will amount to less than one-fifth of this sum. The expenditure tax, properly administered, and in the absence of the present loopholes, should yield at least 15–20 crores of rupees at the current schedule of rates. In its present form it will hardly yield one-tenth of this sum.

Incentive to Convert Income into Capital Gains

With regard to capital gains the new legislation has the great advantage over the old one in that capital gains are now integrated with other forms of income for income tax purposes. But they are not liable to super-tax, which means that they are only liable to a maximum rate of tax of 27·5 per cent., whilst other kinds of unearned income are liable to a maximum rate of 84 per cent.[1] There is therefore still a very considerable incentive for

---

[1] I cannot, incidentally, see the advantage of maintaining the distinction between earned and unearned income once the wealth tax is introduced—it means using two separate instruments for the same purpose. It is true that the present wealth tax rates are very moderate. The effective rates are only one-third of the Swedish rates and yield only about two-thirds of the schedule of the rates which I recommended. But it is better in that case to increase the rates of the wealth tax than to maintain the surcharge on unearned incomes.

converting income into capital gains, and thereby reducing the effective taxation of those who are in a position to benefit from it to well below the rates applicable to other tax-payers. Moreover, while the new law disallows certain of the exemptions provided in the original Act, the important loophole of exempting transfers of property through *inter vivos* gifts and through inheritance remains open, which means (if American experience is any guide) that only about one-third of the capital gains made by each generation come effectively within the tax net.

The effective rate of taxation of capital gains, even in the absence of any evasion, will thus not be 27½ per cent., but something more like 10 per cent.

There is undoubtedly some force in the contention that a high rate of tax on capital gains (such as the combined maximum rate of income tax and super-tax at present) might have highly undesirable economic effects. But this provides an argument not in favour of a discriminatory treatment of capital gains, but in favour of reducing the rates of taxation on ordinary income. There is no real justification for continuing the discrimination between income which takes the form of capital gains and other income; they both generate the same spending power, and both represent the same taxable capacity. The maintenance of the high marginal rates of income tax thus serves neither the interests of equity nor of revenue if it provides the justification for the continuance of the differential treatment of capital gains or for the maintenance of other equally serious loopholes in income tax legislation.

Elastic Definition of Expenses

Of the latter the wide and elastic definition of deductible expenses in the case of business profits is undoubtedly the most important. So long as the owners, directors and managers of businesses are able to pass off so much of their living expenses as business expenditure the incidence of taxation is bound to remain highly arbitrary, and the effective rate of taxation on the business community will remain much below the apparent rate. In my report I suggested that the range of deductible expenses should be confined to "expenses wholly, exclusively and unavoidably incurred in earning the profits of the year" (as against the present rule which permits the deduction of all such expenses which are "wholly and exclusively laid out or expended for the purposes of trade"). This would undoubtedly strengthen the hands of the Revenue in disallowing expenses of various kinds, though the extent to which it would succeed in bringing the treatment of business incomes fully into line with that of contractual incomes would depend on the interpretation given to it by the Courts. It is a matter for consideration therefore whether, in addition to a stricter general rule for deductible expenses, the deduction of particular types of expenses (such as the so-called "expense accounts," entertainment outlays, private cars, etc.), should not be explicitly prohibited.

A further source of loopholes arises from the non-integration, or incomplete integration, of total family wealth and income. To close this it would be necessary to aggregate a minor's income and property with that of the parents, and to include agricultural income and property within the scope of the Union income tax, wealth tax and capital gains tax. This latter reform may require a constitutional amendment which, however, might well be carried with the support of the States, if the revenue resulting from the extension of these taxes to agriculture were earmarked to the States.

Tax Evasion

Even if these loopholes are plugged, the administration of the system will not become effective until far-reaching reforms are introduced for checking tax evasion. The compulsory disclosure of Benami holdings,[1] the abolition of the system of blank transfers of shares and of bearer shares are essential ingredients of this. The introduction of a comprehensive reporting system on capital transactions and of a single comprehensive return for direct taxation are other necessary ingredients. These are matters within the purview of the Direct Taxes Administration Inquiry Committee recently set up and it is very much to be hoped that their recommendations will pay due regard to these basic requirements

[1] [Under Indian law, property can be registered in the name of a nominee (called "benamidar") without declaring the beneficial owner who, however, can protect his rights by keeping the deed to the property in his possession.]

of the efficient administration of an integrated tax structure.

In closing I should like to refer to two particular matters on which the Government of India has frequently been criticised for its failure to follow my original recommendations. One relates to the failure to reduce income tax to the maximum rate of 45 per cent. and the other to the extension of the wealth tax to companies.

45 per cent. Income Tax

I fully maintain the view that with a system of direct taxation of the kind I suggested, the maximum rate of income tax should not exceed 45 per cent. It should be evident, however, that this system has by no means been fully adopted; nothing has been done to tighten up business taxation, while the new taxes, owing to the truncated form in which they have been adopted, will only produce a fraction of the yield which they would have produced otherwise. In their present form, and with the present administrative techniques, the new taxes will hardly yield 20 crores.

In the absence of these gaps in legislation and with an efficient system of administration, they should produce at least 50 crores more—quite apart from the gain in income tax revenue, resulting from lower tax evasion, and the disallowance of certain classes of business expenses. As against that the loss of revenue resulting from the reduction of income tax to the ceiling rate of 45 per cent. would only amount to 18 crores. I doubt whether the interests which agitate for the latter would willingly exchange the present high rates of surtax for these further legislative and administrative changes which would involve them in additional taxation amounting to several times this sum.

Wealth Tax on Companies

As regards the wealth tax on companies, I would agree that this does not serve the same purpose of securing equity in the distribution of the burden of taxation as the wealth tax on individuals. On the other hand it is no more inequitable than the taxation of the profits of companies as such—they both involve the taxation of legal entities over and above the taxation of individuals who own them, and on principles which are unrelated to the taxable capacity of the owners. But considered as an alternative to a higher rate of profits taxation on companies, it has this to be said in its favour that its economic effects are distinctly more favourable than those of the profits tax. For it penalises firms who earn a low rate of profit on the capital which they employ and favours those firms whose earning power is high. It thus rewards efficiency and penalises inefficiency, and in the present stage of India's development, it is well worth while to offer special inducements to companies who use the resources at their command efficiently.[1] For this reason I should favour putting more of the burden of taxation on companies in the form of a wealth tax, and less in the form of a profits tax—i.e. of raising the wealth tax rate (which at $\frac{1}{2}$ per cent. is very low) if the combined income-and-profits tax rate on companies were correspondingly reduced.

[1] Many other features of the present company tax legislation, such as the excess dividend tax, run completely contrary to this and these ought to be abolished and the whole system of company taxation rationalised and simplified without delay.

11

THE ROLE OF TAXATION IN ECONOMIC DEVELOPMENT[1]

I. FISCAL ASPECTS OF DEVELOPMENT POLICY

1. Problems of taxation, in connection with economic development, are generally discussed from two different points of view,
which involve very different, and often conflicting, considerations:
the point of view of *incentives* and the point of view of *resources*.
Those who believe that it is the lack of adequate incentives which
is mainly responsible for insufficient growth and investment are
chiefly concerned with improving the tax system from an incentive point of view through the granting of additional concessions
of various kinds, with less regard to the unfavourable effects on
the public revenue. Those who believe that insufficient growth
and investment are mainly a consequence of a lack of resources
are chiefly concerned with increasing the resources available for
investment through additional taxation, even at the cost of worsen-
ing its disincentive effects.

2. In my opinion, a great deal of the prevailing concern with
incentives is misplaced: except in particular cases, such as in the
matter of tax concessions granted to foreigners which *may* increase
the inflow of capital from abroad[2], it is limitation of resources,
and not inadequate incentives, which limits the pace of economic
development. Indeed, the importance of public revenue from the
point of view of accelerated economic development could hardly
be exaggerated. Irrespective of the prevailing ideology or the
political colour of particular governments, the economic and
cultural development of a country requires the efficient and
steadily expanding provision of a whole host of non-revenue-
yielding services—education, health, communications systems,
etc., commonly known as "infrastructure"—which require to be
financed out of government revenue. In addition, taxation (or

[1] Paper presented to the Conference on Fiscal Policy of the Organisation of American States in Santiago, Chile, December 1962.
[2] But see below, para 13.

other compulsory levies) provides the most appropriate instrument for increasing savings for capital formation out of domestic sources.[1]

3. A feature that is common to most "under-developed" countries is the shortage of revenue which makes it impossible for them to provide essential public services on the required scale. The common assumption is that these countries are unable to lift themselves out of their predicament because of their very poverty. No doubt the "taxation potential" of a poor country—the proportion of its gross national product that can be diverted to public purposes without setting up intolerable political and social pressures—is generally lower, and in many cases appreciably lower, than that of a rich country. But more important, in my view, is the low "coefficient of utilisation" of that potential—due to bad tax laws, bad tax administration, or both—which in turn is only partly to be explained by lack of knowledge, understanding, or of administrative competence—it is also the result of resistance by powerful pressure groups who block the way to effective tax reform. Accelerated development in all such cases is predominantly a political issue: expert advice can point the way, but oevrcoming resistance to more effective policies for mobilising resources must depend on the collective will, operating through political institutions.

4. The inadequacy of public revenue has two important consequences. It forces undue economies precisely in those fields of public expenditure (like health and education) which are more easily sacrificed in the short run, but are the most important from the point of view of long run development. It also yields persistent budgetary deficits which force the monetary authorities to follow very restrictive credit policies (to protect the balance of payments and to limit the pace of inflation) which, in turn, have highly undesirable effects on the pace of economic growth, without fully compensating for the effects of the weakness

---

[1] The only alternative is inflation which, by comparison, is a clumsy and ineffective instrument for mobilising resources, since a large part of the "enforced" reduction in the consumption of the mass of the population, brought about by the rise in prices in relation to incomes, is wasted in the increased luxury consumption of the profit-earning classes. Also, it is difficult to conceive of inflation as more than a temporary instrument for mobilising resources: once wages rise in consequence of the rise in prices, the rate of price-inflation is accelerated, without securing any further savings.

in the state of public finances on the stability of the currency.

5. Many underdeveloped countries suffer, not only from lack of revenue, but also from an irrational scale of priorities in the allocation of public funds. Too much may be spent on the (real or fancied) needs of defence, or for ostentatious purposes of various kinds—such as public buildings and ornaments, lavish diplomatic missions, etc. There is nothing much we can say about all this, beyond noting the fact; and for the rest of this paper we shall consider the problem entirely from the revenue side: what determines a country's "taxation potential," and how can that potential be more fully exploited?

6. The "taxation potential" of a country, as above defined, is obviously greatly dependent on (i) real income per head; (ii) the degree of inequality in the distribution of income; (iii) the sectoral distribution of the national income, and the social and institutional setting in which the output of particular sectors is procured; (iv) the administrative competence, etc., of the tax-gathering organs of the government.

7. It is a commonplace to say that taxes can only be paid out of the "economic surplus"—the excess of production over the minimum subsistence needs of the population. Moreover, in so far as such surplus is not consumed by the people to whom it accrues, but is saved and invested, it can only be made available for the purposes of public expenditure at the cost of reducing the rate of capital accumulation of the community. This is likely to react adversely on the country's economic development except in so far as investment is diverted from inessential or "luxury" purposes (such as luxury housing) to purposes important for development. It would be more correct to say therefore that the taxation potential of a country depends on the *excess of its actual consumption over the minimum essential consumption of the population*, and on its investment which serves the needs of future luxury consumption.

8. In practice however the "minimum essential consumption" of a community cannot be defined or measured; it is not just a matter of the strict biological requirements of subsistence (which themselves vary greatly with climate and location), but of social conventions and habits, and the actual standard of living to which the bulk of the population of any particular community has

become accustomed. Since governments ultimately depend on the consent of the people whom they govern, it is impossible, as a matter of policy, to compress, by means of taxation, the actual standard of living *of the mass of the population* outside fairly narrow limits,[1] though in a progressive country, with a rising income per head, it is always possible to raise the taxation potential over a period by slowing down the rate of increase in consumption.

9. It can happen, on the other hand, that the amount of food or other necessities produced in a country is limited, not by the availability of natural resources (land), or by knowledge or ability, but by the customary way of life of the agricultural population, who prefer a maximum of leisure and a minimum of material income, and therefore work just hard enough to cover their immediate and traditional needs. In such circumstances, additional taxes levied on them would tend to make them work harder and produce more—i.e. to reduce their leisure, rather than their standards of material consumption. Taxation would then act as an incentive to produce more (as opposed to forcing the people concerned to consume less) and this may not encounter the same kind of resistance, particularly if the increase in taxation is a gradual one. From this point of view, the countries of Africa— where, in general, shortage of land is not a critical factor in agricultural production—are more favourably placed than the underdeveloped countries of Asia.

10. Excluding, however, the case where taxation may itself serve as an instrument for increasing real income per head, the taxation potential of a country will be strongly dependent on the prevailing inequality in the distribution of the national income, which in turn is closely linked to the relative importance of income derived from property, as against income derived from work, and to the degree of concentration in the ownership of property. As between two countries with the same real income per head, the accustomed standard of living of the bulk of the popula-

---

[1] If this were not so, and the taxation potential depended only on the absolute level of income, it would vary enormously with the actual level of real income per head. Supposing this potential were 10 per cent. in a country with an income per head of 60 dollars a year, it would be no less than 82 per cent. in a country whose income per head is 300 dollars a year. Yet even the richest countries with incomes per head of over 1,000 dollars a year find it very difficult to raise more than 30-35 per cent. of their G.N.P. in taxation.

tion will evidently be the lower, and the share of unnecessary, or luxury, consumption larger, in the country in which a larger share of total incomes accrues to a minority of wealthy individuals.[1]

11. From this point of view the underdeveloped countries of different regions of the globe (or even individual countries within the same region) show the widest differences. At one end of the scale a country such as India, with one of the lowest incomes per head of population, has a high ratio of property income in total income (a ratio that is comparable to that of the country with the highest income per head, the United States) and in consequence has a relatively high taxation potential in relation to real income per head.[2] At the other end of the scale there are some under-developed countries (particularly in Africa) in which incomes derived from property ownership are relatively insignificant and in which a wealthy property-owning class can hardly be said to exist.

12. The share of the national income of underdeveloped countries accruing to property is largely dependent on the pressure of population on the land, and on the prevailing system of land ownership. In the relatively over-populated countries of the Middle East and Asia, a considerable share of income accrues (or has accrued, until recently) to a wealthy land-owning class who not only pre-empt an undue share of the national income for their personal ends, but whose very existence bars the way to the development of a more efficient agriculture. Even in countries where the ratio of population to natural resources is relatively favourable (as in many of the countries of Latin America), where the fertile or accessible land is firmly held by feudal absentee owners, incomes derived from the ownership (as distinct from cultivation) of land account for a considerable share of incomes produced. This results in a high ratio of resources being devoted

[1] This is not to suggest that either the inequality of incomes or the inequality in standards of consumption could be eliminated by taxation. It is not possible or expedient to prevent the owner of the successful business from enjoying the fruits of his success during his lifetime—any more than it is possible to prevent scarce talent from earning its high reward in a Socialist state. But clearly, not all forms of economic privilege fulfil any positive social function—absentee landlords for example—and the experience of Western Europe and North America has shown that the consumption of the entrepreneurial class can be reduced within wide limits by means of progressive taxation without interfering either with incentives or the means of continued growth and accumulation. (It is consumption, rather than savings out of profits, which shows wide differences between countries, according to the nature of their tax systems.)

[2] Although the "coefficient of utilisation" of that potential appears to be rather low.

to unnecessary consumption. The same is true of countries, in the earlier stages of industrialization, where fortunes made in the course of industrial development virtually escape taxation, and where, in consequence, a much higher share of the profits earned in industry and commerce is devoted to personal consumption.[1] In view of this, expressed as a proportion of G.N.P., the "taxation-potential" of the semi-developed countries of Latin America (with incomes per head of $200–$300 a year) must be fully as large as that of the highly developed countries, although their actual tax revenue is typically only one-half as large.[2]

13. There are some underdeveloped countries which, while they lack a domestic property-owning class, have important foreign enterprises in their territory (for the exploitation of valuable minerals or the produce of plantations), so that a considerable share of their gross *domestic* product accrues to non-residents. Since the right of a country to tax all income arising within its jurisdiction is now firmly established, this provides a source of taxation

---

[1] In a study of Chile some years ago [reprinted in the second volume of these *Essays*, pp. 225–279] I found the following percentage allocation of the gross national product between various categories of expenditure:

Chile: Allocation of Gross National Product in 1953 by Categories of Expenditure, in Percentages

Gross domestic investment (public and private) 12		
of which		
Gross fixed capital formation 9		
Increase in stocks 3		
Government current expenditure 11		
Personal consumption 77		
of which		
Wage and salary-earners (69 per cent. of active population) .. 37		
Self-employed (31 per cent. of active population) 18		
Recipients of profits, interest and rent 22		

Total 100

The total share of property in G.N.P. was 34 per cent. of which direct and indirect taxation took up little over 12 per cent. (i.e. 4·5 per cent. of G.N.P.) and about one-fifth (or 7·5 per cent. of G.N.P.) was saved. If an effective system of taxation had existed which compressed property owners' consumption by one-half, this would have released resources sufficient to double Government current expenditure, or alternatively to increase gross fixed capital formation by 125 per cent.

In the highly industrialized countries of the U.S. and the U.K., the share of the G.N.P. accruing in the form of gross profits, interest and rent is much smaller (less than 25 per cent. in 1953) and the proportion paid in taxation much greater. Property-owners' consumption accounted for only about 7·5 per cent. of G.N.P. in the U.K. in 1953 as against Chile's 22 per cent.

[2] Tax revenue accounts for 9 per cent. of G.N.P. in Mexico, 14 per cent. in Chile, 10 per cent. in Brazil, 16 per cent. in Venezuela (excluding oil royalties).

that is essentially similar to that of a wealthy domestic property-owning class. There is a danger however that owing to the comparative ease with which this source can be tapped (by means of export duties, or taxes on income and profits) such taxation may be carried to the point where it inhibits the development of export industries which may be vital to the development of the economy.[1] On the other hand, many underdeveloped countries have recently been competing with one another in according all kinds of tax privileges and immunities to newly established foreign enterprises in an attempt to attract foreign capital to their own territory, with adverse consequences on their ability to collect revenue. Whilst it can plausibly be argued that an underdeveloped country gains from the inflow of foreign capital even if the income accruing from the investments is left untaxed—owing to the wage and salary incomes generated as a result, and the increased export earnings—it is an uncertain matter how far the total flow of capital investment from the developed to the underdeveloped areas is enhanced in consequence of such policies, and, if it is not, such "beggar-my-neighbour" policies of stimulating development deprive the underdeveloped countries of revenue without any compensating benefit.[2]

14. Underdeveloped countries differ also as regards the relative magnitude of the "non-monetised" or subsistence sector, and the "monetised" or market-exchange sector, as well as the nature of the prevailing type of enterprise in each. The most appropriate forms of taxation will differ as between an economy where commercial and manufacturing activities are carried on by small traders and one where they are concentrated in the hands of large-scale business enterprises. Similarly, the prevailing forms of land tenure, the nature of social and family relationships, the extent of economic inequality, etc., call for differing methods of taxation of the subsistence sector. The general tendency in most underdeveloped countries is to throw a disproportionate share of the burden of taxation on the "monetised" or market sector and an insufficient amount on subsistence agriculture. The reasons

[1] It is said, for example, that the excessive taxation of the foreign owned copper mines of Chile was largely responsible for the decline in the share of Chile in the world copper market.

[2] This point will be further discussed in paragraphs 36-8, below.

for this are partly administrative and partly political—taxes
levied on the agricultural community are far more difficult to
assess and collect and are socially and politically unpopular
because they appear unjust—the people in the "subsistence
sector" are, individually, always so much poorer than the people
in the market sector. Yet for reasons set out in paragraphs 17-18,
below, it is the taxation of the agricultural sector that has a vital
role to play in accelerating economic development; the disproportionate taxation of the "monetised" or market sector tends to
retard economic progress by reducing both the sources of and the
incentives to accumulation.

15. The general conclusion is that the efficient utilisation of the
taxation potential of an underdeveloped country raises problems
which vary with the circumstances of each country, though certain
features may be common to all of them. The extent and importance of a domestic landowning class; the nature of enterprise in
the secondary and tertiary sectors; the role and importance of
foreign enterprise; and finally the competence and integrity of
tax administration; are the main issues in this connection.

16. In the remaining sections of this paper we shall consider
separately the issues raised by (i) the taxation of the agricultural
sector; (ii) the role of indirect (commodity) taxation; (iii) direct
taxation of income and capital; (iv) the taxation of foreign
enterprises; (v) compulsory savings; and (vi) problems of tax
administration.

II. THE TAXATION OF THE AGRICULTURAL SECTOR

17. The most important common feature of underdeveloped
countries is that a high proportion of the total population is
occupied in the so-called "primary" or subsistence agricultural
sector; indeed, the proportion of the population engaged in the
provision of food supplies for domestic use is the best available
index of the stage of economic development of a country. In the
poorest and most backward economies it reaches 80-90 per cent.;
in the relatively poor but semi-developed economies it is around
40-60 per cent.; in the highly developed areas it is 10 per cent. or
less. This means that, as development proceeds, the proportion of
the working population engaged in producing food for domestic

consumption is steadily reduced, and the proportion engaged in manufacturing, commerce and services is steadily increased. In order to make this possible, the proportion of food produced on the land which is *not* consumed by the food producers must steadily increase; this, in turn, inevitably involves that each family engaged in food production should sell a steadily larger part of its output for consumption outside the agricultural sector. Unless this happens, it is impossible for the non-agricultural sector to expand so as to occupy an increasing proportion of the community's manpower. Such an expansion of the "agricultural surplus" cannot be relied upon to arise automatically as part of the over-all process of growth in the economy. Economic incentives do not operate in the same way in the "subsistence sector" as in the case of industry and commerce. A shortage of food is not likely to call forth increased production; a rise in the price of locally-produced food may even lead to a *decrease* of the amounts which are offered for sale, since it may cause the agricultural families to reduce their amount of work (or increase their own consumption) if their own needs for things which can only be procured with money can now be satisfied in exchange for a smaller quantity of foodstuffs. But since, on account of the nature of food as a primary necessity, a very large proportion of the urban worker's income is spent on food—a proportion moreover which is all the higher the higher are food prices relative to urban wages—it is the marketable supply of foodstuffs which limits the effective demand for the products of the non-agricultural sectors. Hence it is the growth of the demand for labour outside agriculture which is limited by the proportion of food production which goes to the market (as against the food consumed by the food producers themselves), and not the other way round.

18. It follows that the taxation of agriculture, by one means or another, has a critical role to play in the acceleration of economic development since it is only *the imposition of compulsory levies on the agricultural sector itself* which enlarges the supply of "savings" in the sense required for economic development. Countries as different in their social institutions or economic circumstances as Japan and Soviet Russia have been similar in their dependence on heavy agricultural taxation (in the case of Japan, through a

land tax; in the case of Soviet Russia, through a system of compulsory deliveries at low prices) for financing their economic development.

19. An annual tax on land, expressed as a percentage of the value of the produce per acre, is the most ancient form of taxation both in Europe and in Asia. Up to the beginning of this century the land tax still provided the principal source of revenue in the countries of the Middle East, in India and in many other areas. (In Europe, its relative importance had been declining for a century or so, as a result of the diminished relative importance of agriculture in the total national income.) Since that time, however, political pressures, combined with monetary changes, have succeeded almost everywhere in "eroding" the weight of this tax almost completely, and its rehabilitation now faces heavy political and administrative obstacles. Yet there can be little doubt that, with heavier agricultural taxation, the rate of development of all these countries could be much accelerated.

20. The main political objection to this tax is that it is socially unjust in its incidence, since (taking needs into account) it hits the poor far more heavily than the rich farmer. However, it would be possible to avoid the anti-social features of the tax by making it a *progressive tax*, varying with the total size of family holdings. Since, in most countries that are relatively over-populated and in which land is scarce, the distribution of the ownership of land is very uneven (with something like one-half of the available land being owned by 10 per cent. or less of the agricultural families in typical cases) it is quite possible to exempt the very small farmer from this tax altogether and yet collect adequate revenue by making its incidence progressive on the owners of the larger holdings. Nevertheless, a progressive land tax naturally raises the most fierce resentment in all countries where a landowning class exists, and, to my knowledge, it has not yet been put into practice anywhere.

21. Another objection frequently made against a land tax is that it requires relatively frequent periodic reassessment of each individual holding—a task which is extremely costly and difficult to perform. It would be possible, however, to assess the potential fertility of individual pieces of land *in relation to the national or*

regional average on the basis of more or less permanent criteria (such as average annual rainfall, irrigation, slope and inclination of the land, porousness or other qualities of the soil, etc.), and once this work of evaluation of "potential relative fertility" is accomplished, it need not be repeated at frequent intervals. On the other hand the actual assessment to tax of each holding could be changed year by year by estimating the average value of output per acre for the country or region as a whole,[1] and multiplying this by the coefficient which relates the fertility of any particular acre to the national average.

22. It would be technically feasible, therefore, to revive the ancient land tax in a way that would make it both more effective and more in keeping with present day conceptions of equity by (i) a system which assessed the potential yield of any particular piece of land not in terms of the actual value of output, but in relation to the yield of the *average* land in any particular region; (ii) by making the tax a progressive one, the effective rates of which varied with the total value of land-holdings of the family unit. Such a tax would preserve the merit of the ancient land taxes in that it would be a tax on the "potential output" rather than on the actual output of any piece of land, meaning by "potential output" the *output which the land would yield if it were managed with average efficiency*. Thus the inefficient farmer whose production is less than the average for the region and for the type of land concerned would be penalised, whereas the efficient farmer would be correspondingly encouraged. Such a tax on potential output is far superior in its economic consequences to any tax based on actual income or profit; and it is technically feasible to impose it in the case of agriculture (where the nature and quality of land provides a measurable yardstick) in a way which is not feasible for other types of economic activity. It would thus give the maximum incentive for efficient farmers to improve their land and expand their output; it should also greatly encourage the transfer of land ownership from

[1] One way of doing this is by making an estimate of the total output of foodstuffs for the country or region and then dividing it by the estimate of the number of cultivable acres in that region. Once statistical estimates had been made for a sufficient number of years, the average value of the produce per acre could be calculated as a moving average of, say, the past five years. In years of drought the tax could be remitted altogether either on a local or a national scale, as the case may be.

inefficient to efficient hands, and thereby raise the average productivity of land nearer to that obtained by the best-managed farms.[1]

23. Another important advantage of a tax on these lines is that it would operate as a potent instrument of land reform, and its efficiency in this respect could be enhanced to any desired extent by increasing the rate of progression of the tax. It could be made to operate so as to induce the owners of large estates—particularly when the tax schedule is expressed in terms of *effective* rates, rather than *marginal* rates—to sell part of their holding in order to bring themselves into a lower tax bracket, thereby making the distribution of land ownership more equal and at the same time creating a freer market in land. In many countries, agricultural stagnation is largely the result of absentee ownership, and of the unwillingness of existing owners to part with any of their possessions, even if they are incapable of putting their land to good use. By making the land market more fluid, a progressive land tax would enhance the chances of able and energetic cultivators to get hold of the land.

24. In some underdeveloped regions—as, e.g., in most areas of Africa—the traditional social customs and the prevailing system of land tenure etc. have made the establishment of a system of an annual land tax hitherto impossible. Instead, resort was generally had to an inferior substitute—the poll tax—which is levied simply on the basis of the numbers of adult males in each region. The great advantage of the poll tax is the ease of assessment; and, in countries where there is not much economic inequality in the rural areas, this tax is not so obnoxious as it would be in older, over-populated countries where a high degree of economic inequality prevails. Nevertheless, a poll tax can never fulfil the same functions as a land tax based on the *potential* fertility of land. A poll tax, unlike a land tax, does not give the same incentives to improve cultivation; it does not make for greater fluidity in the ownership and/or occupation of the land. And because it can take into account economic inequality, a land tax is not only capable of yielding a much larger revenue than a poll tax, but it should also be politically more acceptable.

[1] A tax reform on these lines would of course be the more efficacious in raising agricultural productivity if it were combined with other measures for improving agricultural productivity—e.g. the provision of cheap credit facilities, the institution of agricultural extension services, etc.

25. The importance for economic development of an efficient system of taxation of the agricultural or subsistence sector of the community cannot be over-estimated. In the absence of a direct tax on the subsistence sector—whether in the form of a land tax or a poll tax—this sector can only be taxed indirectly through taxes on commodities which are bought by the agricultural sector. Such methods of indirect taxation can never fulfil the same function, however: they do not provide the same incentives for increased production or an increase in marketable supplies, and may even tend to retard the development of the rural regions. Since, moreover, indirect taxation cannot differentiate between various classes of consumers, and since only a small part of the real income of the subsistence sector may be absorbed by the consumption of products bought for money, the scope for such indirect methods of taxing the subsistence sector is strictly limited.

III. TAXES ON COMMODITIES

26. Whilst commodity taxes are not an adequate method for taxing the agricultural sector, they are bound to be one of the principal methods of taxing the economy at large and one of the principal sources of government revenue. As a method of taxing the "monetised" or exchange sector they are superior to direct taxes wherever the economy largely consists of small enterprises, with few employees in each; in these circumstances income tax is not a convenient or efficient instrument for taxing either the profits of the employer, or (through the P.A.Y.E., or deduction-at-source method) the wages and salaries of employees. To assess and collect taxes on commodities which pass through the frontier is relatively simple, particularly where imports and exports pass through a port. And, to an extent not always realised, such taxes may fall partly on the profits of *producers* or *suppliers* (domestic or foreign) and not only on the *consumers* of the taxed commodities.

27. Thus, in the case of commodities imported for domestic consumption, where particular imports are under the control of a single company, or a limited number of companies (either because the bulk of the local market is controlled by a single great merchanting house, or because the imports are controlled by

world-wide concerns, as with oil and petrol), the price to the domestic consumers tends to be fixed at the "optimum monopoly" price; so that it may not pay the importer to pass on the full incidence of the tax to the local buyer. In this case, the import duty is partly a method of taxing the profits of the importer (which is often a foreign company) and only in part a method of taxing the domestic consumer.

28. Similarly, in the case of exports of minerals or plantation products, an export duty may be a more effective method of taxing the profits of producing companies than an income tax, particularly where the local operating company is a subsidiary of a foreign company which is also its trading partner, so that the profits shown by the local company may be arbitrary. The danger is, however, that once export duties are imposed, the exigencies of revenue might lead them to be fixed at excessive levels with the result that the development of export industries is inhibited.[1]

29. Though it is possible to vary the rate of commodity taxes according to the degree of luxuriousness of the commodity, thereby introducing a certain progression into the tax system, the revenue potentialities of taxes on luxurious goods are limited, since total imports may be small and consumption may be substantially reduced by heavy taxation. To get maximum revenue, it is necessary to tax articles of mass consumption—cotton cloth, sugar, flour, beer, tobacco, kerosene, etc.—and this raises all the political difficulties associated with a reduction in the accustomed standards of living of the mass of the population. This is not a peculiar feature of such taxes, but of taxation in general. It is impossible to increase the amounts raised in taxation suddenly or substantially, without public resistance—whatever form the taxation takes—though of course any community is more ready to accept sacrifices the more it is convinced of their necessity.

30. There is finally a *general tax on sales* or on turnover, levied either at the retail stage, the wholesale stage, or at all stages of production and distribution. Varying forms of such taxes are a common feature of numerous countries, both developed and underdeveloped. The objections commonly made against such

---

[1] The expansion of the Ceylon tea industry is said to have been severely hampered through excessive taxation by means of export duties.

taxes are that they cause a great deal of distortion (particularly when they are levied at all successive stages); that they encourage the creation of vertical combinations, and that they are difficult to enforce; when the degree of evasion is large, it is productive of inefficiencies as well as of inequities in the tax system.

31. There is, however, one particular variant of such a tax which has much to recommend it, since it is capable of providing a firm base for the administration of the whole tax system; this is the *value-added tax*, i.e. a tax on the sales minus the purchases (of fuel and materials and possibly also of capital expenditure items) of each enterprise. Such a tax has already proved successful in some countries (e.g. in France or in Brazil) and its introduction is now under consideration by a number of European countries. A value-added tax is really a tax on the gross income generated by each enterprise (in the form of profits, interest, rent, wages and salaries) and for that reason it could be treated as a species of direct tax, as well as a streamlined form of a sales tax. Apart from the fact that it avoids the distorting features of the general sales tax, it is a more favourable tax, in its economic benefits, than a corporation profit tax, and could also be regarded as a partial substitute for the latter. It must be remembered that from a macro-economic point of view there is not much difference in the overall incidence of the value-added tax and of the corporation tax: both tend equally to be "shifted" if either is introduced in the place of the other, leaving the total amount of profits after tax in the economy the same. But the distribution of after-tax profits between individual enterprises is very different in the two cases. A value-added tax of equivalent yield would improve the position of those enterprises which paid most of the profits tax and worsen the position of those that paid little of it. In other words, it would alter the distribution of profits as between efficient and inefficient units; it would increase the reward of efficiency, and penalise inefficiency. The prevailing system of a high rate of profits tax combined with numerous exemptions—for depreciation, promotional expenditure, past losses, etc.—is really a tax on marginal profits and has the effect of "shielding" inefficient units from competition, and thereby limiting the growth of efficient units. Hence the substitution of a value-added tax for a

profits tax (even if it were partial) would have the same effect as the strengthening of price competition: it would tend to improve the allocative efficiency of the economy.

32. However, the most important advantage of a value-added tax probably lies in its *self-reinforcing character*, assuming the tax is universally applied to all enterprises and is appropriately administered. The tax could be defined as a tax on the receipts from sales less such expenditure (in the appropriate categories) as is properly certified by vouchers made out by the seller of goods, which must indicate the tax code number of the seller. Provided that the rate of tax is not too low (say, of the order of 10-15 per cent. rather than 2-3 per cent.) so that it is in the interest of each taxpayer to claim all exemptions for purchases, it would be simple, with the aid of modern electronic computers, to build up an independent source of comprehensive information on the total volume of sales of every enterprise (and of the total income of all kinds generated by them) from the information supplied by purchasing enterprises. This would provide a proper framework for the administration of all direct taxes (and not only the value-added tax). Moreover, it could have the great advantage, from the point of view of general economic planning, of providing an up-to-date transactions matrix (a continuing input/output table) for the whole economy, which in turn would form an invaluable basis for the calculation of the whole set of national accounts.[1]

IV. DIRECT TAXES ON INCOME AND CAPITAL

33. The role which progressive direct taxes on income and capital should play in the tax system necessarily varies with the stage of economic and social development. The experience of a wide variety of countries shows that taxes on income or profits can only be successfully imposed on large-scale enterprises or on the employees of such enterprises. In many undeveloped areas the bulk of income tax revenue comes from a few large business firms and from Government employees. The extension of the tax to small traders, artisans or professional persons meets with serious

---

[1] Cf. also "A Memorandum on the Value-added Tax," printed on pp. 266 ff. below.

administrative difficulties—as there is no way of ascertaining income where no proper books are kept, no regular accounts prepared or audited. It has often been suggested that a more promising way of bringing small and medium traders within the scope of direct taxation would be by means of a tax assessed on the value of their property—by means of a net wealth tax—since property (whether in the form of land and buildings, plant and equipment or stock-in-trade) is more difficult to conceal than income. However, in the few underdeveloped countries where graduated taxes on net wealth have been introduced (such as India and Ceylon) they operate with a large exemption limit, and they are intended as an additional form of taxation on wealthy individuals and not as a tax on small and medium business, so that there is no actual experience to show how successful such a tax would be in practice.

34. In "semi-developed" countries which possess large-scale enterprises engaged in industry and commerce, and where a wealthy domestic capitalist class exists, progressive taxes on income and wealth are potentially very important both for mitigating the growing economic inequalities between different classes (and the political and social tensions which are attendant on this) and for reducing the share of national resources devoted to socially unnecessary luxury consumption.[1]

35. There is hardly any "semi-developed" country, however, where an efficient system of personal taxation can be said to exist (with the exception of taxes on salaries and wages). In most countries of Latin America, for example, though nominal tax rates mount to fairly high levels—to levels comparable to those in the U.S. or the U.K.—the proportion of large incomes effectively paid in taxation, according to all available evidence, is considerably lower than that falling on small or medium incomes. This is partly due to defective tax legislation—e.g. many countries follow the so-called "cedular" system of income taxation which

[1] This objective cannot be attained by a graduated system of commodity taxation alone. Since the same commodities are bought by people of very different wealth—the richer people buying more *kinds* of goods and services, and not just more "luxurious" goods—and since many of the things on which the rich spend money cannot be effectively taxed—domestic service, foreign travel, antiques, etc.—the spending power of the wealthy classes can never be tapped by means of commodity taxes to anywhere near the same extent as by means of progressive taxes on income or wealth.

imposes a separate tax on different sources of income (and which leaves important sources entirely untaxed) instead of a single comprehensive tax on all income, as in the U.S. or Western Europe. In part it is due to prevailing legal institutions which permit anonymity in the ownership of wealth (mostly on account of the prevailing system of "bearer shares" in the case of companies, or the system of "benami" in India) and which prevent any effective taxation on incomes derived from capital or on wealth (either in the form of inheritance taxes or of annual taxes on capital). It is also due to sheer inefficiency (and, to an unknown extent, perhaps also of corruption) in administration, which prevents the existing provisions from being effectively enforced even to the limited extent to which the existing system of tax laws would permit.

36. In the context of Latin America the most important reform is undoubtedly the creation of a single uniform tax on the total income of individuals from all sources, based on a comprehensive notion of income which embraces all such gains or benefits which increase an individual's potential net worth over a period. Some Latin American countries already levy, in addition to the cedular tax, a supplementary tax—the "global complementary tax"— on the aggregate income of individuals. As the evolution of the British income tax has shown, however, it is not necessary to levy two separate taxes in order to have an effective progressive tax on total income. It is possible to merge the existing cedular system (whilst preserving its administrative advantages) into a single comprehensive tax by making provisional assessments under each schedule (with the maximum use of the deduction-at-source system) and adjusting the final liability on the basis of the over-all return. Whichever method is used, however, there is no justification for retaining different tax schedules and rates of progression for the different sources of income—except in so far as it is desired to differentiate between incomes from work and incomes from property; but this latter objective could be better secured through a supplementary tax on net wealth, discussed in paragraph 39, below. With regard to the profits of companies, on the other hand, it is best to follow the U.S. system of a separate corporation profits tax levied at a flat rate, which is separate from

the income tax liability of shareholders on the dividends distributed to them.

37. Effective income tax reform in Latin American countries has, in my opinion, four major requirements:

(a) The first is that the tax should be made comprehensive. It should encompass capital gains as well as income which takes the form of dividends, interest, etc. It should extend to income from land and houses, including the imputed rent of owner-occupiers. It should avoid exemptions, such as interest on government bonds or on mortgages, which at present undermine its effectiveness in so many countries.

(b) The second requirement is that it should treat the family rather than the individual as the basic economic unit for purposes of personal taxation. This means that the income of husband and wife and minor children should be aggregated for tax purposes (as is the case in France), but there should be generous personal allowances which differentiate the effective burden according to the size of the family. It is a matter for consideration whether this is best done by the adoption of the French "quotient system" (which divides total income according to the number of adult units, and taxes each separately) or by some variant of this which sets a minimum and a maximum to the tax allowance for each member of the family.

(c) The third requirement is that, as far as possible, tax should be deducted at source on each particular kind of income at some standard rate (which is preferably the maximum rate), any excess deductions being repayable when the final liability is computed. To protect the interests of the taxpayer, it is advisable that the government should pay interest on excess deductions for the whole period during which the taxpayer is out of pocket.

(d) The fourth, and perhaps the most important requirement, is that the rate schedule should be both simple and moderate. There is no point in starting to levy tax at a very small rate; 10 per cent. should be regarded as the minimum chargeable rate for the excess of income above the exempted amount; and there is no point in having too many steps. I think the schedule should provide for no more than 6-8 separate income brackets, any incomes in excess of a certain level being charged at a uniform rate. The rate of tax on the successive levels of income should rise by steps of 5 per cent. to a maximum of 40 to 45 per cent. It is an essential precondition of an effective and loophole-free system that the maximum rate of tax should not be an immoderate one; marginal rates of over 50 per cent. militate against the introduction of effective tax reform. Where nominal tax rates mount to very high levels (to 80 or 90 per cent. in a number of cases) it is, in practice, impossible to extend the tax to all forms of income (for example, to capital gains) or to get rid of the numerous exemptions. It is also impossible to secure the compliance of the taxpayer and to administer the tax laws effectively— high tax rates are often no more than an excuse for maintaining an inefficient system—and the amount of revenue lost to the State through a defective tax system is likely to be many times the revenue actually collected from individuals who are subject to the high marginal rates of tax.

38. It would go far beyond the scope of this paper to consider these requirements in more detail—the more so since the detailed requirements of tax reform vary considerably with the circumstances of each particular country. I am convinced, however, as a result of studying the problem in a number of countries,[1] that in all countries which have attained the stage of development at which the need for an effective system of direct personal taxation arises, there are no insuperable technical or administrative obstacles to its introduction, provided that the need is adequately recognised, and that the opposition from vested interests to the necessary legal and institutional reform can be overcome.[2]

---

[1] Two of these studies have been published. Cf. *Indian Tax Reform*, Report of a Survey (Ministry of Finance, New Delhi, 1956), and *Suggestions for a Comprehensive Reform of Direct Taxation*. Sessional Paper IV—1960 (Government Publication Bureau, Colombo, Ceylon).

[2] The most important of the necessary legal reforms is the abolition of the widely prevalent system of anonymity in mobile property (i.e. bonds, obligations, or ordinary

39. Apart from a tax levied on the income of individuals and of companies, an effective system of direct taxation also requires that there should be taxes levied on personal wealth, which could be administered conjointly with the income tax. Such a tax should be levied in two different forms. The first is a relatively small annual tax on the net wealth of the individual (which is now administered in a number of European countries, and in India and Ceylon) which is the most appropriate method of tapping the additional taxable capacity inherent in the possession of wealth as such. Clearly, as between different individuals who have the same income, the man who possesses property as well as income is better off, and has a higher taxable capacity, than the man who has no property. Since different individuals possess disposable wealth and money income in widely differing proportions, a tax assessed on net wealth, which is additional to income tax, is a much fairer method of allowing for such differences than the alternative method of charging income derived from property (the so-called unearned income) at a higher rate than income from work. Also, it has been the experience of many countries that a combined system, which levies an annual tax both on wealth and on income, improves the efficiency of the tax administration considerably, since it makes evasion and concealment more difficult than a system which levies tax either on income alone or on wealth alone. Here again an effective system requires that such an annual tax on wealth should be levied at moderate rates (starting at 0·5 per cent. per annum, with a total exemption for property under 10,000-20,000 U.S. dollars) and that the maximum rate should not exceed 1·5 or at most 2 per cent. per annum.

40. The other form of taxation on wealth arises in connection

shares.) So long as wealth can retreat into complete anonymity by the simple act of transferring the ownership of physical assets to legal entities, the titles to which are in the form of bearer shares, it is impossible to impose an effective and comprehensive system of income taxation or to have an effective wealth tax or inheritance tax. Whilst dividends can be taxed through some form of "coupon tax", the taxation of the gains made on the sale of securities is, in practice, impossible, and so is the effective taxation of gains on the sale of real property, since the owners of real property are also free to conceal their wealth through the device of owning property through holding companies. It would be possible to gain most of the advantages of a system of registered securities (such as obtained in the U.K. or the U.S.) by a provision which compels the holders of securities to keep them permanently deposited with certain designated banks which would keep an up-to-date register of all depositors, and would thus record the changes in the ownership of all securities.

with the gratuitous transfer of property from one generation of owners to the next. This generally takes the form of an inheritance tax which is levied in connection with the passing of property at death, though a number of countries recognise that gifts *inter vivos* form an easy method of inheritance tax avoidance, and levy a complementary tax on *inter vivos* transfers (usually called the gift tax) as well. The ideal system would be to levy a single tax on all gratuitous transfers which is payable by the individual recipient of the gift, bequest, or inheritance, and which is levied on a progressive scale, depending not on the size of the individual gift or legacy, but on the total wealth of the donee. Most countries recognise the need for inheritance taxes as a means of counteracting the tendency to an increasing concentration of wealth through the accumulation of successive generations. A system which levies the tax according to the wealth of the recipient, rather than the wealth of the donor, is evidently fairer, and is more conducive to the promotion of a wider distribution of ownership. However, its administration raises greater difficulties; and it can only be recommended as a feasible proposition to those countries which are prepared to maintain a comprehensive record of the personal balance sheets of all wealthy individuals. This is in any case necessary for the effective taxation of incomes derived from property (including the taxation of capital gains) and for an annual tax on net wealth, as well as for a tax on gratuitous transfers.

41. Apart from taxes on income, some Latin American countries impose considerable pay-roll taxes in connection with their social security systems. These raise difficult problems of their own which cannot be gone into here. It should however be pointed out that wide differences in the social security taxes of different countries (in the same way as wide differences in the systems of income and profit taxation) can be a potent source of distortion in the allocation of resources between countries; and if the countries of Latin America move towards economic integration, in an analogous way to the countries of the European Economic Community, it would be highly desirable to introduce greater uniformity in their systems of social security taxes as well as in their systems of taxation of income and profits.

V. TAXATION OF FOREIGN ENTERPRISES

42. The tax treatment of foreign enterprises and of foreign investment raises two distinct problems for under-developed countries. The first concerns the question of how far under-developed countries should go in the offer of special concessions—in the form of immunity from taxation, etc.—in order to attract foreign capital and enterprise to their country. The second relates to the most appropriate method of taxing the profits of foreign enterprises when they are not exempt. Both questions raise difficult problems as a result of developments which have occurred since the Second World War.

43. Foreign investment in its various forms holds out the best hope of accelerated development to many underdeveloped countries; it may be indispensable at critical stages of development when industrialization gives rise to greatly enlarged imports of equipment and materials but before there is any corresponding increase in export capacity to pay for these. Foreign enterprise may be indispensable also in imparting the know-how necessary for the efficient development of local industries. Moreover, in the case of many countries, the production and export of valuable minerals found in their area holds out the only hope of generating the "economic surplus" which is a necessary precondition for their internal development. For many countries, the production of minerals for export forms a considerable share of the gross national product and is the principal source of their public revenue. It is evidently in the interests of underdeveloped countries that the production of such minerals be developed, and that this should be followed up by the development of processing facilities which give rise to industrial development; it is better to export aluminium than crude bauxite, or refined copper than copper ore; it is better for oil-producing areas to have their own oil refineries, so as to export their oil in refined form. Most underdeveloped countries have neither the money nor the know-how to undertake such developments on their own; moreover, the marketing of many of these commodities is closely controlled by large international concerns.

44. On the other hand, it is broadly true that the amount of investment which the large international concerns are ready to

undertake, both in mining and in processing depends on their over-all view of the requirements of the world market, and their estimate of the annual growth of world consumption. It is therefore *a priori* unlikely that any special concessions (in the form of "tax holidays," etc.) granted by the producing countries are likely to have any appreciable effect on the *total* flow of international investment. They can have important effects, however, on its allocation: since most basic minerals are to be found in many different regions, it is naturally in the interests of international capital to develop them in those countries which offer the most favourable prospects, both from the point of view of production cost and also from the point of view of the tax treatment of the resulting gains. But this in turn tends to bring about an unhealthy competition in the offer of special concessions to foreign capital. Whilst any one country may stand to gain by the offer of such tax concessions, the very fact that various countries are in competition with one another for a larger slice of such investments will cause any new concession offered by one country to be copied by the others, so that in the end they are all deprived of the prospect of obtaining their due share from these developments, without any compensating benefit—the competing concessions will largely cancel each other out.

45. The situation is basically different when the concessions offered to foreign enterprise serve the purpose of developing domestic industries largely catering for the internal market. In such cases tax concessions may well have the effect of increasing the *total* flow of international investment—some particular project of developing a local textile mill, a cement factory or an assembly plant may appear sufficiently attractive when tax concessions are offered when it would not be attractive without them.

46. This question of how far underdeveloped countries *as a group* should go in offering privileged tax treatment to foreign investment (or, for that matter, to domestic enterprise) is therefore a complex one, which cannot in general be answered one way or the other. In cases where the concessions serve the purpose of increasing the aggregate flow of investment it is clearly to their interest, to forego additional tax revenue, even for a considerable number of years, since their rate of economic development may be

greatly enhanced as a result. But in other cases it is not; and, in view of the haphazard multiplication of tax privileges of various kinds in recent years, there is a clear case for international discussions possibly leading to conventions or agreements which would eliminate the element of unhealthy competition which undoubtedly exists at present. It is in the interests of under-developed countries as a group that the tax treatment—both the scope and the rates of taxation of enterprises and the nature and extent of tax holidays, etc., granted—should, as far as possible, be uniform, and that individual countries should not offer additional concessions except in agreement with the others.

47. The second important issue concerns the manner in which the profits of foreign enterprises engaged in production for export (or in the import trade) are to be taxed. The most satisfactory method is a tax on the profits arising from local operations. An export duty, as we have noted, can be a potent form of taxation, but it is not a satisfactory substitute for taxation on the basis of profits: if the export duty is heavy, it may have an inhibiting effect on development; if it is light, it cannot secure adequate revenue. Taxes based on profits are less discouraging to the foreign investor, precisely because their burden depends on the gains actually made; if the operations turn out to be unsuccessful (either because there are unexpected costs in local operations, or because the market conditions are unfavourable) the entrepreneurs are relieved of them.[1]

48. The problem with profit taxation, on the other hand, is to ascertain the true profit in all those cases where the resident operating companies are merely branches or subsidiaries of international concerns whose trading operations are not at "arm's length"—since they sell to (or buy from) non-resident companies belonging to the same group. The prices in such transactions are, in fact, internal accounting prices of the concerns; it is well known that an international concern operating through a chain of subsidiaries can easily "shift" its profit from one place to another by changing the price which the subsidiaries (or associated companies) charge to one another. So long as profits are everywhere

[1] It is for this reason that export duties, in many cases, are fixed in terms of some sliding scale, the incidence of which varies with the prices actually realised in relation to some average.

subject to tax and so long as the rates of taxation are not too different, the incentive for such "profit shifting" will not be strong, particularly when the rates of taxation are heavier in the countries where the parent companies are situated than in the under-developed countries where the branches and subsidiaries operate. But, since the war, international companies have made increasing use of the so-called "tax-havens"—they have established holding companies or subsidiaries in territories where the profits are not subject to tax (or only at nominal rates), or in countries which do not bring into charge the profits earned in the overseas operations of their resident companies.[1] The result has been that an increasing proportion of the profits made by such concerns has been syphoned into such tax-havens, thus depriving both the producing and the consuming countries of revenue.[2]

49. Thus the profits made in the extraction and processing of minerals may be understated by invoicing exports at unduly low prices. The profits made in the importation and local distribution of foreign commodities or services may be understated by invoicing imports at unduly high prices.[3]

50. Sooner or later, the arbitrary allocation of profits in the production or distribution of commodities which enter into international trade will make it necessary for countries to look *beyond* the accounts of the local companies and, if necessary, to impute profits to them based on an appropriate share of the total world profits of the companies which operate local branches or subsidiaries. Here again there is a fruitful field for international co-operation. If it were possible to get agreement between the

[1] For a description of the facilities offered by such "tax-haven" countries, cf. Gibbons, *Tax Factors in Raising International Business Abroad*, Harvard Law School, International Program in Taxation, Cambridge (Mass.) 1957.

[2] This problem is not peculiar to underdeveloped countries but affects the countries of the parent companies as well, as is shown by the current efforts of the U.S. administration to get U.S. tax legislation amended so as to bring the profits of foreign subsidiaries and associated companies within the scope of the U.S. corporation tax.

[3] In the case of the international oil industry, the tendency has been to fix the price-structure in such a way that the profits arising from the whole complex of international operations are concentrated on the production of crude oil, and not in refining and distribution of oil products. The reasons for this are partly to be sought in tax considerations (since the royalties paid to the governments of the oil producing countries qualify as a tax offset in the "parent" countries) and are partly political and strategic. But the result has been that the oil-producing areas have obtained more revenue than could have been obtained if a free competitive market had existed; whereas the oil consuming countries (both developed and underdeveloped) have been deprived of revenue (other than in the form of import duties or excise taxes).

various countries as to how they should deal with such problems, they could be dealt with far more effectively than if each country tried to act in isolation.

51. A related problem, which is perhaps best considered here and which has considerable importance for Latin American countries, is the question of the taxation of income received by residents from abroad. The majority of Latin American countries leave such income untaxed at present (though it is subject to with-holding taxes paid in the foreign country where the income originates). On the other hand, the prevailing practice in most countries with a developed global income tax is to tax the foreign income of residents as well as the income which originates in the country and accrues to non-residents; though, in the major-ity of cases (and as a result of the numerous double taxation agreements concluded since the war) the tax which is levied on the income in the country of origin is allowed as a credit against the domestic tax liability of the recipient of the income.

52. There is undoubtedly a strong case on equity grounds for extending the liability to income tax to income received from abroad and it is known that the residents of many Latin American countries own very substantial amounts of capital abroad. Indeed one of the frequent arguments against an effective tax reform is that it would "drive" capital abroad, to the detriment of the economy. The difficulty is the practical one of compelling residents to declare their foreign assets and the income received from these. The effective solution of this problem requires the co-opera-tion of the governments of those foreign countries where the assets are held. Some countries already provide such information on a mutual basis under international tax treaties, and such countries could no doubt be induced to provide the same service to Latin American governments as well. The question should also be explored how far it would be possible to follow the British system under which all foreign nominative securities (outside the Sterling Area) must be registered not in the owner's own name, but in a "recognised marking name", the name of one of the local financial institutions which deducts income tax at source from the dividends, etc., paid to the individual owner. If the co-operation of the U.S. and of some European countries could be

obtained in disclosing to particular Latin American governments the assets held in their territory by Latin American nationals, the governments should be in a position to ensure a fair degree of compliance with such a provision.

VI. COMPULSORY SAVINGS

53. A relatively new form of raising internal resources for development purposes which has recently been introduced in a number of countries (e.g. Turkey, Ghana, British Guiana, Brazil and some others) is compulsory savings. This obliges individuals and businesses to apply a certain percentage of their incomes to the purchase of interest-bearing but non-negotiable bonds which are repayable (together with accrued interest) after five, seven or ten years. The scheme is usually administered in conjunction with income tax, or (as in the case of Ghana) in conjunction with the purchase of cash crops by a marketing board. The advantage of the scheme, as against straightforward taxation, is that as people are merely asked to postpone their consumption and not forego it altogether, considerations of equity do not require the same kind of differentiation or graduation as in the case of income tax, and, in consequence, more substantial amounts can be raised at relatively modest rates. Thus the compulsory levy is generally imposed on wage and salary earners at a flat rate of 3 or 5 per cent. on the *whole* of income, though the obligation only extends to people whose incomes are above certain minimum levels. There may be a similar obligation on businesses and professional persons, generally with a higher rate of contribution.

54. It is possible to combine such a scheme with a lottery scheme (such as the "premium bonds" in the U.K.) which might make it more attractive to the majority, who are given a chance to win large cash prizes even before the bonds are due for redemption. But the lottery element makes the administration of this scheme far more complicated; also, it was found in some cases that there was a great deal of moral opposition (by the churches, trade unions and farmers' organisations) to a compulsory lottery.

55. It is possible also (though this requires far more administrative preparation) to make the scheme into a universal contributory pensions scheme, drawn up on an actuarial basis, whereby

the repayment of the compulsory loan takes the form of a pension upon retirement, graduated according to the amount of the contributions made during working life. A compulsory savings scheme which results in a universal old age pension scheme is likely to be far more popular than a scheme where the contributors are supplied with non-negotiable bonds repayable after a fixed number of years.

56. A scheme of this kind is only appropriate to underdeveloped countries which have already attained a stage of development which makes it possible to bring a considerable section of the population within the scope of direct taxation; or where there is a major cash crop (such as cocoa in Ghana) which is purchased by a central marketing board at fixed prices.

VII. THE PROBLEM OF TAX ADMINISTRATION

57. It cannot be emphasised too strongly that the efficacy of the tax system is not just a matter of appropriate tax laws, but of the efficiency and integrity of tax administration. In many under-developed countries the low revenue yield of taxation can only be attributed to the fact that the tax provisions are not properly enforced, either on account of the inability of the administration to cope with them, or on account of straightforward corruption in the administration. No system of tax laws, however carefully conceived, is proof against collusion between the tax adminis-trators and the taxpayers; an efficient administration consisting of persons of high integrity is the most important requirement for exploiting the "taxation potential" of a country.

58. One important condition for this is that the government departments concerned with the administration of taxes should not be over-burdened, and this in turn requires that complicated taxes should be avoided unless there is an administration able to cope with them. Yet in many countries there are hundreds of different taxes with a negligible yield—the cumulative result of the gradual accretion of imposts which have long since lost their justification, but which have never been formally withdrawn— the administration of which is a great deal more costly than the amounts collected. Indeed, there is no other field where bureau-cracy can be so cumbrous and absurd as in the administration of

taxes; and in many countries there needs to be an infusion of a new spirit, which makes it possible to apply modern techniques of business administration, before any major reform can be accomplished.

59. Many underdeveloped countries suffer both from an insufficiency of staff and from the relatively low grading of the staff of the tax administration departments. Persons of ability and integrity can only be found for these jobs if sufficient recognition is given to the importance of the tasks which they are asked to perform, and this should be fully reflected in their status, pay, prospects of promotion, etc. Any additional outlay incurred in improving the status and pay of the officials of the revenue department is likely to yield a very high return in terms of increased revenue.

12

WILL UNDERDEVELOPED COUNTRIES LEARN TO TAX?[1]

I

THE importance of public revenue to the underdeveloped countries can hardly be exaggerated if they are to achieve their hopes of accelerated economic progress. Whatever the prevailing ideology or political colour of a particular government, it must steadily expand a whole host of non-revenue-yielding services—education, health, communication systems, and so on—as a prerequisite for the country's economic and cultural development. These services must be financed out of government revenue. Besides meeting these needs, taxes and other compulsory levies provide the most appropriate instruments for increasing savings for capital formation out of domestic sources. By providing a surplus over recurrent expenditure, they make it possible to devote a higher proportion of resources to building up capital assets.

This is not to say that poor countries could or should finance their development programmes entirely by their own effort. The advanced countries with high incomes have an obligation to assist in the process by providing aid, and this obligation has been amply recognised—if not adequately implemented—in recent years. However, foreign aid is likely to be fruitful only when it is a complement to domestic effort, not when it is treated as a substitute for it.

The fact is that in relation to gross national product the tax revenue of the underdeveloped countries is typically much smaller than in the advanced countries. Whereas the "developed" countries collect 25 to 30 per cent. of their G.N.P. in taxation, the underdeveloped countries typically collect only 8 to 15 per cent.

Is this an ineluctable consequence of their poverty? Since taxation can be paid only out of the surplus of income over the

[1] Originally published in *Foreign Affairs* (New York), January 1963.

minimum subsistence needs of the population, most people believe that the proportion of the national income which a poor country can divert to communal purposes through taxation—without setting up intolerable social tensions—is much smaller than in a rich country. Two considerations show, however, that this is not the whole, or the main, explanation.

In the first place, though underdeveloped countries show enormous diversity in their economic and social set-up, they all— excepting the more primitive countries of Africa or Polynesia— show a degree of inequality in the distribution of income comparable to, if not greater than, that of the "developed" countries of Western Europe or North America. The statistical evidence is sketchy and not very reliable; yet such as there is all tends to show that the degree of concentration in the ownership of property is quite as great in the poor or semi-developed countries of the Middle East, Asia, or Latin America as in the countries of advanced capitalism. The share of the national income which accrues to property owners of all kinds is probably appreciably larger in countries like Mexico, Chile, India, Turkey or Persia than in the United States or in Britain.

Hence, while their average income per head is low, the fraction of their national income which accrues to a small minority of individuals is frequently greater than in the rich countries; and a much higher proportion of that income is devoted to personal consumption, and a lower proportion to savings. This is partly a reflection of the failure of their taxation systems, but partly it follows from the fact that—depending on the degree of underdevelopment and the pressure of population on the land —a considerably greater part of wealth comes from the ownership of land, and a smaller proportion from industrial or commercial capital; and the owners of land, unlike the owners of industrial or commercial enterprises, are high spenders, not high savers. In a study which I made of Chile some years ago (one of the countries for which detailed national income statistics are available), I found that the proportion of the G.N.P. which was "taken up" by the consumption of property-owners was over 20 per cent.— probably three times as high a proportion as that of the United States. This shows that the *level* of the national income per head is not a good indicator of taxable capacity: a poor country may have a high taxation potential if a relatively large part of its resources is nevertheless devoted to unessential or luxury consumption.

The second important consideration is that the incidence of taxation in most underdeveloped countries is regressive—far more regressive (or far less progressive) than that of the developed countries. Indirect taxes, the bulk of which normally fall on articles of mass consumption, make up a much higher share of the total revenue, and far more of the income tax revenue falls on salaries and wages, upon which is collected by the deduction-at-source method, and often operates with a very low exemption limit.[1] As far as the mass of the people are concerned, the burden of taxation as measured by the percentage of income taken in tax is probably just as large in the low-income countries (at least in the urban sectors) as in the rich countries.

The shortfall in revenue is thus largely a reflection of failure to tax the wealthier sectors of the community effectively. Though progressive income taxes and inheritance taxes exist on paper in most of the underdeveloped or semi-developed countries—sometimes imposed at high nominal rates, mounting to 80 per cent. or more on the highest incomes—there are few cases in which such taxes are effective in practice. This is evinced by the glaring discrepancy between the amount of incomes of various types—profits, rents, etc.—that can be presumed to exist, judging from national output statistics, and the incomes declared in tax returns or computed on the basis of tax receipts. In the developed countries, the national income estimates based on the "income" and the "output" methods of computation are more easily reconciled, and do not reveal such glaring differences. It is probably not an exaggeration to say that the typical underdeveloped country collects in direct taxation (excluding the taxation of wages and salaries) no more than one-fifth, possibly only one-tenth, of what is due—or rather what would be due if the tax laws themselves did not accord wide legal loopholes through exemptions and omissions of various kinds.

[1] In Turkey, for example, the exemption limit for income tax is around $100 a year for a single person.

This broad generalisation requires, of course, a great deal of qualification when applied to individual countries or regions. There are some countries which have been conspicuously unsuccessful in imposing taxes on the wealthy classes—chiefly, I think, the countries of Latin America—for whom the above picture may even be an understatement. There are others, chiefly the ex-colonies of the British Empire, which have only recently gained independence but inherited relatively high standards of tax administration from their colonial days: for these it may be an exaggeration. Some countries have made notable efforts in recent years to improve both their legislation and their tax administration. In others the situation is deteriorating, owing to the paralysing effect of corruption, or to the steady erosion of ancient taxes; there the weight of direct taxation may be less now than it was 50 or 100 years ago.

II

Another source of untapped taxable capacity in many under-developed countries is to be found on the land. The agricultural or "subsistence" sector, which typically accounts for one-half or more of the national output, virtually escapes taxation at present,[1] owing to the "erosion" of the ancient land taxes of the countries of the Middle East and Asia. It is true that the peasantry is poor everywhere and its capacity to pay is limited. It is also true, however, that in most places—at least in most of the over-populated regions—only a proportion of the produce accrues to the cultivator, the rest accrues to the owner of the land, or to some intermediary tenant; and as has been known since the time of Ricardo, the incidence of land taxes necessarily falls on the landlord. Despite recent measures of land reform in countries like India, the distribution of land-holdings remains very uneven, with no more than one-half, or possibly two-thirds, of the land in the hands of genuine owner-cultivators.

The land tax is one of the most ancient forms of taxation in both Europe and Asia, and up to the early part of this century it

---

[1] This is not meant to apply, of course, to plantation agriculture or to the production of cash crops for export by native farmers who may be heavily taxed through export levies or through the price policy of a marketing board.

still provided the principal source of revenue in the countries of the Middle East, India and Japan. Since that time, however, political pressures, combined with monetary changes, have succeeded in virtually eliminating it; the tax continues to be collected in most places, but on the basis of completely out-of-date valuations. Its rehabilitation now faces heavy political and administrative obstacles. Traditionally, the land tax was one-tenth of the value of the produce of the land. But its current yield in India is only about 1·5 per cent.; in Turkey only 0·2 per cent. Yet, as the economic history of Japan demonstrates, the taxation of land can be a very potent engine of economic development, though its importance cannot be measured adequately by its money yield. This is because the land tax yields not just revenue, but the right kind of revenue; it enlarges the supply of foodstuffs to urban areas, and thus the amount of employment that can be offered outside agriculture without creating inflation. It also promotes agricultural efficiency. It encourages the more efficient use of the land as well as the transfer of ownership from relatively inefficient to efficient cultivators.

It is possible, moreover, to "streamline" this tax in accordance with more modern notions of equity by making it a progressive tax, graduated according to the total value of the land held by an individual and his family, so that the burden is concentrated on the large landowners. A scheme recently proposed in Turkey by the State Planning Organisation would have exempted holdings of less than 2 hectares altogether, while larger holdings would have borne a graduated charge rising from 5 per cent. on holdings of less than 10 hectares to 15 per cent. on holdings of 50 hectares or more. Since the top 1·5 per cent. of agricultural families own more than 21 per cent. of the land (and a further 14 per cent. of families another 31 per cent.), this scheme would have made it possible to collect the revenue needed for the new five-year development plan by a levy which, without being exorbitant, would have avoided the anti-social features of the old land tax. However, the Cabinet, which approved the development plan, has refused to sanction the scheme for financing it, and recently it was reported that all the top officials of the Planning Organisation have resigned in protest. In countries where a powerful landowning class exists, the prospects for effective land taxation do not appear more promising than the prospects for land reform.

III

When countries pass to a higher stage of development, as the more advanced regions of Latin America have done, industrial and commercial wealth (which is less tangible) assumes increasing importance. The taxation of that wealth raises more complicated problems, while any genuine measure of reform designed to tap it meets with the same kind of political resistance.

The effective administration of income tax on individuals or corporations requires a carefully-thought-out legal code and a corps of capable and honest administrators. It is often argued that these taxes are really too difficult for the less developed countries to cope with, and it would be better if they concentrated on simpler forms of taxation. But the fact is that there is no suitable alternative. A graduated system of commodity taxation can never succeed in mitigating growing economic inequalities (and the political and social tensions which are associated with this process), or in reducing the resources devoted to socially unnecessary luxury consumption, in the same manner as progressive taxes on income and wealth. The same commodities are bought by people of very different means—the richer people buying more kinds of goods and services, and not just more luxurious goods; and many of the things on which wealthy individuals spend money cannot be effectively taxed—for example, domestic service, foreign travel, antiques, and so on.

It is also argued that the progressive taxation of industrial and commercial wealth, unlike that of landed wealth, slows down the rate of development by reducing both the means and the incentives to accumulation. In the United States or in Britain, the argument runs, progressive taxation was imposed only after the process of industrialisation was largely completed—not in the middle of the Industrial Revolution. It does not follow, however, that if the system of progressive taxation had been imposed earlier the course of economic development would have been very different. It is true that profits have always been the main source of industrial and commercial capital accumulation. But experience has shown that taxes on profits affect consumption out of profits far more than business savings. The reason for this is that, for a successful businessman or corporation (in developed or undeveloped countries alike), the requirements of business expansion take precedence over the desire for higher consumption; the money that the owners take out of a business is generally no more than what is left after the business' own needs are satisfied. Otherwise it would be difficult to explain why fast-growing businesses should invariably plough back so much more of their profits than slow-growing businesses, or why the proportion of profits distributed as dividends should be so much less in countries where the taxation of profits is high than where it is low.

If the effects of increased public spending are taken into account, and not only the reduction in private spending, and if public money is wisely spent (admittedly this is not something that can be taken for granted), it is difficult to maintain that the reduction in inequality through progressive taxation puts a brake on economic development. It may do the very opposite. For, in countries where luxury spending is not effectively curbed, the pattern of investment gets distorted. Too much of the capital accumulation is taken up by the expansion of industries and services which mainly cater for the rich. This kind of "growth" merely serves to make the rich even richer; it does not improve the standard of living of the masses of the population.

There are basic differences in the way capitalism developed in North America and the way it is now developing in the countries of Latin America. They cannot be explained merely by the differences between fiscal systems. Long before progressive taxation was invented, a whole set of attitudes and circumstances forced American business to concentrate on developing products for the mass market; the Woolworths and the Fords made their fortunes by providing goods within the reach of the many and not for the better satisfaction of the few. In Latin America development takes a different course. I know of no Latin American millionaire who made his fortune in the five-and-ten business. But vast fortunes were made in providing luxuries for a class whose members prospered largely by catering for each other. Whatever the true cause of such differences, it becomes vastly more important to apply progressive taxation, as a deliberate corrective to spontaneous economic forces which produce steadily growing inequality.

IV

Nor would it be correct to say that an effective system of progressive taxation cannot work because of the lack of administrative competence or honesty of officials, or the lack of a sense of social obligation of taxpayers. It is true that in most underdeveloped countries—though conditions vary a good deal—revenue officials are grossly underpaid, revenue departments are frequently understaffed, and are short of men of ability and training. Straightforward corruption must be widespread. However, it is impossible to find out how much of the shortfall in revenue is due to this, as against sheer inefficiency or incompetence, or a laxity in the enforcement of the law which is tolerated, if not inspired, in higher quarters.

But the experience of many countries which suffered from much the same evils in the past shows that corruption and inefficiency *can* be eradicated if sufficient attention is given to the creation of corps of permanent officials[1] whose pay, status and prospects of promotion are high enough to attract the best talent, and also high enough to establish the professional standards and etiquette associated with a public service that enjoys a privileged social status. The example of the Chinese Maritime Customs has shown what the creation of a well-paid body of permanent officials could accomplish, even in a country where corruption was as deeply ingrained as it was in Imperial China. Of course, no underdeveloped country has the manpower resources or the money to create a high-grade civil service overnight. But it is not sufficiently recognised that the revenue service is the "point of entry"; if they concentrated on this, they would secure the means for the rest.

It is true that the prevailing systems of income taxation in the United States, Britain, or Canada rely heavily on the voluntary compliance of the taxpayer; for important categories of income,

---

[1] In many Latin American countries the top-ranking officials of the tax administration—including district commissioners or even their deputies—are not permanent civil servants at all, but are appointed on the spoils system, changing with each administration.

the revenue authorities mainly depend on the taxpayers themselves to supply information, the accuracy and completeness of which is not automatically or systematically checked. But there is no technical necessity for this. One could conceive of a system in which transactions in capital assets and income payments of all kinds are systematically reported, in the same way as wage and salary payments are now reported. With the aid of modern business machines, it would be possible to keep a record of the ownership of all property—land and houses and stocks and shares—and to keep a running check on changes in the personal balance sheet of all wealthy individuals. Each taxpayer could be asked to give a statement of his net worth each year, and not only of his income, and the return on this wealth could be independently checked if all property were registered and all changes in property registration were automatically reported in the name and the tax-code number of the beneficial owner. Tax administrators know that the discovery of changes in an individual's net worth over a period is the most effective method of bringing to light concealment of income. In advanced countries, such investigations are made sporadically, as a spot-check on returns or in cases where fraud is suspected; there is no reason why they should not be made systematically in countries where taxpayers are less honest or compliant.

V

It would be wrong to assume, therefore, that there are insuperable technical obstacles to the introduction of any effective system of progressive taxation. It is not beyond the wit of man to devise laws and administrative procedures which would oblige even the most recalcitrant (or cunning) Latin American or Middle Eastern millionaire to surrender a reasonable share of his income or wealth to the state in taxation. But that is not to say that, in the countries where such reforms are most needed, they have much chance of acceptance. The secrecy and anonymity of property is regarded as sacred and is safeguarded by the system of "bearer" shares which effectively hides the identity of the shareholders of companies and which enables even the ownership of real property to be concealed through holding companies. Any suggestion that ownership should be disclosed and regularly reported to the government—as is done, for example, in the Scandinavian countries—would be unthinkable.[1] No doubt, secrecy of property ownership is a far more valuable safeguard in countries which are politically unstable than in the settled democracies of Western Europe or North America. But political instability is itself a consequence of economic and social conditions which result from the unbridled greed of an oligarchical ruling class.

To the detached observer, fiscal reform undoubtedly appears as the most appropriate instrument for transforming the feudal or quasi-feudal régimes which inhibit the healthy evolution of so many of the underdeveloped countries and prevent them from following the path towards the kind of mass-prosperity civilisation which has evolved in Western Europe and North America. But the advocacy of fiscal reform is not some magic potion that is capable of altering the balance of political power by stealth. No doubt, expert advice on tax reform can be very useful in making men of good will—ministers or officials—conscious of the precise nature of the legislative and administrative changes that are required. But what can actually be accomplished does not depend merely on the individual good will of ministers or on the correct intellectual appreciation of the technical problems involved. It is predominantly a matter of political power.

In a successfully functioning democracy, the balance of political power is itself a reflection of a continuous social compromise between the conflicting interests of particular groups and classes, which shift automatically in response to varying pressures. But experience has shown that in underdeveloped countries, with a predominantly ignorant and illiterate electorate, parliamentary institutions do not, in general, work in this way. Periodic elections and multi-party systems are not instrumental in securing continuous or peaceful social adjustment. Power remains in the hands of certain dominant groups, irrespective of whether one party or

---

[1] In Turkey, one of the acts of the military dictatorship that followed the Menderes régime was to introduce a measure for a single compulsory declaration of personal wealth. But Parliament insisted that these declarations should be deposited in sealed envelopes with public notaries and should not be opened for at least two years. There is now strong pressure in Parliament for a further provision to the effect that after two years have elapsed, the envelopes should be returned unopened to the taxpayers. In Mexico when it was suggested that some similar provision would be needed for the proper enforcement of inheritance taxes, the Congress responded by abolishing the inheritance tax altogether.

another is in office or whether there is an elected government or a dictatorship of some kind. The history of the last ten years produced plenty of examples—in Asia or in Latin America—of dictatorships replacing parliamentary systems, or vice versa, without significantly altering the underlying balance of power in society.

In many areas of the Middle East and of Latin America, revolutionary pressure continues to build up, as a result of blind opposition to overdue social reforms. Ostensibly it is motivated by fear of Communism: in reality it serves to bring Communism nearer. The problem which has to be solved, and to which no one has yet found a satisfactory answer, is how to bring about that change in the balance of power which is needed to avert revolutions without *having* a revolution. Can it be brought about by outside pressure —by making internal social and economic reforms the quid pro quo for external aid, as in the Alliance for Progress? Or can it be brought about by some organised attempt at the political re-education of backward ruling classes—a kind of Westernised version of Chinese brainwashing? History does provide cases— nineteenth-century England is an obvious one—of a ruling class voluntarily relinquishing privileges for the sake of social stability. It did so in an instinctive appreciation of its long-run interests. But when ruling classes evince no signs of such instinct, can they be made to acquire it?

13

A MEMORANDUM ON THE VALUE–ADDED TAX[1]

1. The purpose of this memorandum is to discuss the possible advantages of a value-added tax, introduced in replacement of other taxes, from three points of view: (i) the administration of the tax system and as an aid to economic planning; (ii) income distribution and economic efficiency; (iii) as an aid to exports. Under the last head, we shall also consider the merits of introducing a value-added tax for the purpose of the payment of a general subsidy on wages to employers.

I. OUTLINE OF THE PROPOSED SYSTEM

2. A discussion of this kind is best conducted in terms of a fairly concrete proposal. It will therefore be assumed, for the purposes of the argument, that the proposed tax is (1) universal, extending to trading enterprises of all kinds; (2) that it is levied on the sales of each enterprise, *less* its purchases from other enterprises, but with no deduction for income payments by the enterprise in the form of salaries and wages, interest or rents, professional services, fees of consultants, etc.; (3) that all expenditures on goods and services purchased are deductible, irrespective of whether they are in the nature or a current expense in the operations of a particular business or of a non-recurrent (capital) nature; (4) that both the sales and purchases of a given period are calculated on a cash basis and no allowance is made for changes in the value of stock carried; (5) that all imports are liable to the tax, but exports are exempt; (6) that the rate of tax will be an appreciable one, of the order of 10 per cent. of the "value added."

3. A tax of this kind can be looked upon in two ways. On the one hand, it could be regarded as a proportionate direct tax on the gross income generated by each enterprise (i.e., on the "net output" as defined in the Census of Production), but with exemption for gross investment in the form of capital expenditure

---

[1] A memorandum submitted to the *Committee on Turnover Taxation* in July 1963.

or additions to stocks. On the other hand, it could be regarded as a universal and uniform tax on that part of the national expenditure which represents consumption, as against investment.[1]

4. It is possible, of course, to conceive of a tax of this kind on numerous other lines—the French tax, for example, is levied on manufacturers and wholesalers only; it exempts farm products and certain commodities such as newspapers, and applies at a reduced rate to certain foods, fuel, public utilities, services, etc. It would be possible also to confine the deduction to such purchases—broadly materials and fuel—which are actually embodied in the commodities or services sold (in which case the tax would be the equivalent of a single-point sales tax on *all* expenditure).

5. The kind of tax suggested here has been chosen on both economic and administrative considerations. From an economic point of view, a tax which falls only on consumption expenditure is greatly to be preferred to one which falls on both consumption and investment; it is also simpler to administer because the purposes for which goods and services are purchased by enterprises do not have to be scrutinised. There are great advantages also in a universal tax applying to enterprises of all kinds. Because the goods or services supplied by a particular enterprise normally enter into the production of a number of different final products, it is more difficult to introduce exemptions with a value-added tax than with a single-point sales tax.[2] Also, such exemptions would be more difficult to justify if the tax were conceived as a universal business tax in substitution for existing taxes on business profits, and not simply as a substitute for existing commodity taxes,

---

[1] The French value-added tax—where the seller is meant to "pass on" the tax directly and is required to show it separately on his invoice to the buyer—is more in the nature of a universal sales tax, with appropriate credits for double taxation. But if it is conceived as a universal business tax—which is in partial or full replacement of other taxes on business—it is more appropriate to levy it on the difference between the annual sales and purchases of the enterprise, and administer it in the same manner as the present Inland Revenue taxes; provided only that this method of administration does not create added difficulties (in view of G.A.T.T. rules) for the refunding of the tax on exported commodities. From the point of view of the ultimate incidence of the tax, the two methods of administration should not make any difference—in both cases the tax will be ultimately fully passed on to the final buyer of consumption goods—though in the case of an annual tax the effect may be more delayed than in the case of a sales tax which is collected monthly or quarterly.

[2] The exemptions in the French system give rise to anomalies, since the exempt enterprise gets no credit on its purchases and may therefore be in a worse competitive position than if it were subject to the tax. (It is known that the French oil refineries requested the Government that the tax should be extended to them.)

such as a purchase tax: and, as will be argued below, it is only in the former case that its introduction could be expected to yield significant economic advantages.

6. It would not be practicable to extend the tax to house rents or to certain services, such as professional services, life insurance, or domestic service, and these could be exempted without impairing its efficacy or simplicity of administration. If, however, food, fuel and light were also to be exempted, the tax could no longer be regarded as a universal business tax, and its administration would give rise to serious complications and anomalies.[1] It would therefore be preferable to make the tax universal, but to use part of the proceeds for subsidising the prices of these items to the final consumer.[2]

7. Since personal consumption expenditure (excluding housing and certain services) is now running at the rate of £16,500 millions per annum and the public authorities' current expenditure (excluding wages and salaries) is well over £2,000 millions, a universal value-added tax of 10 per cent. might bring in something of the order of £1,800–£2,000 millions.[3] This would make it possible to abolish the purchase tax (which now yields £550 millions), the profits tax on companies (yielding £400 millions), as well as the income tax on the undistributed profits of companies (which yields some £600 millions)[4] and still leave say, £300–500

---

[1] Thus the greater part of the output of enterprises producing fuel and light are sold to other enterprises; if therefore the fuel and light industries were exempted, the range of deductible expenses by other enterprises would have to be correspondingly curtailed, whilst the exempt enterprises would not be able to claim relief on their purchases of goods and services which were subjected to the tax (such as imported goods).

[2] If the tax were administered as a multi-point sales tax (as in France) such consumer subsidies could take the form of charging a low rate of tax on such items (say, 1 or 2 per cent.) at the point of sale to the final consumer, but giving a refund, at the full rate, for the taxes levied on the goods and services purchased by the enterprises selling to the consumers.

[3] The French value-added tax (which applies at a zero rate to certain items and at rates varying between 6 per cent. and 20 per cent. to others) now yields 36 per cent. of the national tax revenues, and 13 per cent. of total private consumption expenditure— which in terms of a U.K. equivalent, would imply a tax yielding some £2,400 millions.

[4] The abolition of the profits tax and the income tax on the undistributed profits of companies means, of course, that companies as such would be totally relieved from direct taxation; the income tax that would still be payable on interest and dividends distributed would become a simple withholding tax, a method of collecting the personal income tax, just like P.A.Y.E. Such a far-reaching reform would necessitate special measures to deal with (a) unincorporated enterprises which would be subject to the value-added tax—this could be done by relieving such enterprises of income tax on profits reinvested in stocks or in the form of capital expenditure; (b) businesses in company form which are not subject to the value-added tax (like one man companies

millions over for subsidies on the consumers' expenditure on food, fuel and light. Since total personal expenditure on these items is now running at around £6,000 millions, this means that a 10 per cent. value-added tax would, broadly, finance the abolition of the purchase tax, and the taxes on company profits, even if the tax on that part of consumers' expenditure which goes on food, fuel, and light (along with housing and certain personal services) were in greater part refunded. There would also be some consequential increase in Government expenditure in so far as the prices of goods and services purchased by the Government on current account rose in consequence (though on the argument later advanced in this paper, this may not be a substantial item). On the other hand, if the value-added tax were adopted in replacement of the existing taxes on business profits, there would also be a strong case, on distributional grounds, for introducing additional taxes on individuals (such as a tax on capital gains and a wealth tax) and (possibly as a temporary measure) an additional non-refundable tax on increased dividend payments. In one way or another, therefore, the introduction of a value-added tax would require a thorough recasting of the whole of our existing tax system, the nature of which is best seen in the light of an analysis of its effects on prices and on the distribution of the product of industry between wages and profits.[1]

2. ADMINISTRATIVE ADVANTAGES

8. The most important administrative advantage of a universal value-added tax is its self-reinforcing character which would provide the revenue authorities with an invaluable weapon against tax-evasion, and not only in the enforcement of this particular tax, but of other taxes as well. The problem of tax-evasion is generally regarded as quantitatively far less important in Britain than in other countries, whose standard of tax morality and administrative competence is known to be lower. But it cannot be said that straightforward tax-evasion does not exist in this country—

selling personal or professional services, or certain types of financial enterprises), to whom the current income and profits taxes (or some equivalent) would still have to be applied.
    [1] Most of these considerations would not apply to the scheme described in paragraphs 38-9, below, in which a value-added tax is combined with the payment of a general subsidy on wages, and not in substitution for other taxes.

particularly among smaller enterprises—and it is in the nature of successful tax-evasion that it is an "unknown factor": its quantitative importance or unimportance cannot be reliably estimated, except as a result of a systematic attempt to detect it. A universal value-added tax, with the aid of modern electronic computers, would make it possible to obtain continuing comprehensive information on the sales and purchases of each enterprise from the returns furnished by other enterprises and thus provide a systematic check on the returns made by each taxpayer. For this purpose, it would be necessary that standard vouchers (containing the tax code number of both the seller and the buyer) should be made out with every transaction between enterprises; that copies of such vouchers should be furnished by each enterprise with the periodic returns, and that the information given on the vouchers should be fed into electronic computers so as to build up an estimate of the sales of each enterprise from the purchases of other enterprises, and of the purchases of enterprises from the sales of others. (The latter type of information would only be necessary at the wholesale stage, so as to provide a check on the returns of retailers.)

9. Apart from these advantages in the better enforcement of taxes—which may or may not be considered sufficiently important to justify the introduction of a comprehensive reporting system of this kind—this system would also provide an invaluable aid to economic planning and forecasting. For it would furnish an up-to-date "transaction-matrix" of the whole economy—showing the flow of transactions between each of the economic "sectors", classified also according to regions—in a degree of detail and comprehensiveness that could not be obtained otherwise.[1] The importance of this to planning, and to economic policy generally, needs no emphasis.

3. EFFECTS ON ECONOMIC EFFICIENCY AND ON INCOME DISTRIBUTION

10. By far the most important question in connection with a value-added tax consists of its effects on economic efficiency,

---

[1] For this purpose each enterprise should be provided with a code number consisting of three sets of numbers: the first indicating the tax office (or district), the second the nature of the business (according to the standard industrial clasification), and the third its actual number in the tax register of the district.

and this in turn is closely related to the question of its incidence. How far, and in what respects, is the incidence of this tax different from that of the existing taxes on business profits? The answer to this question, as we shall find, provides the key to an analysis of the broader economic effects.

11. The classical theory of public finance asserts that the only taxes which can be passed on in the form of higher prices are those which affect all units of production more or less equally, and which therefore enter into costs at the "margin of production." On this basis a value-added tax would be passed on in much the same way as a commodity tax,[1] whilst a tax on profits would not. The most thorough exposition of this view is found in W. H. Coates' famous memorandum to the Colwyn Committee.[2] Since that time, the classical view has been challenged by economists from two different directions. One of these is based on recent "macro-economic" theories of profits, which conclude that the aggregate profit, *net* of tax, generated by the economy is determined on the one hand by business capital expenditure and on the other hand by the propensities to save of businesses, wage- and salary-earners, and the government; and that a tax on profits can only affect the volume of profits *after tax* in so far as it influences one or more of those factors. If it does not, its incidence must be shifted, through higher profit margins, to the general consumer. The other is based on recent theories of imperfect competition and oligopoly, which challenge the orthodox view of how prices are determined in a competitive market. It is this latter approach which is more directly relevant to the issues under discussion and therefore best considered first.

12. We may begin by examining the classical view. This is based on the "marginal" theory of pricing, according to which the price established in the market corresponds both to the marginal cost of production of each firm, and to the (average) cost of the

---

[1] This is true quite irrespectively of the differences in the ratio of "value-added" to price among different firms in an industry (which are quite as large as the differences in the ratio of profit to value added, and mainly reflect differences in the efficiency of raw material and fuel utilisation), simply because with a uniform tax the difference made by the tax to the cost of purchased materials, etc., per unit of output, would exactly cancel the differences in the tax paid by the firms themselves on account of a higher or lower ratio of "value-added" to price.

[2] *Report of the Committee on National Debt and Taxation*, 1927, Cmd. 2,800, Appendix XI.

least efficient or "marginal" firm. Since the "marginal" firm (or the "marginal unit" of production of any other firm) earns *no* profit, the market price cannot be influenced by a tax which is levied on profit.[1] As against this, the so-called "business school" contended that it is the "normal cost" of "representative firms" which determines prices; and this "normal cost" includes a "reasonable net profit, after all outgoings, including taxes."[2]

13. Coates thought that the issue between these two schools was largely a question of fact: it turned on whether the industries of the country were "mainly in the hands of representative concerns," whose costs were very similar, or whether they were in the hands of "concerns in varying circumstances and abilities showing results, varying from losses, or small profits, up to large profits, per unit of business." He then proceeded to show by means of copious statistics, derived from income tax returns, that in each of seven industry groups examined, the profit/turnover ratio had shown a wide dispersion between different firms and that an appreciable proportion of total sales came from firms which made either a loss or very little profit.

14. However, the validity of the "marginal" theory does not turn on the question whether the profits of different firms are similar or dissimilar, but on two other factors which are themselves interrelated: on the question whether firms operate under conditions of *rising* or *falling* short period costs, and on whether they operate under *perfect* or *imperfect* competition. It is only under *perfect* competition, when each firm faces an unlimited market, and in consequence sells the maximum amount that it is willing to sell at the given price, that the "marginal" firms, by providing an indispensable part of the market supply, "settle the general price."[3]

[1] It may be worth quoting Coates' exposition of this theory at some length: "Concerns which are on the point of withdrawal from the market have been contributing their supplies to the total offered, and their influence on the supply side has been a factor in the conditions which determine price, for, on the economic argument, this tends to be settled in any given unit of time by the demand which is effective in relation to the total quantity on offer. The addition to supply, which their activities have produced, will, by its enlargement of supply, have tended to depress the price to meet the effective demand. Yet the price influenced by this marginal production of the weak producers will have been insufficient to yield those producers a residiuum of profit. Into that price can enter no element of any tax which is levied on profit, for, in the conditions which exist, no tax will be levied on those weak producers whose incremental supply on the market is a factor in the determination of price" (*loc. cit.*, p. 71).
[2] Coates, *loc. cit.*, p. 70   [3] Coates, *loc. cit.*, p. 68.

This in turn implies that the infra-marginal firms operate under conditions of rising unit costs, which alone limits their output: for it is the inability of the low-cost firms to provide enough for the need of the market that enables the high-cost firms to survive. Under these conditions, variations in market supply in response to changes in demand mainly result from the activities—the appearance or disappearance—of marginal firms, and not from variations in the output of infra-marginal (and relatively low-cost) firms.

15. In reality, however, these conditions are not applicable to the most important sectors of the economy, in particular to the whole field of manufacturing industry. Unit costs are normally falling, not rising, even in the short period—as witnessed by the fact that an increase in production is accompanied by a rise in the ratio of (gross) profit to turnover, even at a constant price. Changes in market demand induce variations in the level of activity of *all* firms, and not only the marginal firms. This is evidence that conditions of imperfect competition prevail and the output of the infra-marginal firm is limited by demand, and not by the capacity to produce.

16. Under these conditions the general level of prices is set, not by the high-cost "marginal" firms, but by the profit margins of those firms (not necessarily the most efficient or the lowest cost firms) possessing the most up-to-date plant and equipment. In any industry, there is a minority of exceptional firms, earning abnormally high profits on the capital employed, owing to their superior management. But apart from these (which fall into a special category) the differences in labour and material cost per unit of output mainly reflect the age of equipment, so that the lowest-cost operating units—amongst the firms run by normal managerial efficiency—are those which possess the most recent equipment, whilst the "marginal" firms are those operating the oldest surviving equipment. The profits earned by such "normal firms" on new plant will correspond to the required rate of profit on new investment. In these circumstances, it will be the price charged on output produced with the most up-to-date equipment that will determine the age of marginal equipment, and thus the costs incurred at the margin, and not the other way round. If these prices were lower, more of the high-cost operating units

would become extra-marginal (i.e. more ancient equipment would be scrapped) and a higher proportion of output would come from relatively low-cost sources.[1] It may be that, at any one time, the capacity of the low-cost firms is limited, so that they could not provide a much higher proportion of market supply, without expanding their own capacity. But the point is that they could step up the rate of expansion of capacity through investment fairly easily, if they thought that there was sufficient demand at prices which offered an adequate profit. It is the opportunity of earning a "satisfactory" profit, not savings or finance, which mainly limits the rate of infusion of new capacity into industry.

17. The "required" rate of profit is very high (in relation to the rates of interest) simply because, in a world of continual technical progress and obsolescence and the continued change in marketing conditions associated with it, *business firms expect the profits derived from today's equipment to be much smaller and more uncertain in the more distant years than in the early years*; they depend therefore predominantly on the margin of profits expected in the initial years of operation of a new plant in deciding whether a project involving new capital expenditure is worthwhile or not. The useful life of new plant and equipment may be reckoned at 15–20 years or longer: but, because of the uncertainty of the more distant future, business men reckon that any new project "must pay for itself" in the first few years of operation. Hence they will require a high initial rate of return and, to ensure this, they use the rule-of-thumb method of a fixed "pay-off period" in deciding how much new investment to undertake. If this pay-off period is 3 years, this means that profit net of *all* outgoings (including taxes which are no different for purposes of this calculation than other outgoings, but before deducting the depreciation provision) must average 33⅓ per cent. a year in the first three years of operation. If the pay-off period is 5 years, the trading profit net of all taxes

---

[1] In actual fact any one firm may possess a multitude of plants (or operating units) of varying ages and its profit/turnover rate will reflect this. It may still be true that it is the required margin of profit on the output produced with the aid of the most recent equipment which will govern the prices charged on the output of the whole industry—simply because if the price were higher than this it would be worth while to infuse new capital into the industry, and sell its output at a lower price; if the price were lower than this, new investment would dry up, and the age of equipment would be prolonged (which would be associated with a rise in price).

must average 20 per cent. a year over the five year period.[1] The choice of a pay-off period in turn depends on the expected rate of technological improvement in an industry. The more "dynamic" the situation in which an industry finds itself—the more important the rate of improvement of design, the greater the likelihood of new substitutes being invented—the shorter this pay-off period will be. The shorter the pay-off period, the higher the supply price of commodities produced with the aid of new equipment; and since this supply is elastic, it determines in turn the prices which firms can obtain on goods produced with more ancient and less efficient equipment. Old equipment works for what it can get; it will continue to be operated so long as profits are higher than zero, or at any rate so long as the scrap value of equipment is less than the discounted value of the profits from its operation.

18. It is in this manner that taxes on the profits of businesses get "passed on" in the form of higher prices. Suppose that in a particular industry the normal "pay-off period" for new investment (whether for replacement or expansion) is three years. If we suppose that the labour cost per unit of output on the operation of new equipment is the same as the material and fuel cost, and the initial capital expenditure (per unit of output) is one and a half times the sum of the labour and material cost, i.e. investment per worker is three times the annual wage—the required gross profit (net of taxes) is one-third of the gross price (or the "turnover") or one-half of the "value added" (this implies that the capital/output ratio will be 1 when "output" is reckoned *gross*, and 1·5 when it is reckoned *net*, i.e. as the value added). If the taxes accruing on *gross* profits amount to $33\frac{1}{3}$ per cent., the required

---

[1] The assumption that for the purpose of this calculation profits are reckoned *net* of taxes is sometimes disputed. But if they were reckoned gross the whole method of estimating the worthwhileness of investment projects by reference to a "pay-off period" would not make sense; the interest of the investor is in knowing how long it would take to recover the cost of the investment, and he can only recover the part of the profit that is left after payment of taxes. It is possible that, owing to the complications of estimating the actual tax burden on future profits, (particularly under the British system) business men make a notional, or "average," allowance for taxes; and if they do so, it may be simpler to allow for the tax in fixing the length of the pay-off period itself, rather than use two separate rules of thumb in making their calculations. Thus, if some businessmen say that they use the criterion of "two years' gross profit before tax," this may not mean (unless they act irrationally) that they do not take taxes into consideration; if the taxes were reduced or abolished, the period of the pay-off might be appropriately adjusted.

gross profit before tax will be 43 per cent., instead of 33⅓ per cent. of turnover, and 60 per cent., instead of 50 per cent. of the value added.[1] If these taxes amount to 20 per cent., the required margin will be 38·5 per cent. of the turnover and 55 per cent. of the "value added."[2]

19. The main effect of the higher margin which enters into the price calculations of "price leaders" as a result of business taxation is to increase the dispersion of unit costs and labour productivity among the different firms of an industry. This is due to the fact that if the margin charged on goods produced with the most recent equipment is higher, the permissible cost differential between the lowest and highest cost firms will be greater; old equipment can be operated for a longer period; the rate of introduction of new equipment will be reduced, and at any one time a larger proportion of total supply will come from relatively inefficient firms.[3]

A Numerical Example

20. To explain this process further it may be easiest to resort to a highly simplified example, illustrated with the aid of diagrams. Let us suppose that in a particular industry (which we suppose to be fully integrated, so that the value added *equals* the price) the productivity of labour, operating on *new* equipment, is increasing at a constant rate of 5 per cent. a year owing to continuous technological improvements, while the cost of equipment (in terms of output) per unit of output capacity remains unchanged, and the productivity differences between firms are solely due to the difference in the age of equipment utilised. Let us assume further that, in the absence of taxation, the required profit in the initial year (the profit necessary to induce businesses to invest new capital in the industry) is equal to the labour cost—

[1] This is because with a 33⅓ per cent. tax, the gross profit per unit of output must be raised by 50 per cent. to yield the same net profit; if the required profit is one-half of the value added, the tax will raise the latter by 25 per cent.; hence the new share of gross profit will be 75/125 = 60 per cent.

[2] The proper method of reckoning is to take the tax charged on the net profit (*after* capital allowances) and express it as a percentage of the *gross* profit, since this will govern the effect of the tax on the supply price of commodities. When the charge on the net profit is around 50 per cent., the effective charge on the gross profit (having regard to the effect of capital allowances) may be no more than 20–25 per cent. See also paragraphs 21 and 24 below.

[3] As will be argued in paragraph 26 below this will mean at least a temporary reduction in the rate of growth of productivity and a permanent reduction in the average *level* of productivity in relation to that associated with the most recent equipment.

i.e., it is 50 per cent. of the value added.[1] On the supposition that the price charged on goods produced with the aid of the most recent equipment determines the price obtainable on goods produced with older and less efficient equipment, the price will fall annually by 5 per cent. relatively to wages-per-man, owing to the competition of newly installed equipment.[2] We may assume that the behaviour of demand for the goods produced by the industry is such that total demand for the product increases at the same rate as the price is reduced, so that if the physical efficiency of equipment of any given vintage remains unchanged over time —i.e., the productivity of the labour operating it remains constant —the total labour force engaged by the industry will also be constant over time. But a certain proportion of the labour force will be "transferred" each year from the equipment which is scrapped on account of obsolescence to newly produced equipment; and assuming that this process goes on steadily year by year, the gain in productivity of the *whole* labour force, resulting from this transfer, will be the same as the annual increase in productivity on newly installed equipment. The gradual "obsolescence" of equipment of any given vintage will reflect itself in the steady reduction of profits earned on it in successive years. Thus on the assumption that the profit is 50 per cent. of turnover in the first year, it will fall to 45 per cent. in the second year, 40·5 per cent. in the third year, 36·5 in the fourth year, and so on, until it falls to zero at the end of the 13th year.[3] On the supposition that equipment will continue to be operated so long as the profit is positive, the economic lifetime of equipment of any given vintage will be 14 years; the equipment installed in any one year will give employment to 7 per cent. (1/14th) of the labour force (but of a higher fraction of output) while the other 93 per cent. (or 13/14ths) will be distributed between the equipment produced in the 13

---

[1] This will be the case, e.g., when the capital investment per operative is three times the annual wage, and the pay-off period is three years, or when the capital per worker is five times the annual wage and the pay-off period is five years, and so on. (We ignore for simplicity the fact that the price-wage relationship is expected to change over time, so that more than a third of the cost would be required to be recovered in the first year with pay-off period of three years, etc.)

[2] In reality this takes more frequently the form of a rise in wages (in relation to prices) rather than an absolute fall in prices, but this makes no difference to the argument.

[3] This is because $100e^{-0.05t} = 50$, when $t = 13·86$.

preceding years. This situation is illustrated in Figure 1 (p. 280) where output per man and wages per man are measured on the vertical axis, while the equipments of different vintages operating at any one time are shown horizontally. The height of each column above the W line indicates the profits made on the equipment of each vintage at a particular time; the diagram can also be interpreted as showing the profit-history of any particular vintage of equipment from its installation in Year 0 until its disappearance at the end of Year 13. It is important to bear in mind that while the "required profit" on new equipment determines the price for *all* production, it is the competition of older equipment which limits the amount of new equipment that can be profitably installed. The introduction of new equipment will be limited each year to an amount which absorbs only 7 per cent. of the labour employed by the industry simply because, at the price ruling, demand will be limited to that amount—the rest of the demand will be satisfied from the older equipment which it is profitable to operate at that price. The difference in labour productivity between the least efficient and the most efficient operating units will be as 1 : 2 and the average labour productivity will be 72 per cent. of the productivity of labour operating the most recent (and therefore most efficient) equipment; and the total profit on all production will represent 30·5 per cent. on turnover.[1]

21. Let us now suppose a tax on profits which amounts to an effective rate of 23 per cent. on the gross profit.[2] This will raise the

---

[1] This is because the share of the profit in total output will depend on the relation between the productivity of labour on equipment of average efficiency and the productivity of labour on the least efficient equipment still in use. If we denote by P the productivity of labour on the *most* efficient equipment, βP that of the *least* efficient equipment, and $a P$ the productivity on *average* equipment, their relation is given by the formula

$$a P = \frac{P(1-\beta)}{\log_e \dfrac{1}{\beta}}$$

while the share of profit in output is given by $\dfrac{a-\beta}{a}$

[2] The figure of 23 per cent. was chosen so as to correspond to the burden of income and profit taxes at the prevailing tax rates and capital allowances in the U.K., for an "average" investment project in manufacturing industry (consisting as to 70 per cent. of plant and machinery and 30 per cent. of building and works), in the case of a 3-year pay-off period. For a 2-year pay-off period the corresponding effective rate would be 27 per cent., and for a 5-year period, 19 per cent. For reasons explained below (paragraph 24) the relief from taxation associated with a withdrawal of business profit taxes in the U.K., would be appreciably less than these figures indicate.

"required profit" from 50 to 65 units and the total supply price from 100 to 115, so that the share of gross profit in turnover on the least-cost production will rise from 50 to 56·5 per cent. This will prolong the economic lifetime of equipment from 14 years to 16⅔ years; for the same reason, the installation of new equipment each year will be limited, after a period of transition,[1] to the absorption of 1/16⅔rds, or 6 per cent., of the labour force, as illustrated in Figure 2. Once this change has worked its way through the age-structure of equipment, the difference in labour productivity between the least efficient and the most efficient operating units will be as 1 : 2·3, and the average productivity of labour will be 68 per cent. of the productivity of labour on the most efficient equipment (instead of 72 per cent.). The share of profit (before tax) as a percentage of *total* output, will be 36 (instead of 30·5) per cent., or 18 per cent. higher, and the volume of pre-tax profits (in money terms) 25 per cent. higher, whereas the rise in the gross margin on the output produced by *new* equipment will be 30 per cent.[2]

22. It follows that, while income and profit taxes on businesses will tend to get "passed on" in higher profit margins, the nature of the mechanism which brings this about will be different from that of sales taxes, and the shift in incidence will not be such as to leave profits after tax unaffected. Thus, while a general tax on sales of 10 per cent. will always raise prices in relation to wages by 10 per cent., a tax on *net* profits of around 50 per cent. may raise prices in relation to wages by a percentage which may vary between, say, 10–20 per cent., depending on the length of the pay-off period and the capital/labour ratio, the allowances for depreciation, etc. While a general sales tax leaves productivity unchanged, a tax on profits, by lengthening the operating life of equipment and thereby reducing average efficiency, will raise prices by more than the associated increase in pre-tax profits. (In the example given above, a rise in price of 15 per cent. involved a

---

[1] The *initial* effect of prolonging the lifetime may be to inhibit new investment altogether for a number of years.

[2] Assuming an effective tax rate of 19 per cent. (as would be appropriate for a 5-year pay-off period), the "required profit" on the output of new installations would rise from 50 to 62 units; the supply price of that output from 100 to 112; the average productivity of labour would be 69 per cent. of that on the latest equipment; and the share of profit in total output 35 per cent.

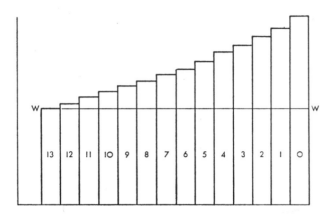

Figure 1

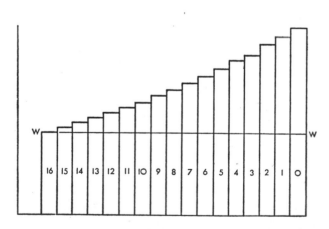

Figure 2

fall in average labour productivity of 5·5 per cent.; which meant that only about three-fifths of the rise in prices was accounted for by the rise in pre-tax profits; the remainder reflected the fall in average productivity).

23. In addition, the duration of the process of tax shifting will be longer. While the effect of a sales tax is direct and immediate, the corresponding effect of a profit tax will be gradual, and its full effect on the structure of production may become manifest only after a period of many years. When taxes are raised, the economic life of equipment is prolonged, and demand reduced as prices rise in consequence—both of which may cause new investment to fall off or even be suspended altogether for a period. In the reverse case the reduction in prices will normally depend on the infusion of new capacity, but particularly when there is a fair degree of spare capacity on equipment of recent vintage, so that the additional load caused by the accelerated scrapping of old equipment, and the additional rise in demand caused by the fall in prices, may be absorbed without requiring large increases in investment. But even if we supposed that there were no appreciable excess capacity, the additional investment needed to balance the reduction in working life might be accomplished in a limited period. In terms of our example, the complete withdrawal of income and profit taxes, which would shorten the lifetime by 3 years, would make it necessary to double the rate of gross investment for a three-year period after which the rate of new investment would fall back to a rate which is only 16⅔ per cent. higher than the initial rate (before the tax was withdrawn).

24. The above results (though based on the tax rates and allowances actually in force in the U.K.) may give an exaggerated impression of the effects of a withdrawal of the profits tax and income tax on companies on prices and productivity. The reason is that the company income tax is levied only on the *undistributed* part of the profit—the tax would continue to be charged on dividend distributions and interest payments. Since some part of any increase in the capital employed by a business is financed out of borrowed capital, and some part of any increase in profits is distributed to shareholders, a reduction of the company income tax by x per cent. has a lesser effect on net profits than a reduction

of profit tax by the same percentage. To calculate the combined burden of the two taxes we must therefore convert the company income tax into its profit-tax-equivalent; this conversion can only be made on certain assumptions—e.g., that the share of dividends in total profits remains constant over time. On that assumption (and taking the 1962 ratio of savings to distribution as the basis), the two taxes represent the equivalent of a single profit tax charged at the rate of 36·5 per cent. (as against the combined nominal rate of 53·75 per cent.). This means that, taking into account the investment and initial allowances now in force, the effective burden of company taxation on the profits arising from the operation of new capacity is only 16½ per cent. in the case of a three-year pay-off period, and 13 per cent. in the case of a five-year pay-off period (as against the 23 per cent. and 19 per cent. assumed earlier),[1] that is to say, it is only about one-half to two-thirds as high as the proportion taken in taxation in profits *as a whole*. Hence on the assumptions made in paragraph 18 concerning the capital/labour ratio on new investments (which may not be too unrealistic for manufacturing industry) the ultimate effect of the complete withdrawal of these taxes may be a reduction of prices relative to wages by 6–8 per cent., which would be associated with a rise in *average* productivity (according to the formula on paragraph 20, footnote) of 2½–3½ per cent. A withdrawal of the *present profit tax alone*, on the same assumptions, would reduce prices by only 2½–3½ per cent., with an associated rise of ¾–1 per cent.

Further Considerations

25. The above argument was conducted on the assumption that businessmen's cost and price calculations are made by reference to a fixed "pay-off period"—a period which may vary as between industries according to their assessment of uncertainty due to technological change or of other factors affecting the market situation, but which is not influenced by the existence or the weight of profit taxation. Though there is a fair amount of

---

[1] Our previous figures may be more relevant however to the United States, where the rate of the corporation profit tax levied in addition to personal income tax) is 52 per cent.

evidence that this is, in fact, the prevailing method of calculation in connection with investment decisions, it is possible that other methods are used as well—e.g., that businesses wish to secure a certain net return on the capital invested over the whole of the expected lifetime of the equipment after providing for depreciation and obsolescence; the required rate of net return depending not on the prevailing rates of interest, but on the rate of return achieved on investment in fixed assets in industry generally. These two methods yield substantially the same results (though not identical results, for the weight of taxation taken into consideration is not the same in the two cases) provided it can also be shown that the *net* rate of return on investments is determined by factors which are not directly influenced by profit taxation. The latter proposition is in accord with the recent dynamic theories of growth (and also with certain empirical studies made in the U.S.) but its consideration raises complex issues of economic theory that are beyond the scope of this paper.

26. Our argument also assumed that the rate of technological progress—as measured by the annual increase of efficiency of newly created equipment, at a given capital/output ratio—was not affected by the increase in the average life of equipment, and the consequent reduction in the ratio of annual investment to the outstanding capital stock. On this assumption, the increase in the operating life of the equipment and the consequent increased dispersion of productivity has no permanent adverse effect on the *rate* of economic growth: the rate of growth of productivity will be lowered only temporarily whilst the process of adjustment is going on. It is only the average *level* of productivity in relation to the productivity associated with the best techniques currently available—in other words the average productivity at any given *point* of time—that will be permanently reduced by this change.

27. As a matter of fact, it is not likely that the slowing down of the rate of capital formation and the consequent reduction in the proportion of current resources applied to investment, should leave the rate of technological progress unaffected. Learning is the product of experience: the more new "machines" are made, the more experience is gained in the development of new ideas and new methods, the faster the rate of increase in efficiency will

tend to be.[1] If this is taken into account, it is quite possible that the long-run rate of *growth* of productivity should be reduced in consequence of profit taxation, and not only the average level of productivity; and if it is, these long-run consequences might be more important than the effects which we have analysed. Since, however, the magnitude of these effects is completely unknown and incalculable, we shall take no further account of them.

The Macro-economic Aspects

28. So far the problem has been considered from a "micro-economic" point of view—by analysing the effects of the imposition or withdrawal of taxation on the price behaviour of the firm, and on the cost and output structure of an industry. It still remains to consider the problem from a "macro-economic" point of view—i.e., by examining the effects of taxation on the over-all distribution of the national product between profits and wages. The latter type of analysis looks at the problem from a different angle, and the results of these two methods of investigation are not always easily reconciled.

29. Recent theories of the determination of the share of profits in a capitalist economy focus attention on the residual character of profits, and on the fact that profits are the main source of business savings.[2] The aggregate volume of profits made will be such as to generate sufficient savings to finance investment—which is only another way of saying that prices (in relation to costs) will settle at the point where effective demand balances the available supply. This type of theory can best be expressed in the following equation:

$$P = \frac{1}{s_p}(I + B - S_w - S_g)$$

where P stands for aggregate profits generated in the economy after taxes, s_p for the proportion of profits saved, I for gross business investment, B for the balance of payments on current account, S_w for the net excess of non-business savings over non-business investment[3] and S_g (government savings) for the net

[1] This is at last becoming increasingly recognised. Cf., Kenneth Arrow, "The Economic Implications of Learning by Doing," *Review of Economic Studies*, June 1962.
[2] This is due to the fact that two-thirds or more of (gross) profits are saved, as against 5–10 per cent. of other types of income.
[3] Non-business investment is mainly in residential housing.

excess of Government revenue over Government expenditure. With the exception of P and I, all the items could take on negative as well as positive values.

30. The above equation is formally an identity; it assumes significance only in so far as the equation succeeds in isolating the mutually invariant elements, and P can be considered as a dependent variable, determined by the behaviour of the others. On these suppositions, the imposition of taxes on profits can only affect P by changing one or more of the values on the right hand side of the equation.

31. On our previous argument, the effect of a profit tax (as against an equivalent sales tax) will be to reduce business investment I, (since it will reduce the proportion of extant equipment which is annually replaced); it will also, by raising cost, reduce B (the balance of payments on current account) and for both of these reasons it would tend to reduce P, and hence the share of profits, for any given level of output. It may also induce companies to lower dividend payments in relation to profits (after tax) which would be the equivalent of a rise in the propensity to save out of profits (a rise in s_p) thus reducing P further. The joint effect of these factors may more than balance the tax charge, so that pre-tax profits might even be reduced, rather than raised. By the same token a withdrawal of profit taxes by raising I and B and possibly lowering s_p would increase P, this might more than offset the change in tax, thus causing pre-tax profits to rise.

32. The seeming contradiction between these two methods of analysis can be resolved however if we take into account that these macro-economic effects operate through changes in the level of activity and employment; and not (or not necessarily) through changes in prices in relation to wages. As was mentioned in paragraph 15 above, the actually realised profit in relation to turnover varies with the level of activity, not on account of any consequential change in the price/wage relationship, but on account of the fact that labour costs per unit of output are falling as capacity is more fully utilised, and vice versa.[1] As shown in Figure 3, there is a falling average labour cost curve for the

[1] In an unpublished study on variations of productivity and real wages in the U.K., R. R. Neild found that short-period variations in demand caused variations in productivity and profits, but left the price/wage relationship unaffected.

typical firm, *given* the rate of money wages, so that given the price, the share of profit in output will be an increasing function of the level of production. It is perfectly possible in this case that the price should be raised in relation to wages (and in relation to the cost curve) on account of the tax, and at the same time the share of profit in output should be reduced with a lower degree of utilisation of capacity. (In the diagram this will be the case when the price increases from p to p', if at the same time production is reduced from N to N'.) If, on the other hand, we assume that the

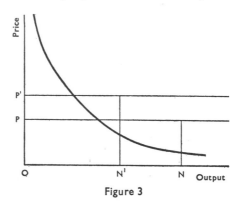

Figure 3

government follows a full employment policy, the tendency towards a fall in industrial activity and employment will be offset by fiscal policy—i.e., the fall in I and B, and the possible rise in s_p will be offset by a deliberate reduction in S_g. In that case the necessary compensatory change in S_g will be such as to make the resultant change in P for any given volume of income (Y) consistent with the results of the "micro" analysis as given in paragraphs 21–2. This, we may recall, did *not* involve that the imposition of a tax on profits left P/Y unchanged, for the rise in profits before tax was less than the amount taken in tax, over the whole range of operating units taken together. In the same way, a withdrawal of the tax on profits, assuming that it is accompanied by a compensatory change in S_g necessary to maintain full employment without inflation (which would take the form of a higher budgetary surplus), would still involve a considerable increase in the share of profits in the national income, and would thus make for greater inequality in the distribution of incomes.

33. This conclusion is strengthened if we now take into account that not *all* profit differences between "firms" are due to the use of equipment of varying ages; in great part they simply reflect differences in the efficiency of management. According to recent estimates made by Mr. Frank Brechling for N.E.D.O., the differences in output per head between firms employing the lowest 10 per cent. and the highest 10 per cent. of the labour force in 1958 (as measured by productivity) have been as large as 1 : 4, in the average of 21 industries examined, and they have been associated with differences in the share of profits in value added which varied from an average of 18 per cent. in the former group to 75 per cent. in the latter. Since, for the average industry, the annual growth of productivity due to technological progress cannot be put higher than 3–5 per cent., whilst the average operating life of industries' equipment cannot be put higher than 20–30 years, the factors analysed above cannot account for *larger* productivity differences than 1 : 2, or at most 1 : 2·5; the remainder must therefore be due to factors which are not affected (or not in the same way) by profit taxation. This means that in the case of the most successful firms, the reduction in the gross profit margin, due to the withdrawal of the tax, will be proportionately much less than the tax charge of which they are relieved, and they will be making substantially higher profits.[1]

Summary of the Above Argument

34. We may sum up the results of the above analysis. If a value added tax of a uniform rate of 10 per cent. were substituted for the existing profits tax and the income tax on undistributed profits (as well as for the purchase tax), the "supply price" of manufactured goods (excluding the tax) relative to money wages would tend to fall, partly as a result of a reduction in the margin of profit on sales, and partly of a consequential increase in average efficiency. The full effects of these changes would not be felt immediately but only after an interval of a few years. On the basis

[1] Thus if we suppose that the required margin of profit on goods produced with new equipment, but by firms operating with average managerial efficiency, is 50 per cent. *net* of tax, and the withdrawal of tax will lead to a 10 per cent. cut in prices in relation to wages, the exceptional firm making an 80 per cent. profit will have its profits cut by some 12 per cent.—say, from 80 per cent. to 70 per cent., but since the tax previously paid on the gross profit might well have amounted to 35 per cent. (or more) on the gross profit, its post-tax profits will still be 50 per cent. higher than before.

of the assumptions made in paragraphs 18 and 20 concerning the capital/labour ratio on new investments and of the length of the pay-off period and of the assumptions made in paragraph 24 concerning the effective burden of the profit and income taxes now in force, the ultimate reduction would be of the order of 6–8 per cent. of the value added by domestic activities, or (allowing for import content) 5–6½ per cent. in the prices charged to consumers. This means that, allowing for the effects of the withdrawal of the purchase tax (which may be put at 3 per cent.), a 10-per-cent. value-added tax may ultimately only raise prices to the general consumer by no more than 1–2 per cent.[1] Nevertheless, the change would imply a considerable shift in the burden of taxation from the owners of enterprises to wage- and salary-earners; a shift that would manifest itself, not so much in a reduction in real wages and salaries, but in the failure of real wages to rise with the consequential rise in average productivity, and in the rise in the share of profits. It would thus increase the inequality in the distribution of incomes, which would become further enhanced with the passage of time. For it would greatly speed up the accumulation of personal fortunes by men who are successful in business and thereby promote an even greater concentration in the ownership of wealth. It would also augment the share of national resources devoted to luxury consumption. From an equity point of view, or a socio-political point of view, such a change could therefore only be contemplated if it were coupled with a considerable increase in the range and effectiveness of the taxation of personal wealth—e.g. by the introduction of a progressive wealth tax, an effective tax on capital gains and a gift tax—and possibly some restraint (by means of a special tax or other means) on increases in dividend payments.

35. Further, the question must also be considered whether the advantages in terms of industrial costs, productivity and prices which could be expected to follow from the abolition of the existing taxes on business profits could not equally be attained by some less radical change in the tax system. Thus if business calculations of profitability depended entirely on the profits

---

[1] This is without taking into account the possible improvement in the rate of technological progress, referred to in paragraph 26 above.

expected over the pay-off period, allowing firms to write off capital expenditure completely before any tax is charged—in other words, a 100 per cent. initial allowance—would have the same effect on the supply price of commodities as the complete remission of taxes on profits; indeed the concessions recently made in the form of higher initial and investment allowances should already secure a substantial part of such advantages.[1] But even if business calculations of profitability depended on the expected net return over the whole life of the investment, and not only on the profits in the initial years of operation, it is possible to offset the effects of the tax charged on future profits by subsidies on investment, given in the form of investment allowances. There is always therefore *some* combination of initial and investment allowances which should secure the same effects on prices and productivity as the complete withdrawal of taxes on profits.

36. There is finally the question as to how far the introduction of a universal value-added tax would be justified if it were intended only as a replacement for the existing profits tax and purchase tax or only for the purchase tax.[2] The economic advantages of a withdrawal of the profits tax alone are probably not significant enough to justify the introduction of an entirely new tax on that score— they may amount to only 2–3 per cent. in terms of prices, and 1 per cent. or less in terms of productivity, which does not seem a sufficient advantage to compensate for the added administrative burdens involved. The same is true if the proposed tax were intended to replace the present purchase tax.[3] The only possible advantage

---

[1] In the absence of the present initial and investment allowances, the effective burden of the present profits tax and the income tax on undistributed profits would amount to 27 per cent. for a three-year pay-off period and 22 per cent. for a five-year pay-off period.

[2] As was shown in paragraph 7 above, a universal value-added tax at the rate of 10 per cent., levied on all expenditure except housing and certain services, would bring in sufficient revenue to make up for the abolition of all three taxes, and still leave £300–500 millions for offsetting the effects of the tax on the cost of food, fuel, and light by means of consumer subsidies. On the same basis (i.e. that the part of the tax falling on food, fuel and light expenditure is refunded) the withdrawal of the purchase tax and the profit tax alone would require a value-added tax of around 7 per cent.; of the purchase tax alone, 5 per cent.

[3] It is true of course that the French value-added tax was introduced as a substitute for a multi-stage turnover tax, and not as a substitute for profit taxation; its early advocates emphasised the economic disadvantages of a "cascading" turnover tax as well as the advantages, from the point of view of general tax enforcement, of the self-reinforcing features of a universal value-added tax. However, there are no "multi-stage" sales taxes in the U.K., whilst tax evasion is probably not sufficiently widespread or important to justify the introduction of such a system on that score.

from an economic point of view, might be that our present purchase tax levies a sales tax on a limited range of articles at a relatively high rate; in many cases these are commodities the production of which is subject to important economies of scale; if the rates of tax were reduced by spreading the net more widely, the domestic consumer would ultimately benefit through the lower costs of production of these goods, and this would more than offset the increase in prices of other commodities which are now exempt from tax. As against this consideration, there is the fact that a general sales tax is bound to be more regressive (or less progressive) in its incidence, as between different classes of consumers, than the present purchase tax.

IV. THE EFFECT ON EXPORTS

37. The effects on exports and the balance of payments of the scheme considered will partly depend on the consequential change in the level of money wages. Since, as was argued above, the benefits of the withdrawal of taxes on business profits in lowering industrial prices may only occur gradually, whereas the value-added tax could well raise the prices paid by domestic consumers almost immediately, it is quite possible that the introduction of the scheme will cause wages to increase during a transitional period faster than they would have done otherwise. If this happens, the effect on export costs will be adverse in the short run, and this may cancel out the benefits of the scheme on exports in the long run.

38. Assuming, however, that the rate of increase in money wages is not affected by the scheme (partly because the value-added tax is not passed on immediately, and partly because the cost of living is held down by subsidies) the withdrawal of income and profits taxes would ultimately lower the supply price of manufactured goods (excluding the element of imported materials and components) by 6–8 per cent. (relative to wages). Hence the substitution for the existing taxes on profits of a value-added tax which is fully refunded on exported goods (in the same way as under the French system) would be the equivalent of a devaluation of the pound by 6–8 per cent. Both of these factors—assuming an average import content of 20 per cent. in exports—might lower export

prices by 5–6½ per cent. In other words it would bring about the same competitive advantage as a general reduction in money wages by 6–8 per cent., relative to our industrial competitors. (In the same way, a value-added tax imposed in replacement of the profits tax only would bring about the same advantage as a general reduction of money wages by 2½–3½ per cent.) But it would have the merit—as against devaluation, or a general cut in money wages—that it would be associated with a rise in the average productivity of labour in industry which would tend to offset (or possibly more than offset) the loss in real income due to the adverse change in the terms of foreign trade which the reduction in our export prices would entail. As against this, while the effects of a devaluation on export prices would be immediate, the corresponding effects of the withdrawal of taxes on profits would come about gradually, over a period of years.

39. A value-added tax which was imposed in substitution for purchase tax only would make no important difference to exports,[1] since exported goods are already exempt from purchase tax. It is sometimes argued that the very fact that the exporter gets a cash refund on the value of goods exported equivalent to the tax on the *full* f.o.b. value of the goods, and which is therefore normally considerably larger than the tax for which he is liable on domestic sales (on account of the value added by his own operations) would itself provide an incentive to the manufacturer to seek out export markets—quite apart from any incentive provided by a reduction in export costs. There may be something in this, but it is impossible to judge how much weight should be attached to such psychological incentives.

40. In order to promote exports effectively one could adopt a scheme on rather different lines, which has not, so far as I know, been publicly advocated—the introduction of a value-added tax that is imposed not in substitution for, but in addition to, existing taxes, and the proceeds of which are used for the payment of a general subsidy to enterprises on their wage and salary

---

[1] For the reasons advanced in paragraph 36 above, it might make some difference, in so far as the removal of the purchase tax on durable consumer goods, by increasing domestic demand, would tend to lower their costs of production; assuming, of course, that there is sufficient capacity available to permit higher exports *pari passu* with higher home consumption.

disbursements.[1] As far as the domestic consumer is concerned, such a scheme would not impose any net burden, since the effects of the tax and the subsidy on prices would largely cancel each other. But as the tax would be refunded on exports, export costs would be reduced, and the balance of payments improved by this scheme to the same extent as by a general reduction in money wages (equivalent to the subsidy) or by an equivalent devaluation of the exchange rate.[2] The scheme would not have the advantages of the scheme considered earlier in increasing productivity through accelerated scrapping and replacement, nor the disadvantages in terms of a higher relative share of profits and increased economic inequality.[3] As compared with the existing situation, its effect on productivity would be neutral; it would not decrease productivity any more than a general payroll tax would increase it.[4] But from

[1] A scheme of this kind could be best administered as a combined operation at annual intervals, and entrusted to the Inland Revenue. The net liability of each enterprise would then be computed according to the following formula:

Tax on (Sales *less* Export Sales, *minus* Purchases of goods and services from other domestic Enterprises).

less

Subsidy on (Total Wage and Salary Payments).

When the net liability according to this formula, is negative, the enterprise receives a cash payment from, when positive, it makes a payment to, the Revenue. Export sales are only credited to the final exporter who is actually responsible for shipment. Alternatively it would be possible to operate the value-added tax on the lines of a sales tax (with monthly or quarterly collections) and to operate the wage subsidy scheme in conjunction with income tax.

[2] As was shown in paragraph 7 above, a 10 per cent. universal value-added tax would bring in some £1,800–2,000 millions, of which some £250 million would fall on goods and services purchased by the central government and the local authorities. Total wage and salary payments (including employers' contribution to national insurance, etc.) are now running at the rate of some £17,000 million a year, of which some £2,700 millions are paid by public authorities (excluding trading services). Hence assuming the government pays no subsidy to itself for its own employees, the revenue from a 10 per cent. tax would suffice for the payment of a subsidy on the wage and salary bill of all enterprises at the rate of 12·5 per cent., which—according to the now generally accepted precepts of Keynesian economics—would reduce the price-level of the gross *domestic* product (i.e., the money value added by domestic activities) by an equivalent percentage. This means that, assuming an average import content of 20 per cent. on both domestic consumption and exports, it would reduce the price-level (excluding the tax) of goods and services to the final buyer, home or foreign, by 9·7 per cent.

[3] The net effect of a combined value-added tax and a wage subsidy is to leave the share of profits more or less the same, since the increased profits made on exports will tend to be offset by a lower *net* profit on domestic sales. (This is because, owing to the subsidy, the tax cannot effectively be passed on to the consumer in this case; while the subsidy on wages will lower the amount of profits, in money terms, earned on the sale of any given volume of investment goods.) A straightforward devaluation, on the other hand, would raise the share of profits and reduce real wages.

[4] Though a detailed demonstration of this would be lengthy and complicated, it might suffice to point out that while, on the one hand the combined scheme would operate as a tax on gross profits (since a tax on value added, *less* a subsidy on wage and salary payments of an almost identical rate comes to the same thing as a tax on gross

the point of view of exports and the balance of payments it would be just as effective as devaluation; moreover, since the rates of tax and subsidy could be changed at fairly frequent intervals (at least annually) according to balance of payments requirements, the scheme would confer much the same advantages as a system of flexible exchange rates. Furthermore, for a reserve currency country like Britain, there are important advantages in any scheme which gives the benefits of devaluation on current transactions without affecting the gold value of sterling balances.[1]

41. The introduction of such a scheme would probably be regarded as a thinly disguised devaluation by other countries (which in a sense it is) and, no doubt, attempts would be made to declare it as inconsistent with Britain's existing international obligations under the G.A.T.T. (or possibly the Bretton Woods agreements). However, any such claim would be unjustified. For a general wage subsidy is not the same thing as a direct subsidy on exports; in its external effects (in combination with the new tax) it is identical with that of a devaluation, or of a general cut in money wages, neither of which are in any way inconsistent with the G.A.T.T.; while a general cut in money wages is certainly not inconsistent with the rules of the I.M.F. From the point of view of its internal effects it is preferable to either alternative (since it avoids the inflationary effects of the former, and the deflationary effects of the latter) but this is no concern of the Contracting Parties of the G.A.T.T., or of any other international body. Moreover, by introducing some differentiation in the rate of subsidy payable according to different regions—e.g. by paying a higher rate of subsidy on labour employed in the North and a lower rate of subsidy on employment in the South—such a system could also be made to serve as a potent instrument of regional economic planning.

profits) and would thereby tend to raise the supply price of commodities produced with new equipment, lengthen the economic life, and reduce average productivity; on the other hand, the wage subsidy, by lowering the prices of investment goods, would do precisely the opposite—remembering that, under the scheme proposed here, investment expenditure would be effectively relieved of the value-added tax, in much the same way as exports—and when the tax rates are nearly the same as the subsidy rates, these two effects will offset each other. In other words the disincentive to investment caused by the additional tax on profits made on operating new equipment will be cancelled by the incentive to investment caused by the lower costs of investment.

[1] Also it would be less likely to be imitated by other countries owing to political prejudice against a system involving the payment of wage subsidies.

INDEX TO AUTHORS